First World War
and Army of Occupation
War Diary
France, Belgium and Germany

7 INDIAN (MEERUT) DIVISION
Headquarters, Branches and Services
Commander Royal Artillery
9 August 1914 - 31 December 1914

WO95/3933/1

The Naval & Military Press Ltd
www.nmarchive.com
Published in association with The National Archives

Published by

The Naval & Military Press Ltd

Unit 10 Ridgewood Industrial Park,
Uckfield, East Sussex,
TN22 5QE England
Tel: +44 (0) 1825 749494

www.naval-military-press.com

www.nmarchive.com

This diary has been reprinted in facsimile from the original. Any imperfections are inevitably reproduced and the quality may fall short of modern type and cartographic standards.

© **Crown Copyright**
Images reproduced by permission of The National Archives, London, England, 2015.

Contents

Document type	Place/Title	Date From	Date To
Heading	7 Meerut Div C.R.A. 1914 Aug-1915 June		
Miscellaneous	Meerut Division Aug-Dec 1914		
Heading	War Diary of C.R.A. Meerut Division Volume I From 9/8/14 To 31-10-14		
War Diary	Mussoorie	09/08/1914	10/08/1914
War Diary	Meerut	11/08/1914	01/09/1914
War Diary	Bombay	02/09/1914	15/09/1914
War Diary	S.S. Torilla	15/09/1914	12/10/1914
War Diary	Marseille	13/10/1914	18/10/1914
War Diary	En Train	19/10/1914	20/10/1914
War Diary	Orleans	21/10/1914	27/10/1914
War Diary	En Train	28/10/1914	28/10/1914
War Diary	Merville	29/10/1914	29/10/1914
War Diary	Locon	30/10/1914	31/10/1914
Miscellaneous	Headquarters 7th Indian Division	28/08/1914	28/08/1914
Miscellaneous	Appendix 2		
Miscellaneous	Appendix 3	07/09/1914	07/09/1914
Miscellaneous	Appendix 4		
Miscellaneous	Appendix 5		
Heading	War Diary of C.R.A. Meerut Division From 1st November 1914 To 30th November 1914 Volume I		
War Diary	Locon	01/11/1914	30/11/1914
Miscellaneous	To The Adjutant 4th Brigade R.F.A.	02/11/1914	02/11/1914
Miscellaneous	Messages And Signals		
Miscellaneous	Messages Signals And Field Telegraphs		
Map	Map		
Miscellaneous	Appendix 8 (a)		
Miscellaneous	Messages Signals And Field Telegraphs		
Heading	War Diary of C.R.A. Division From 1-11-14 30/11/14 Volume		
Map	Map		
Miscellaneous	Messages, Signals And Field Telegraphs		
Miscellaneous	Instructions		
Miscellaneous	Messages, Signals And Field Telegraphs		
Miscellaneous	Report By O.C. 2nd Battery On Periscope	10/11/1914	10/11/1914
Miscellaneous	Operation Orders	10/11/1914	10/11/1914
Map	Map		
Miscellaneous	Appx 16		
Miscellaneous	Messages Signals And Field Telegraphs		
Miscellaneous	A Form Messages And Signals		
Miscellaneous	Messages Signals And Field Telegraphs		
Map	Map		
Operation(al) Order(s)	Operation Order No.2 By Lieut General C.A. Anderson C.B. Commanding Meerut Division	10/11/1914	10/11/1914
Operation(al) Order(s)	Operation Order No.3 By Lieutenant-General C.A. Anderson C.B. Commanding Meerut DIvision	13/11/1914	13/11/1914
Miscellaneous	Messages Signals And Field Telegraphs		
Miscellaneous	A Form Messages And Signals		
Miscellaneous	Headquarters Meerut Division	25/11/1914	25/11/1914

Operation(al) Order(s)	Operation Order No.3 By Brigadier General A.B. Scott C.B. D.S.O. Commanding Royal Artillery Meerut Division	30/11/1914	30/11/1914
Heading	War Diary of Headquarters Divisional Artillery Meerut Division From 1-12-14 To 31-12-14 Volume II		
War Diary	Locon	01/12/1914	25/12/1914
War Diary	Ham	26/12/1914	31/12/1914
Operation(al) Order(s)	Operation Order No.6 By Lieutenant-General C.A. Anderson C.B. Commanding Meerut Division	01/12/1914	01/12/1914
Miscellaneous	Headquarters, Meerut Division	01/12/1914	01/12/1914
Miscellaneous	A Form Messages And Signals		
Map	Map		
Miscellaneous	Appendix 30		
Operation(al) Order(s)	Operation Order No.7 By Lieutenant-General C.A. Anderson C.B. Commanding Meerut Division	10/12/1914	10/12/1914
Operation(al) Order(s)	Operation Order No.8 Lieutenant-General C.A. Anderson C.B. Commanding Meerut Division	11/12/1914	11/12/1914
Operation(al) Order(s)	Operation Order No.4 By Brigadier General A.B. Scott C.B. D.S.O. Commanding Royal Artillery Meerut Division	10/12/1914	10/12/1914
Miscellaneous	Appendix 33		
Miscellaneous	A Form Messages And Signals		
Miscellaneous	G.O.C. R.A. Meerut Div.	14/12/1914	14/12/1914
Operation(al) Order(s)	Operation Order No.15 by Br General F.E. Johnson D.S.O. Commanding Lahore Divisional Artillery	15/12/1914	15/12/1914
Miscellaneous	Operation Orders	15/12/1914	15/12/1914
Miscellaneous	Appendix 37	16/12/1914	16/12/1914
Operation(al) Order(s)	Operation Order No.9 By Lieut-General C.A. Anderson Commanding Meerut Division	18/12/1914	18/12/1914
Operation(al) Order(s)	Operation Order No.6 By Brigadier General A.B. Scott C.B. D.S.O. C.R.A. Meerut Division	18/12/1914	18/12/1914
Miscellaneous	Appendix 40		
Miscellaneous	A Form Messages And Signals		
Diagram etc	Diagram		
Miscellaneous	A Form Messages And Signals		
Miscellaneous	20th Battery RFA 9th Bde RFA States		
Miscellaneous	A Form Messages And Signals		
Miscellaneous	Messages, Signals And Field Telegraphs		
Miscellaneous	Messages And Signals		
Miscellaneous	A Form Messages And Signals		
Miscellaneous	Messages Signals And Field Telegraphs		
Miscellaneous	A Form Messages And Signals		
Miscellaneous	Messages Signals And Field Telegraphs		
Miscellaneous	Appendix 59		
Miscellaneous	Messages Signals And Field Telegraphs		
Miscellaneous	A Form Messages And Signals		
Miscellaneous	Messages, Signals And Field Telegraphs		
Miscellaneous	Appendix 64		
Miscellaneous	Messages, Signals And Field Telegraphs		
Operation(al) Order(s)	Operation Orders No.7 By Brigadier General A.B. Scott C.B. D.S.O. C.R.A. Meerut Division	25/12/1914	25/12/1914
Miscellaneous	March Table		
Operation(al) Order(s)	Operation Order No. 10 By Lieutenant General C.A. Anderson C.B. Comdg Meerut Division	24/12/1914	24/12/1914
Miscellaneous	March Table		

Operation(al) Order(s)	Operation Order No. 11 By Lieutenant General C.A. Anderson C.B. Comdg Meerut Division	25/12/1914	25/12/1914
Miscellaneous	March Table		
Miscellaneous	8th Battery RFA	15/12/1914	15/12/1914
Miscellaneous			
Miscellaneous	Headquarters Divisional Artillery Meerut Division	15/12/1914	15/12/1914
Miscellaneous	Appendix 70		
Miscellaneous	Summary Of Intelligence Up To 10.p.m. 24th December 1914	25/12/1914	25/12/1914
Miscellaneous	Summary Of Information Up To 9.30.a.m.	23/12/1914	23/12/1914
Miscellaneous	Summary Of Information Up To 10.00.p.m.	21/12/1914	21/12/1914
Miscellaneous	Summary Of Information Up To 10. p.m	20/12/1914	20/12/1914
Miscellaneous	Summary Of Information	20/12/1914	20/12/1914
Miscellaneous	Information Summary Up To 6.p.m	10/12/1914	10/12/1914
Miscellaneous	Airman's Report 10.am.	19/12/1914	19/12/1914
Miscellaneous	Summary Of Information Up To 10.p.m	18/12/1914	18/12/1914
Miscellaneous	Summary Of Information Up To 11.p.m	17/12/1914	17/12/1914
Miscellaneous	Summary Of Information Received From C.R.A. Lahore Division	17/12/1914	17/12/1914
Miscellaneous	Summary Of Information Up To 8.a.m	17/12/1914	17/12/1914
Miscellaneous	Summary Of Information Up To 9.a.m	15/12/1914	15/12/1914
Miscellaneous	Summary Of Information Up To 10.a.m	14/12/1914	14/12/1914
Miscellaneous	Information Summary Up To 11.p.m	13/12/1914	13/12/1914
Miscellaneous	Summary Of Information Up To 9.p.m 12.12.14	13/12/1914	13/12/1914
Miscellaneous	Information Summary Up To 10.a.m	12/12/1914	12/12/1914
Miscellaneous	Information Summary Up To 10.a.m	11/12/1914	11/12/1914
Miscellaneous	Information Summary 10/12/14	10/12/1914	10/12/1914
Miscellaneous	Information Summary Up To 9.a.m	09/12/1914	09/12/1914
Miscellaneous	Information Summary Up To 7.p.m	08/12/1914	08/12/1914
Miscellaneous	Information Summary Up To 7.p.m	06/12/1914	06/12/1914
Miscellaneous	Airman's Morning Report	06/12/1914	06/12/1914
Miscellaneous	Information Summary Up To 9.pm.	05/12/1914	05/12/1914
Miscellaneous	Information Summary Up To 6.pm.	04/12/1914	04/12/1914
Heading	War Diary December 1914 Hd. Qr. Divisional Artillery Meerut Division		
Map	Map		
Heading	War Diary December 1914 Hd Qr. Divisional Artillery Meerut Division		
Map	Map		
Heading	War Diary December 1914 Hd. Qr Divisional Artillery Meerut Division		

7 MEERUT DIV

CRA

1914 AUG — 1915 JUNE

MEERUT DIVISION
AUG - DEC 1914

C. R. A.

IV BDE RFA
IX BDE RFA
XIII BDE RFA

Div. Ammn. Column

A.G.6

121/2168

War Diary
of Secret Division
G.R.A Volume I

from 9/8/14 to 31·10·14

Pg. 1-15

Headquarters Divisional Artillery
7th Indian Division.
I.E.F. "A"

VOLUME. I.

Army Form C. 2118

WAR DIARY
—of—
INTELLIGENCE SUMMARY.

(Erase heading not required.)

Instructions regarding War Diaries and Intelligence Summaries are contained in F.S. Regs., Part II, and the Staff Manual respectively. Title pages will be prepared in manuscript.

Hour, Date, Place.	Summary of Events and Information.	Remarks and references to Appendices.
11.30.P.M. 9th August 1914 MUSSOORIE.	1st day of Mobilization for "Overseas Expeditionary Force "A". No staff as yet appointed. Lt Colonel E.P. SMITH. R.A. officiating as C.R.A. No peace office establishment allowed. Field Staff Office in peace so kept in the office of the O.C.R.F.A. Brigade at MEERUT, which has proved unsatisfactory – books not up to date.	App.9
12.noon 10th August 1914 MUSSOORIE	Mobilization progressing. No staff as yet appointed. Arrangements for supply of equipment being made locally at MEERUT. Arrangements also being made to obtain clerk, signallers and orderlies and horses from out-stations, other than MEERUT.	App.9
12.noon 11th August 1914 MEERUT.	Following N.C.O.s and men joined as signallers and orderlies to C.R.A:- 5 from 73rd Battery R.F.A at Lucknow, 1 from 10th Battery R.F.A. at BARRACKPORE, from 26th Battery R.F.A at ALLAHABAD 1 Clerk from 92nd Battery R.F.A at DINAPORE also joined.	App.9
Forenoon 12th August 1914 MEERUT	Captain R.K. LYNCH-STAUNTON.R.H.A appointed Staff Captain to C.R.A who to Brig General A.H.SHORT. R.A. at present in England, and expected to join unit en route to base.	App.9
12.noon 13th August 1914 MEERUT	Eight riding horses for signallers, orderlies and clerk joined from No.8 Ammunition Column R.F.A at FYZABAD.	App.9
12.noon 14th August 1914 MEERUT.	Officiating C.R.A leaves MUSSOORIE with his improvised base office and one Soldier Clerk (lent by 7th Division) for MEERUT the mobilization station.	App.9

Army Form C. 2118.

2

WAR DIARY (continued)
INTELLIGENCE SUMMARY.
(Erase heading not required.)

Instructions regarding War Diaries and Intelligence Summaries are contained in F. S. Regs., Part II, and the Staff Manual respectively. Title pages will be prepared in manuscript.

Hour, Date, Place.	Summary of Events and Information.	Remarks and references to Appendices.
6. a.m. 15th August 1914. MEERUT	Officiating C.R.A. with office (as on 14th) arrived.	App.2
9. a.m. do.	Equipment and Field Staff Office collected. Field Staff Office in unsatisfactory condition. It is also found on receipt of "Tables of Books, forms and Stationary taken into the field by the Army in India" that practically the whole of the Books, forms and Stationary in the Field Staff Office are obsolete. Up-to-date forms etc. indented for to the Contractors for Stationary and Govt Printing Calcutta. The N.C.O. of the 9th Battery R.3.A appointed clerk to C.R.A. having been found inefficient a Staff Sergeant from the Headquarter office 7th Division is applied for in his stead - but not joined.	App.3
4. p.m. 16th August 1914 MEERUT	Still awaiting forms and stationary to complete Field Staff Office. No news of C.R.A. who is expected to join unit en route to base. C.R.A's Clerk not joined. 1 public and 4 private followers required to join unit on mobilization are unobtainable. Otherwise unit ready to move to base.	App.2
6. a.m. 17th August 1914. MEERUT	Staff Sergeant A.E. WHICKER, India Miscellaneous List, forms no clerk to C.R.A. Mobilization Store Tables of R.A. units applied for by wire.	App.2
4. p.m. 18th August 1914 MEERUT	Forms and stationary still awaited from Contractors Govt Printing and Stationary. Contractor Govt Printing intimates (by wire) that Mobilization Store Tables of R.A. units have not been issued.	App.9.
4. p.m. 19th August 1914	Forms and stationary still awaited.	App.2
4. P.M. 20th August 1914	As for 19th instant.	App.2

Army Form C. 2118.

3

WAR DIARY (continued)
or
INTELLIGENCE SUMMARY.

(Erase heading not required.)

Instructions regarding War Diaries and Intelligence Summaries are contained in F. S. Regs., Part II, and the Staff Manual respectively. Title pages will be prepared in manuscript.

Hour, Date, Place.	Summary of Events and Information.	Remarks and references to Appendices.
4.p.m. 21st August 1914 MEERUT	Unit complete and ready to move. C.R.A. (Brig General SHORT) expected to join unit at overseas base.	WD.9
4.p.m. 22nd August 1914 MEERUT	Awaiting orders to move. Arrangements made with Railway Authorities for stock to convey unit by ordinary train to seaport - seaport at present unknown.	WD.9
4.p.m. 23rd August 1914 MEERUT	Awaiting orders re date and place of embarkation of unit for overseas Expeditionary Force.	WD.9 WD.9
4.p.m. 24th August 1914 MEERUT	As for 23rd instant.	
11.p.m. 25th August 1914 MEERUT	As for 23rd instant. Wire received by Divisional Commander giving names of Officers who will join units en route to base - Brig General SHORT R.A. (C.R.A.) not mentioned.	WD.9
9.am 26th August 1914 MEERUT	Wire sent to M.S. Chief India asking if any news of General Short - having reference wire received by Divisional Commander on 25th instant.	WD.9
4.p.m. 27th August 1914 MEERUT	As for 23rd instant.	WD.9
3.p.m. 28th August 1914 MEERUT	Orders received for unit to embark on S.S. "MONGARA" (B.I.S.N.Co) at Bombay on 2nd September 1914.	See Appendix 1. WD.9
4.p.m. 29th August 1914 MEERUT	All arrangements made for move of unit to Bombay - but timings of train not yet known. As no news of permanent C.R.A. G.O.C 7th Division decided that Lt-Colonel E.T.P. SMITH. R.A. should be prepared to accompany unit as C.R.A.	WD.9

Army Form C. 2118.

WAR DIARY (continued)
or
INTELLIGENCE SUMMARY.

(Erase heading not required.)

Instructions regarding War Diaries and Intelligence Summaries are contained in F. S. Regs., Part II, and the Staff Manual respectively. Title pages will be prepared in manuscript.

Hour, Date, Place.	Summary of Events and Information.	Remarks and references to Appendices.
11.p.m. 29th August 1914. MEERUT	Intimation received that Brig. General H.F.MERCER, C.B, D.S.O, A.D.C, R.A. appointed C.R.A. 7th Division, also as that officer cannot arrive BOMBAY until 4th September 1914 unit will embark on S.S.TORILLA (B.I.S.N.Co) at BOMBAY on 4th September 1914.	WD.2.
6.p.m. 30th August 1914. MEERUT	Definite arrangements made for unit (less horses) to leave MEERUT by 2.11 hours train on 1st September 1914, arriving Colaba (BOMBAY) (B.B+C.I.Ry) at 8.30 hours on 2nd September 1914. Horses leave for BOMBAY by 18.11 train as Railway Authorities unable to take them by fast passenger train leaving at 2.11 hours on 1st September 1914.	WD.2. WD.3.
6.p.m. 31st August 1914. MEERUT	Unit waiting to move.	

W. Shpred-Bande
Captain
for Brigadier General
Commanding Royal Artillery
7th Indian Division
I.E.F. "A"

Army Form C. 2118.

Headquarters Divisional Artillery
7th Indian Division
I.E.F. "A"

Volume II

WAR DIARY
or
INTELLIGENCE SUMMARY.

(Erase heading not required.)

Instructions regarding War Diaries and Intelligence Summaries are contained in F. S. Regs., Part II, and the Staff Manual respectively. Title pages will be prepared in manuscript.

Hour, Date, Place.	Summary of Events and Information.	Remarks and references to Appendices.
3. a.m. 1st September 1914 MEERUT.	Unit leaves for BOMBAY, except Brig General MERCER who joins unit at BOMBAY direct from SIMLA. Horses were despatched to BOMBAY on 30th August 1914.	AAQMG
10.30 a.m. 2nd September 1914 BOMBAY	Unit complete (except Brig General MERCER) arrives and ready to embark on 4th instant. Unit proceed to Cooperage Reizef Camp near Colaba (BOMBAY).	AAQMG
4. p.m. 3rd September 1914 BOMBAY.	Unit ready to embark. Intimation received that unit will not embark till 8th or 9th instant as S.S. TORILLA will not be properly fitted out till those dates.	Verbal from Embarkation Authorities. AAQMG AAQMG
4. p.m. 4th September 1914 BOMBAY	Unit awaiting embarkation.	
9. a.m. 5th September 1914 BOMBAY	Unit awaiting embarkation. Brig General MERCER joins. Wire sent to Chief General Staff India urging increase to Staff owing to increase in number of batteries each Division.	× Appendix 2. AAQMG
6. a.m. 6th September 1914 BOMBAY	Brig General A.B. SCOTT, C.B., D.S.O., R.A. appointed C.R.A. 7th Indian Division vice Brig General MERCER appointed to Army Staff Indian Division.	AAQMG
3. P.M. 7th September 1914 BOMBAY	Embarkation Commandant BOMBAY intimates that no troops will embark from BOMBAY for the Overseas Expedition until 15th instant.	Appendix 3. AAQMG
6. P.M. 8th September 1914 BOMBAY	Brig General Scott joins. Unit complete awaiting orders for embarkation.	AAQMG

Army Form C. 2118. 6

WAR DIARY (continued)
INTELLIGENCE SUMMARY.
(Erase heading not required.)

Instructions regarding War Diaries and Intelligence Summaries are contained in F. S. Regs., Part II, and the Staff Manual respectively. Title pages will be prepared in manuscript.

Hour, Date, Place.	Summary of Events and Information.	Remarks and references to Appendices.
6.p.m. 9th September 1914 BOMBAY	Awaiting orders for embarkation. Chief General Staff India wires that Artillery units will be rearmed at port of disembarkation with rifles suitable for Mark VII ammunition – present weapons needed in INDIA.	⁺Appendix 4. MR.2.
6.p.m. 10th September 1914 BOMBAY	Awaiting embarkation	MR.2.
6.p.m. 11th September 1914 BOMBAY	Awaiting embarkation	MR.2.
6.p.m. 12th September 1914 BOMBAY	Awaiting embarkation.	MR.2.
6.p.m. 13th September 1914 BOMBAY	Awaiting embarkation.	MR.2.
6.p.m. 14th September 1914 BOMBAY	Five rifles of Staff returned to FEROZEPORE Arsenal under telegram received from Chief General Staff on 9th instant. Verbal orders received to embark on S.S. TORILLA at 2.p.m. on 15th instant.	MR.2.
2.p.m. 15th September 1914 BOMBAY S.S. TORILLA	Unit embarked in monsoon weather.	MR.2.
9.am. 16th September 1914 S.S. TORILLA	Moved to mid stream and anchored off BOMBAY. Rations on boardship for horse per day:- 3 lbs oats, 5 lbs bran, 12 lbs grass.	MR.2.

Army Form C. 2118.

WAR DIARY (continued).

INTELLIGENCE SUMMARY.

(Erase heading not required.)

Hour, Date, Place.	Summary of Events and Information.	Remarks and references to Appendices.
6 P.M. 17th September 1914 S.S. TORILLA.	Horses exercised and groomed during day.	MQ3. MR9.
6 P.M. 18th September 1914 S.S. TORILLA.	As for 17th instant.	
6 P.M. 19th September 1914 S.S. TORILLA.	Lieutenant J.N.M. MAC FARLANE, 100th Battery R.F.A. posted as Orderly Officer but not joined - Application for Brigade Major refused. 2 Orderlies who joined on 11th August 1914 being insufficient taken ashore to rejoin their battery (the 73rd now at BOMBAY having been mobilized).	Appendix 5. MQ3.
11 a.m. 20th September 1914 S.S. TORILLA.	Received 1 N.C.O and 2 Gunners to replace orderlies taken ashore on 19th instant. This gives one spare man - N.C.O. drawn from No.8 Ammunition Column at FYZABAD. 1 Gunner from 10th Battery R.F.A at BARRACKPORE. 1 Gunner from 92nd Battery at DINAPORE. Sailed with other ships forming convoy escorted by H.M.S. SWIFTSURE, H.M.S. FOX and R.I.M.S. DUFFERIN.	MQ.8.
6 P.M. 24th September 1914 S.S. TORILLA.	AT SEA. Run to 12 noon 208 miles. Weather fine. Sea calm. Head breeze - cool. Horses groomed and exercised.	MQ.9.

Army Form C. 2118.

WAR DIARY (continued)
INTELLIGENCE SUMMARY.
(Erase heading not required.)

Instructions regarding War Diaries and Intelligence Summaries are contained in F. S. Regs., Part II, and the Staff Manual respectively. Title pages will be prepared in manuscript.

Hour, Date, Place.	Summary of Events and Information.	Remarks and references to Appendices.
6.p.m. 22nd September 1914 S.S. Torilla	At Sea. Run to 12 noon 228 miles making total 436 miles. Weather still fine and sea calm. Horses Groomed and exercised.	M.R.9.
6.p.m. 23rd September 1914 S.S. TORILLA	At Sea. Run to 12 noon 196 miles making total 632 miles. At 12.45 P.M. 12 ships sighted N.W. These came up alongside at 2.15 P.M and were 10 troopships escorted by H.M.S DARTMOUTH and R.I.M.S. HARDINGE. Weather still fine and sea calm. Horses Groomed and exercised.	M.R.9.
6.p.m. 24th September 1914 S.S. TORILLA	At Sea. Run to 12 noon 216 miles making total 848 miles. Weather & sea same as yesterday.	M.R.9.
6.p.m. 25th September 1914 S.S. TORILLA	At Sea. Run to 12 noon 237 miles making total 1085 miles. Weather & sea same as yesterday.	M.R.9.
6.p.m. 26th September 1914 S.S. TORILLA	At Sea. Run to 12 noon 235 miles making total 1320 miles. Weather & sea same as yesterday.	M.R.9.

Army Form C. 2118.

WAR DIARY (continued)
or
INTELLIGENCE SUMMARY.

(Erase heading not required.)

Instructions regarding War Diaries and Intelligence Summaries are contained in F. S. Regs., Part II, and the Staff Manual respectively. Title pages will be prepared in manuscript.

Hour, Date, Place.	Summary of Events and Information.	Remarks and references to Appendices.
6 P.M. 27th September 1914 S.S. TORILLA	At sea. Run to 12 noon 238 miles making total 1538 miles. Weather fine but climate warmer. Sea calm. Horses groomed and exercised.	
10 P.M. do.	Passed Aden	No 2?
7.45 am 28th September 1914 S.S. TORILLA	Passed Perim Island	
6 P.M. do.	Run to 12 noon 276 miles making total 1814 miles. Weather fine. Climate much warmer. Sea calm. Horses walked and exercised.	
6 P.M. 29th September 1914 S.S. TORILLA	Run to 12 noon 257 miles making total 2071 miles. Otherwise as for 6 P.M. 28th instant	No 29
6 P.M. 30th September 1914 S.S. TORILLA	Run to 12 noon 258 miles making total 2329 miles. Otherwise as for yesterday.	No 2.9

M Offord
Captain
for Brigadier General
Commanding Royal Artillery
7th Indian Division

Headquarters Divisional Artillery
Meerut Division.

VOLUME III

G

Army Form C. 2118.

WAR DIARY

INTELLIGENCE SUMMARY

(Erase heading not required.)

Instructions regarding War Diaries and Intelligence Summaries are contained in F. S. Regs., Part II, and the Staff Manual respectively. Title pages will be prepared in manuscript.

No 3 Section
A.'s Off: at Base
I.E. Force
Passed to French S. Sect:
19.11.14

Hour, Date, Place.	Summary of Events and Information.	Remarks and references to Appendices.
6.p.m. 1st October 1914 S.S. TORILLA	Run to 12 noon 246 miles making total 2575 miles. Weather fine. Climate much warmer. Sea calm. Horses groomed and exercised.	M29.
6.p.m. 2nd October 1914 S.S. TORILLA	Run to 12 noon 255 miles making total 2830 miles. Otherwise as for 1st October.	M29.
4.a.m. 3rd October 1914 S.S. TORILLA	Arrived PORT SUEZ and anchored. Horses groomed and exercised during remainder of day.	M29.
3.a.m. 4th October 1914 S.S. TORILLA	Left PORT SUEZ for PORT SAID.	M29.
3.p.m. 4th October 1914 S.S. TORILLA	Arrived PORT SAID and anchored.	M29.
4.p.m. 5th October 1914 S.S. TORILLA	Left PORT SAID and anchored midstream.	
5.p.m. 6th October 1914 S.S. TORILLA	Sailed from PORT SAID with convoy of other ships. Signal message received that G.O.C. Division wanted interview with C.R.A. on "S.S. City of Poona" at 9.30 a.m. C.R.A. and Staff Capt R.A. (on one of H.M's. Scheering) boarded S.S. City of Poona and discussed question of Ammunition etc with Divisional Staff on board. The Divisional Artillery Headquarters embarked on said ship as Divisional Headquarters could have been settled more easily and at a short mode of time all matter.	M29.
6.p.m. 7th October 1914 S.S. TORILLA	Run to 12 noon 220 miles. Weather fine. Sea calm. Horses groomed and exercised.	M29.
6.p.m. 8th October 1914 S.S. TORILLA	Run to 12 noon 264 miles. Otherwise as for 7th instant.	M29.
6.p.m. 9th October 1914 S.S. TORILLA	Run to 12 noon 231 miles. do.	M29.

VOLUME III

WAR DIARY (continued)
or
INTELLIGENCE SUMMARY.
(Erase heading not required.)

Army Form C. 2118.

Instructions regarding War Diaries and Intelligence Summaries are contained in F. S. Regs., Part II, and the Staff Manual respectively. Title pages will be prepared in manuscript.

Hour, Date, Place.	Summary of Events and Information.	Remarks and references to Appendices.
6 p.m. 10th October 1914 S.S. TORILLA	Run to 12 noon 280 miles. Otherwise as for 7th instant	M.R.2
6 p.m. 11th October 1914 S.S. TORILLA	Run to 12 noon 283 miles. do.	M.R.2
4 p.m. 12th October 1914 S.S. TORILLA	Arrived and docked at Hangar No. 4 New docks, MARSEILLE. Unloading of baggage commenced.	M.R.2
6 p.m. 13th October 1914 MARSEILLE	Horses disembarked at 8 a.m. and unit proceeded to Camp LA VALENTINE, where it arrived at 1 p.m. Shorts for horses and Khaki Khaki (except pantaloons - not available) drawn for all British rank & file, at rate of 1 jacket and 1 cap each.	M.R.2
6 p.m. 14th October 1914 MARSEILLE	Awaiting entrainment for point X. Just commenced to rain. Lieut F.N. MACFARLANE R.A. joined as Orderly officer K.C.R.A.	M.R.2
6 p.m. 15th October 1914 MARSEILLE	Awaiting entrainment for point X. Rained whole day.	M.R.2
6 p.m. 16th October 1914 MARSEILLE	do.	M.R.2
6 p.m. 17th October 1914 MARSEILLE	do.	M.R.2
6 p.m. 18th October 1914 MARSEILLE	Awaiting entrainment for point X. At 5 a.m. 200 horses of 4th Cavalry stampeded. They took with them the 8 British horses of the Subordinate Staff (- Six out of the eight were recovered during the day - two out of the Six were badly lame when they returned to the lines.	M.R.2
6 p.m. 19th October 1914 EN TRAIN	Unit (4 officers (including interpreter), 1 Staff Sergeant, 12 rank + file, 6 officers charges + bridles, 8 horses) left Camp LA VALENTINE at 7.30 a.m. and entrained at Gare du ARENC at 2 p.m. for point X. The 2 missing native horses had not been found when unit departed from MARSEILLE.	M.R.2

Army Form C. 2118.

WAR DIARY (continued)
INTELLIGENCE SUMMARY.

(Erase heading not required.)

Instructions regarding War Diaries and Intelligence Summaries are contained in F. S. Regs., Part II, and the Staff Manual respectively. Title pages will be prepared in manuscript.

Hour, Date, Place.	Summary of Events and Information.	Remarks and references to Appendices.
6. p.m. 20th October 1914 EN TRAIN	Unit en route by train to point X. Halts were made during the day at certain stations for watering and feeding of horses - also for cooking mens food.	AR 29.
11. p.m. 21st October 1914 ORLEANS	Unit arrived at ORLEANS (LES AUBRAIS Stn) at 7.30 p.m. and entrained and proceeded to Camp DES GROUES.	AR 29.
6. p.m. 22nd October 1914 ORLEANS	Bomb. Stay admitted to Hospital with a bad foot. One lame horse admitted to Veterinary Hospital	AR 29.
6. p.m. 23rd October 1914 ORLEANS	Major E. G. Thompson, 17th Lancers joined as Staff Captain - with 2 Batmen and four horses - one (unproven) G.S. wagon (2 horses) and one man of Army Service Corps; also two H.T. Carts, 4 mules and 2 Indian public followers joined for attachment to unit. No 32919 for Smith, 60 Co. R.G.A. (who was sent from Simla (A.H.Qrs) to do clerk to Brig General H.J. MERCER, C.B., R.A. appointed to Army Corps) not being required with Headquarters Indian Army Corps posted to unit as 2nd Clerk, unit having been made up to War Establishment.	AR 29.
6. p.m. 24th October 1914 ORLEANS	Whole of Division (Meerut Division) marched out of camp on a route march, with 1st line transport and TRAIN (less supply section) 2 cobs (remounts) received for Capt F FANE Interpreter. Bombardier Stay discharged from Hospital. One sickhorse to village, any troop. One horse exchanged for one from 93 Bgde, F. A., H. Qrs.	AR 29.
6. p.m. 25th October 1914 ORLEANS	During the day remounts were received to complete establishment of riding horses for subordinate Staff. All available clothing + ordnance stores obtainable were drawn from the advanced ordnance depot to make up deficiencies. Strength of unit today is as follows:-	✱ 1 one horse sent to 93rd An. Col. it not being fit for work required. ✱ 5 for Subordinate staff who had 2 for draught men for Wagons had not received no charger from Indian to India.

P.T.O.

Army Form C. 2118.

3rd Meerut Division Head Quarters

WAR DIARY
INTELLIGENCE SUMMARY
(Erase heading not required.)

Hour, Date, Place.	Summary of Events and Information.	Remarks and references to Appendices.
	Commander Royal Artillery .... Brig. Genrl. A.B. Scott, C.B., D.S.O, R.A.	
	Brigade Major R.A. ... Captain R.K. Lynch Staunton, R.A.	
	Staff Captain ... Major E.G. Thompson, 17th Lancers.	
	Orderly Officer + A.D.C. ... Lieut F.N.M. MacFarlane, R.A.	
	Interpreter ... Captain F. FANE.	
	Chief Clerk + Q.M. Sergt ... Staff Sergt A.E. WHICKER, I.M.L.	
	2nd Clerk ... Gunner J.F. SMITH, 60th Company R.G.A.	
	Signallers (4) Orderlies (3)	
	a/Bombr Stamp R.F.A. Bombr Stary R.F.A.	
	" Chapman R.F.A. Gunner Hart R.F.A.	
	Gunner Horn R.F.A. " Sinnott R.F.A.	
	" Brown R.F.A.	
	BATMEN (8)	
	To C.R.A. { a/Bombr Payne R.F.A. To B.M. { Gunner Bruniton R.F.A. To S. Capt { Private Smith 17th Lancers	
	{ Gunner Dawe { Driver Edmondo { " Smith "	
	To Orderly Officer - Gunner Monckman R.F.A. To Interpreter - Gunner Atherton R.F.A.	
	Cook - Gunner Moody R.F.A.	
	The following are attached to the unit:-	
	Driver of G.S. wagon. Driver Hodgson, Army Service Corps.	
	Driver of A.T. Carts. 2 Indian Drivers of 114th Mule Corps.	
	1 " " Lahore Transport Corps (on loan)	
	with lead pack horse.	
	ANIMALS WITH UNIT	
	12 officers chargers. 10 riding horses. 2 Heavy Draught horses. 1 hack pony. 4 mules = 29 animals.	

Army Form C. 2118.

13

WAR DIARY (continued)
OR
INTELLIGENCE SUMMARY.

(Erase heading not required.)

Instructions regarding War Diaries and Intelligence Summaries are contained in F. S. Regs., Part II, and the Staff Manual respectively. Title pages will be prepared in manuscript.

Hour, Date, Place.	Summary of Events and Information.	Remarks and references to Appendices.
6 p.m. 26th October 1914 ORLEANS	Awaiting orders for entrainment for unknown destination.	MO2
8 p.m. do.	Orders received for unit to entrain at 2.55 p.m. on 27th instant.	MO2 MO2
6 p.m. 27th October 1914 ORLEANS	Unit entrained for unknown destination.	
6 p.m. 28th October 1914 EN TRAIN	do., and en route.	
6 p.m. 29th October 1914 MERVILLE	Passed ROUEN about 6 a.m. ABBEVILLE about 3.30 p.m. ST OMER about 6 p.m. BOULOGNE about 9 p.m. and CALAIS at 11 p.m. Arrived at regulating station HAZEBROUK about 2.30 a.m. Arrived at MERVILLE and detrained at 7 a.m. and proceeded into billets. C.R.A visited C.R.A. 5th Division at GORRE by motor. Rained hard during the evening.	MO2
12 m.n. 30th October 1914 LOCON	C.R.A and Brigade Major accompanied G.O.C. Meerut Division by motor this morning and visited Headquarters 19th, 20th + 21st Infantry Brigades. 4th, 9th + 13th Artillery Brigades were ordered to send their Battery Commanders to spend the day in observing stations of Batteries of 5th Division (now in position) whom they were to relieve. Batteries moved out in the afternoon preparatory to occupying those positions which extend from RUE DES BERCEAUX on the N to ½ mile S. of Rue de l'Epinette on the S (about 4500 yds) BETHUNES. By 10.30 a.m. all Brigade had arrived in MERVILLE and ST VENANT complete with their Brigade Ammunition Columns. Divisional Headquarters moved to LOCON. Heavy firing occurred during night.	MO2

Army Form C. 2118.

VOLUME III

WAR DIARY (continued)
or
INTELLIGENCE SUMMARY.
(Erase heading not required.)

Instructions regarding War Diaries and Intelligence Summaries are contained in F. S. Regs., Part II, and the Staff Manual respectively. Title pages will be prepared in manuscript.

Hour, Date, Place.	Summary of Events and Information.	Remarks and references to Appendices.
6. P.M. 31st October 1914. LOCON.	Heavy firing in the early morning. 4th, 9th, + 13th Brigades R.F.A. occupied the positions vacated by batteries of 5th Division and 110th Heavy Battery occupied position of 108th Heavy Battery. The 4th Brigade R.F.A. was grouped to the 20th Infantry Brigade and the 9th and 13th Brigades to the 21st Infantry Brigade. The 8th Howitzer (4·5 in.) Brigade into attached to the Division also the 2nd Siege and 114 Heavy Batteries. 37 Howitzer Battery attached to 4th Bde R.F.A. 61st & 65th Batteries grouped with 21st Lieut Colonel DUFF's Commanding 8th Howitzer Brigade was put in Command of the Artillery grouped with the 21st Infantry Brigade i.e. 9th and 13th Bdes (18 pr.) and 8th Howitzer Brigade (less 37th Battery) to simplify work of Infantry Brigadier. During the day the MEERUT Divisional Ammunition Column arrived at ESSARS and commenced supply Ammunition in the course of the afternoon. The Airman attached to Divisional Artillery Headquarters sent in his usual morning report to C.R.A. 5th Division who retains the MEERUT allotted the day's tasks to the Heavy Batteries. Divison took over at 10. a.m.	65th Battery grouped with 21st Infantry Brigade. M.29
12 m.n. 31st October 1914. LOCON.	The 9th Bde R.F.A. fired a few registering rounds with their starting zones, their position established for one mile S.W. from RICHEBOURG in the order 19th, 20th, + 28th. The 13th Brigade R.F.A. occupied a front of about 1½ miles N and S. for a point about one mile S.W. of FESTUBERT. P.T.O	

Army Form C. 2118.

(15)

WAR DIARY (continued)

Instructions regarding War Diaries and Intelligence Summaries are contained in F. S. Regs., Part II, and the Staff Manual respectively. Title pages will be prepared in manuscript.

INTELLIGENCE SUMMARY.

(Erase heading not required.)

Hour, Date, Place.	Summary of Events and Information.	Remarks and references to Appendices.
	Positions of batteries as follows:— 8th, 2nd and 44th Batteries in action facing East (roughly). There were two French batteries on the left of the 2nd Battery. Little else to report about this Brigade. 2nd Siege Battery fired bombs near LOISNE engaged hostile battery east of the E of the S in RUE DE MARAIS at 12.30 p.m with Aeroplane observation. Same battery also engaged hostile batteries reported to be 1100 yds S. of L in LORGIES and 600 yards S of the 1st Battery mentioned. Ranges 6,600 and 6,800. R.F.A., or 110 and 114 Heavy Batteries. No information received from 4th Brigade R.F.A., or 110 and 114 Heavy Batteries.	(maps FRANCE 1–80,000 Sheets ARRAS, ST OMER and LILLE.)
LOCON 31.10.14		

M Shyok-Saunter
Captain R.A.
for Commander Royal Artillery
Meerut Division.

APPENDIX 1.

No.20072/22-(Q.C.).   Headquarters, 7th Indian Division.
                        Meerut.   28th August 1914.

From,
    The Assistant Quartermaster General,
        7th Indian Division.
To,
    The Commanding Royal Artillery,
        7th Indian Division.

MEMORANDUM.

Divisional Artillery Headquarters will embark on the "MONGARA" at BOMBAY on the 2nd September 1914.

                        Sd   H.W. Codrington, Lt Colonel.
J.H.   offg A.Q.M.G. 7th Indian Division.

APPENDIX 2.

Copy of a telegram from Brigadier General F. Mercer, C.B., D.S.O., A.D.C., Commanding Royal Artillery, 7th Indian Division, to the Chief of the General Staff, Army Headquarters, India, Simla, No.88-C.R.A.W. dated the 5th September 1914.

Having regard to increase in number of batteries in the two Divisions strongly urge as essential an addition to Divisional Artillery Headquarters to conform with Home Establishment aaa present scale quite inadequate aaa would you consider and wire me decision aaa have written aaa.

APPENDIX 3

No.51/11/E.

Headquarters, Embarkation Commandant.
No.3 Shed, Alexandra Dock.
dated 7th September 1914.

From,

    The D.A.A. & Q.M.G.
        Embarkation Staff.

MEMORANDUM.

It is notified for information that no troops will embark from Bombay for the Over-seas expedition until the 15th instant, except those for the H.T. "DILWARA", notice of which will be notified hereafter.

            Sd. J.A. Cummins, Major
    Depy Asst Adjt and Qr Master General,
           Embarkation Staff.

To, Officers Commanding Units in Relief Camps Bombay etc, etc,

APPENDIX 4.

Copy of a telegram from the Chief of the General Staff, Army Headquarters, India, Simla, to Brigadier General F. Mercer, C.B., D.S.O., Inspector of R.H. & R.F.A. Bombay, No. 3185-W dated the 9th September 1914.

Your telegram of eigth aaa Artillery will be rearmed at port of disembarkation with Rifles suitable for mark seven ammunition present weapons are needed in India.

APPENDIX 5.

Copy of a telegram from the Military Secretary to His Excellency the Commander-in-Chief in India, to Brigadier General A.B. Scott, C.B. D.S.O., Commanding Royal Artillery, 7th Indian Division, No.1712/347 dated the 18th September 1914.

Your telegram of 15th appointment Brigade Major not sanctioned aaa Macfarlanes appointment as Orderly Officer approved and he has be ordered to join.

----

x
Lieutenant J.N.M. Mac Farlane
100th Battery R.F.A.
Neemuch, India.

War Diary 12/2

of

C.R.A. Meerut Division

From 1st November 1914
To 30th November 1914

Volume I

Ref 16/6 50

Headquarters Divisional Artillery
Meerut Division

VOLUME IV

Army Form C. 2118.

No 3 Section
A. G's Office at Base
I. E. Force
Passed to Gen'l S. Sect'n
on 11 – XII – 14

Instructions regarding War Diaries and Intelligence Summaries are contained in F. S. Regs., Part I, and the Staff Manual respectively. Title pages will be prepared in manuscript.

WAR DIARY
of
INTELLIGENCE SUMMARY.

(Erase heading not required.)

Hour, Date, Place.	Summary of Events and Information.	Remarks and references to Appendices.
1st November 1914 LOCON	Position of Divisional Artillery remained same as yesterday and as marked in rough map of LA BASSEE – PONT DU HEM attached. The 4th Brigade R.F.A. & 37th Howitzer Battery remained grouped with 20th Infantry Brigade. The 8th Howitzer Brigade (less 37th Battery) with 9th and 13th Brigades R.F.A. remained grouped with 21st Infantry Brigade under command of Lt Colonel DUFFUS R.F.A. & Heavy Battery and No 2 Siege Battery remained under the command of the C.R.A. 4th Brigade R.F.A. reported that 7th Battery upon reserve. 14th Battery opened fire 4 times. 66th Battery fired at Infantry trenches – the shots effective by scattering the Infantry. 7th Battery located hostile howitzers near LORGIES and silenced them, range of trenches and demolished a house containing machine guns. Captain Vernon R.F.A. mounted on horse while laying telephone wire for Communication with infantry trenches. This officer's devotion to duty brought notice of high authorities. 9th Brigade R.F.A. Brigade Headquarters moved from GORRE to LE TOURET during afternoon. The Brigade supported our Infantry who recaptured 3 trenches during night of 31st/1st. During the night the 19th & 20th Batteries were withdrawn and evacuated in rear of the position took orders to re-occupy their positions at dawn which they did. The 65th Battery withdrew for the night with orders to remain out of action during the 2nd for a day's rest. 13th Brigade R.F.A. 2nd Battery in billets resting. 6th Battery during night 31st/1st a German attack on the Black Watch trenches at 9.P.M was shelled by two Batteries, the O.C. Black Watch on the trenches according to direct fire, the attack quickly repulsed at a range of 1700 X. 44th Battery had 1 section detached to GIVENCHY & Endeavour to enfilade hostile trenches. 61st Battery nothing to report. 2nd Siege Battery at 11.15 engaged hostile battery E of S in RUE DE MARAIN – observation being given by aeroplane – afterwards another battery S of E in LORGIES & was engaged.	⊕ Appendix 28 – Appendix G X The 110th & 114th + Map of FRANCE 50,000 Sheets LILLE ARRAS & ST OMER. Appendix 6 a.

WAR DIARY (continued)
Vol IV
of
INTELLIGENCE SUMMARY.

(Erase heading not required.)

Army Form C. 2118.

Hour, Date, Place.	Summary of Events and Information.	Remarks and references to Appendices.
9.10 a.m. 2nd November 1914. LOCON	110th Heavy Battery engaged battery near LORGIES at 8,900 yds. firing interrupted a good deal by presence of GERMAN aeroplanes over head. Heads of 2 Batteries near BOIS DE BIEZ seen about 5 P.M. 114th Heavy Battery engaged battery near Distillery at RICHEBOURG L'AVOIE at 3 P.M. battery near LORGIES. Divisional Ammunition Column remained at ESSARS - reported unable to obtain any 4.5" Howitzer Ammunition for the 8th Howitzer Brigade (attached to Meerut Division), also no 18pr ammunition issued this day, vide Indian Corps. 39/16.K. Headquarters Divisional Artillery remained with the Divisional Headquarters at LOCON touch being kept with Artillery units by means of mounted orderlies and Divisional Signal Cos telephone lines through Infantry Bde Sections.	× Appendix 7. MR.3 × Appendix 8
10.45 a.m. do.	Report received from the 19th Infantry Brigade that siege guns and shrapnel were directed at the trenches and enemy were advancing against the 2nd Gurkhas, and asked for Artillery support. Information sent to G.O.C. 20th Indian Infantry Bde, who was asked to let Field Artillery groups work him, cooperate if unemployed. Reply received from G.O.C. 20th Infantry Bde that 4th Bhe R.J.A. homed turn on 2 Batteries and possibly 3.	$ Appendix 6
12.55 p.m. do.	Orders sent to 110th Heavy Battery to search and sweep immediately along last E in to G.O.C. 114th Heavy Battery to search and sweep immediately along last E in NEUVE CHAPELLE to N.W corner of BOIS du BIEZ - this was done. NEUVE CHAPELLE to N.W corner of BOIS du BIEZ - this was done.	
1. P.M. do.	In accordance with instructions received from G.O.C Division, (at request of G.O.C 19th Infantry Bde) orders were issued to 114th & 110th Heavy Batteries to demolish NEUVE CHAPELLE village - East of the church. 114th Battery then engaged 2 hostile batteries to the EAST - Observation by Airman - Range 5,700.	
2. P.M. do.	12 rounds fired at 114th Battery by enemy, 114th Battery in accordance with orders Village of NEUVE CHAPELLE Shelled by 114th Battery at 12.6'6' P.M.	

WAR DIARY (continued) VOL IV

Army Form C. 2118.

INTELLIGENCE SUMMARY.

(Erase heading not required.)

Instructions regarding War Diaries and Intelligence Summaries are contained in F. S. Regs., Part II, and the Staff Manual respectively. Title pages will be prepared in manuscript.

18

Hour, Date, Place.	Summary of Events and Information.	Remarks and references to Appendices.
2.30 p.m. 2nd November 1914 LOCON	Heavy shell fire directed at 114th Battery. Lieut. PIERSON R.G.A and B.S.M. GILBERT were killed. Remainder of Battery orderly under cover. Four to five seen near LORGIES. During afternoon 110th Battery shelled enemy.	
3.45 p.m. do.	2nd Siege Battery opened fire on enemy mortar reported by Lt. Norfolk to be in RUE DOUVERT. Only 6 rounds fired. Observation difficult. Heavy Batteries ordered to stop firing during afternoon, owing to expected counter attack near BOIS du BIEZ, which was not to have rendered fire(?) in this sector. Jampson to own own battery.	
7.45 p.m. do	8th Battery opened fire at 7.4 p.m. on Infantry attack which was repulsed. Later fire on trenches at request of O.C. Black Watch, an officer of which regiment observed fire. 44th Battery - 2 sections resting, 3rd section in action near GIVENCHY to enfilade hostile trenches. Fire reported of great value by Infantry Commander. 1 gunner wounded. **GENERAL** The insufficiency of present establishment of telephones most marked: this was emphasised by the fact that when MEERUT Division took over from 5th Division practically all the telephones of R.A. 5th Division had to be handed over in situ. Difficulty of inter-communication with Heavy Batteries. Some telephones had to forgo the use of important trunk observing stations to keep telephones linked up by telephone communication to Divl. Signal Co. Sections at Infantry Brigade Headquarters and these to C.R.A. Insufficiency of establishment of entrenching tools for Batteries in this description of warfare somewhat mitigated by issue of 10 picks & 10 shovels (extra) per Battery.	× Appendix × 6 No. ?
2. a.m. 3rd November 1914 LOCON	Verbal report from G.S.O.(2) MEERUT Division that situation on front of 19th Infantry Brigade very serious and that very active artillery support wanted. During night the 114th Heavy Battery shifted to an alternative position near CHALEON dit L'OISNE. Battery ready for fire at 7 a.m. During night 2nd/3rd 8th Battery searched over German trenches. Battery Commander in touch with Col.'s Dogras and Gurkhas. 8.6's, 8th & 444th Batteries took alarm to hand silenced German Mortar - No. 19. ×	

Army Form C. 2118.

WAR DIARY (continued) VOL IV

INTELLIGENCE SUMMARY.

(Erase heading not required.)

Instructions regarding War Diaries and Intelligence Summaries are contained in F.S. Regs., Part II, and the Staff Manual respectively. Title pages will be prepared in manuscript.

Hour, Date, Place.	Summary of Events and Information.	Remarks and references to Appendices.
7.30 a.m. 3rd November 1914 LOCON	Message sent to G.O.C. 21st Infantry Brigade to instruct 9th Brigade R.F.A. to bring cross fire on to any hostile batteries they cannot locate, shelling 19th Infy Bde. Similar report to G.O.C. 20th Infy Bde with regard to 4th Bde R.F.A.	× Appendix 8(i)
9 a.m.	do. Captain Evans, Black Watch — the C.R.A's airman reported various changes observed in hostile guns.	
10.25 a.m.	do. Orders sent to O.C. 114th Heavy Battery to engage hostile batteries in vicinity of BOIS du BIEZ many aircraft observation.	
10.35 a.m.	do. Orders sent to O.C. 110th Heavy Battery to engage hostile batteries — No.4(a) — vide Appendix 6. This was carried out.	
10.45 a.m.	do. O.C. 2nd Siege Battery was ordered to reconnoitre alternative positions for his battery in vicinity of FESTUBERT and RICHEBOURG ST VAAST so owing to shortage of his flight lyddite shell, he was now reduced to using heavy lyddite and his range consequently reduced to about 4500+. 114th Heavy Battery engaged hostile battery No.22, N.E. of BOIS du BIEZ — observation by aircraft.	× Appendix 6
1.30 p.m.	do.	
3.30 p.m.	do. Orders sent for 37th and 65th Howitzer Batteries to endeavour to locate No.26 near LA QUINQUE RUE between to & No.28 and shell a house + which airman reports many inhabitants & by the Germans; round which airman reports many inhabitants &	
6.30 p.m.	do. Skeleton info 20,000 received + issued to units.	8(a) Appx
7.20 p.m.	do. Report received from 37th Battery that he had put 2 lyddite shells into house No.26 (vide above at 3.30 p.m.) at dusk. 65th Battery reported unable to locate it, orders received after dark, but that he would arrange with 37th for mutual observation of fire at dawn. BEUVRIE Church where 110th Heavy Battery during day the Germans shelled near BEUVRIE Church where 110th Heavy Battery has no observation post, possibly this fire was directed at FRENCH troops in vicinity of BEUVRIE. ×	# Appendix 27

Army Form C. 2118.

WAR DIARY (Continued)
INTELLIGENCE SUMMARY.

(Erase heading not required.)

Vol IX

Instructions regarding War Diaries and Intelligence Summaries are contained in F. S. Regs., Part II, and the Staff Manual respectively. Title pages will be prepared in manuscript.

Hour, Date, Place.	Summary of Events and Information.	Remarks and references to Appendices.
7.30.a.m. 4th November 1914 LOCON	65th Howitzer Battery report light very bad. 8th Battery fired a few rounds to keep down enemy snipers. 114th Heavy Battery in action at daybreak, thick fog, silenced bursts of rifle fire.	
8.50.a.m. do	The enemy appears to be attacking Kemsko with more vigour, night section of 114th Heavy Battery engaged the battery N of village of VIOLAINES after firing a few rounds the shield of N°2 gun broke - putting this gun temporarily out of action.	
12 noon do	65 Howitzer Battery acted in co-operation with the Lincolns, searching fire on target 7b (a new target reported by aeroplane)	× appendix 6
12.30.p.m. do	7th Battery fired at reported gun near cross roads at RICHEBOURG L'AVOUE: 61 Battery fired at same point on information from ?Sgt. Gadivalla that they were being enfiladed.	× appendix 6
1.50.p.m. do	The 2nd Siege Battery was turned on to target Z (Battery) with shrapnel.	× appendix 6
2.30.p.m. do	7th Battery assisted 439th Garhwalis to repulse attack. Shelled target 31 when Garhwalis were attacked. 65th Howitzer Battery on receipt of a message from G.O.C. 20th Infantry Bde. for support against targets 31 (Maxims), 18 (guns) which were heavily engaged by the Seaforths + 139th Garhwalis, engaged these targets with the 9th Brigade, necessitating the 19th + 20th Batteries + 61 Howitzer running up out of their entrenchments for the switch, afterwards were withdrawn for the night to secondary position.	§ appendix 6
2.45.p.m. do	114th Heavy Battery engaged target N°18 (guns) in S.E. corner of BOIS du BIEZ.	# appendix 6
3.6.p.m. do	2nd Siege Battery fired 26 rounds light lyddite at target 8(a) (guns)	# appendix 6
3.30.p.m. do	2nd Siege Battery reported that a light lyddite shell exploded prematurely wounding 2 gunners severely and one officer (one Lieut Moriarty) slightly.	
3.45.p.m. do	61st Howitzer Battery endeavoured to shell target N°19 (Mortar)	* appendix 6
4.30.p.m. do	110 Heavy Battery received orders to move battery to new position during night.	
5.15.p.m. do	Heavy hostile artillery fire on night of 19th Infantry Bde.	
5.30.p.m. do	Infantry fire died down and things appeared quiet. G.O.C. 20th Infy Bde wished for co-operation.	² appendix 9a
9.p.m. do	110 Heavy Battery left LE HAMEL considerable difficulty in getting out of position owing to narrow and greasy mud.	# appendix 6
10.30.P.M. Midnight do	110 Heavy Battery arrived at LES LOBES and occupied a position - ordered about 70° S.E. 109 H. Battery Bde ordered to make a night attack to re-occupy trenches evacuated by 2nd Lincolns. LAHORE Division co-operation. Order sent that no other artillery to fire N of NEUVE CHAPPELLE which (British Infantry) Bde might not clearly.	× appendix 6

Army Form C. 2118.

WAR DIARY (continued) VOL IV

INTELLIGENCE SUMMARY.

(Erase heading not required.)

Instructions regarding War Diaries and Intelligence Summaries are contained in F. S. Regs., Part II, and the Staff Manual respectively. Title pages will be prepared in manuscript.

Hour, Date, Place.	Summary of Events and Information.	Remarks and references to Appendices.
5th November 1914 LOCON		
7-0 a.m.	During early morning the 114th Heavy Battery were marching to new position near LES LOBES and preparing new position there. 7 am 2 guns ready in action, other 2 stuck in edge of a narrow road, were pulled out and disguised — bothered during day by German aeroplanes.	
8-8.30 am	1 Section of 114th Heavy Battery shelled targets 8a and 8b.	× Appendix 6
10.30 am	Ol. 2nd Siege Battery reports LOISNE has shelled (positions of 114th Heavy Battery and 2nd Siege Battery). 66th Battery R.F.A. opened fire in direction of target No 2.5 and silenced enemy.	
11 am	114th Heavy Battery fired 20 rounds at No 2. This provoked a reply from a German × Battery, which searched with 30 rounds for position of 114th Heavy Battery	× This was probably one + the same shelling — possibly slight divergence in times
11.30 am	13th Brigade R.F.A. engaged trenches forward RUE D'OUVERT and members of infantry with observing officers on our trenches reported infantry all day, working well. Ol. Right Sector of Defence (Colonel McC[illegible])	
11.45 am	Ol. 4th Bde R.F.A. reports 37th Battery heavily shelled enemy digging trenches in front of the 1/39th Garhwalis.	
12.17 p.m.	65th Howitzer Battery opened slow rate of fire on trenches in front of RUE D'OUVERT.	
12.30 p.m.	Airman reported to 114th Heavy Battery for observation purposes, and lines were laid out to 2 new targets near VIOLANES.	
1.30 p.m.	114th Heavy Battery engaged targets near VIOLANES and the Distillery; while engaged on these targets which the airman reported correct as to line and range, the battery was subjected to severe shelling from a heavy howitzer (estimated about 8.2) — the range of the battery was found — no casualties no detachments were under cover, but the air bursts hit some men and horses of the Brigade Ammn Col in field beyond. The airman reported the VIOLANES Battery silenced and directed the flash of the Howitzer which had been shelling 114th Heavy Battery according engaged it at × LE HUE, range 9200 × while the airman observed. He put the battery right on so to range and fire. Howitzer ceased firing.	
2. p.m.	37th How Battery attacked 4th Brigade R.F.A. co-operated in action on left of 21st Infantry Bde on their night. 114th Battery had 6 men wounded and four horses killed by fire of heavy German guns while in billet.	

Army Form C. 2118

VOL IV

22

WAR DIARY (continued)

INTELLIGENCE SUMMARY.

(Erase heading not required.)

Instructions regarding War Diaries and Intelligence Summaries are contained in F. S. Regs., Part II, and the Staff Manual respectively. Title pages will be prepared in manuscript.

Hour, Date, Place.	Summary of Events and Information.	Remarks and references to Appendices.
2.30 p.m. 5th November 1914 LOCON	Two shells pitched into No 2 Siege Battery in bivouac - killing 2 gunners, wounding one gunner and one limit conform. Observation impossible owing to heavy mist. Shots were probably overshoots of shells directed at 114th Heavy Battery	
3.10 p.m. do	2nd Siege Battery opened fire on Northern end of RUE D'OUVERT and continued to knock village down, this at request of L'Col DUFFUS acting O.C, R.A. with 21st Infantry Brigade	Appendix 9
3.30 p.m. do	German aeroplane in front of 110th Heavy Battery.	
4 p.m. do	Hostile aeroplane dropped a signal over 28th Battery R.F.A. 5 minutes later the enemy bracketed the battery with 2 rounds of lyddite. Enemy then shortened his range and the 37th Howitzer Battery was heavily shelled by German high explosive shells. One gun right section had shield and both wheels broken, 3 men wounded.	
4.30 p.m. do	Following casualties occurred in the 28th Battery R.F.A. near observation station — wounded MAJOR E.H. PHILLIPS, D.S.O. - killed 2 gunners, one bombardier wounded. MAJOR PHILLIPS had selected a new observing station about 500× S.W of the first which his Captain had occupied during the morning. Returning to his battery with his observing party and having just reached the road, a high explosive shell from enemy burst near the party causing the above casualties. The wounded are doing well.	
6.30 p.m. do	114th Heavy Battery moved to position vacated by 110th Heavy Battery and will be ready to open fire at daybreak tomorrow morning. 114th Battery, I section, remains one day and night intrenched at position close to GIVENCHY Church- enfilading enemy's trenches. Infantry Commander reports doing excellent work.	
6.45 p.m. do	37. How moved out of action to billets near LE TOURET previous to occupying a new position yet to be reconnoitred. This battery has been in action day and night for 12 consecutive days. The 2nd Siege Battery moved after dark to occupy new position near the firing line selected near RUE de CHEVATTE, as owing to the state of the "light" lyddite shell, their effective range has been reduced to about 4500 ✕. Shells to be fired but only day and to night descents in suspect in barrels. The Heavy guns + howitzers moved out +… and the state of the roads has got much worse. The last 24 hours heavy storm.	*Appendix 6 *Appendix 6

Army Form C. 2118.

23

WAR DIARY (continued) VOL IV

INTELLIGENCE SUMMARY.

(Erase heading not required.)

Instructions regarding War Diaries and Intelligence Summaries are contained in F. S. Regs, Part II, and the Staff Manual respectively. Title pages will be prepared in manuscript.

Hour, Date, Place.	Summary of Events and Information.	Remarks and references to Appendices.
5th November 1914 LOCON 10.p.m.	20th Battery R.F.A. fired a few rounds towards the cross roads on the ESTAIRES — LA BASSEE road S.W. of the BOIS de BIEZ.	No.2
11. p.m. do	above operation repeated.	
12 mn. do	above operation repeated. This in the hope of damaging German transport which is reported to frequent this road nightly (by the Infantry).	*Appendix 6
3. am 6th November 1914 LOCON	7th Battery R.F.A. shelled enemy attacking near target N°.31.	
5. am do	In response to heavy musketry fire the 20th Battery opened fire on the enemy opposite our trenches between LAQUINQUE RUE and FESTUBERT.	
6. am do	7th & 66th Batteries shelled trenches in front of left and left centre of 20th Infantry Brigade. Attack was repulsed. During the night the 114th Heavy Battery which had been heavily shelled on the 5th, moved into the position vacated by the 110th Heavy Battery on the 4th at LOISNE. 114th Heavy Battery in action and ready to open fire.	
8. am do	The 2nd Siege Battery also moved into position during the night 5th/6th from LOISNE to near the RUE DES CHAVATTES and by 8.a.m on 6th was in action and wire communication established.	
10. am do	The morning started very thick and foggy and this state of conditions prevailed most of the day, rendering work of aircraft impossible. In fact any observation of artillery fire during the day was quite impossible. 114th Heavy Battery at a range of about 7400* from near LOISNE and the 110th Heavy Battery from its new position near LES LOBES, at about 10,200* each fired 30 rounds lyddite into square 142(J) B.3.d on the rail-skeleton square map 20,000, this area containing targets 47a and 47. During this operation, the position vacated by 114th Heavy Battery last night was shelled by the enemy's big howitzer.	*Appendix 6 *Appendix 27
11. am do	The 9th Brigade R.F.A. (19th, 20th and 28th Batteries) fired 15 rounds each at a rapid rate on the area of targets N°. 8a, 8c and 25.	6 Appendix
12.10. p.m. do	2nd Siege Battery first fired 40 rounds heavy lyddite into square B.14.d of map 142(h)— Sketch squared map 20,000. This square contains targets N°. 8a, 8c and 25— Observation impossible.	

Gulab Singh & Sons, Calcutta—No. 22 Army C.—5.8.14—1,07,000.

Army Form C. 2118
Vol IV

WAR DIARY (continued)
or
INTELLIGENCE SUMMARY.
(Erase heading not required.)

Instructions regarding War Diaries and Intelligence Summaries are contained in F. S. Regs., Part II, and the Staff Manual respectively. Title pages will be prepared in manuscript.

Hour, Date, Place.	Summary of Events and Information.	Remarks and references to Appendices.
4.P.M. 6th November 1914 LOCON	114th Heavy Battery fired 20 rounds lyddite at target No. 2, range about 8000ft, and 110th Heavy Battery fired 20 rounds at target No. 18 at range of 8800ft. Fire opened simultaneously. Observation impossible. Direction by squared map and bearings. This again drew the fire of the German 8.2" howitzer, which put in 30 rounds to the 114th Heavy Battery's late position.	*Appendix 6
5.40.p.m. do	7th Battery shelled trenches in front of 3rd Gurkhas on reinforce to regiment for aid from them.	
8.56 p.m. do	8th Battery shelled ground beyond German trenches to S of 20th Infantry - continued until 7th + 8th Batteries fired on trenches on left centre 1/39th Garhwalis Brigade line infantry had captured.	
9.15. p.m. do	During the day the O.C. 13th Bde R.3. A. reports:- The 2nd Battery endeavoured to shell a "sap" at request of Infantry Commander Right Section, and that the enemy were driven from the trench. 44th Battery moved its billets. 61st Battery fired a few rounds at trenches towards RUE DOUVERT where enemy movement was visible behind houses in the evening. A section of 44th Battery remained in action near GIVENCHY. Major E.H. PHILLIPS, D.S.O., 28th Battery R.3. A. died of wounds received on 5.11.1914.	MB2
7th November 1914 LOCON		
9.30.am. do	Heavy firing during the night opposite 20th Indian Infantry Brigade. Thick and foggy conditions again prevailed though on the whole atmosphere not more promising morning than yesterday. Aircraft observation, however, quite impossible during the morning, when it had been hoped to correct a line for the 110th Heavy Battery and the 2nd Siege Battery. O.C. 114th Heavy Battery heard a howitzer shelling our lines somewhere to the North he therefore endeavoured to create diversion by bringing a section on to LA HUE (target 34)* This appears to have the desired effect.	*Appendix 6
10.a.m. do	7th Battery fired on enemy digging in front of the 1/39th Garhwal Rifles.	
10.10.a.m. do	14th Battery fired on hostile trench No. 31.*	# Appendix 6
11.a.m. do	7th Battery fired on enemy digging in front of the 1/39th Garhwal Rifles.	
12.p.m. do	8th Battery fired on area between LA QUINQUE RUE and RUE de CAILLOUX.	

Army Form C. 2118.

25

WAR DIARY (continued) VOL IV

INTELLIGENCE SUMMARY.

(Erase heading not required.)

Instructions regarding War Diaries and Intelligence Summaries are contained in F. S. Regs., Part II, and the Staff Manual respectively. Title pages will be prepared in manuscript.

Hour, Date, Place.	Summary of Events and Information.	Remarks and references to Appendices.
1. p.m. 7th November 1914 LOCON.	8th Battery registered area between while shields (placed on front side of our own trenches) and got direct hits with percussion on opposite German trenches. This was Right Section of Defence.	
2.30 p.m. do	110th Heavy Battery with aeroplane observation opened fire on H(a)* — fired 8 rounds but owing to mist the line not satisfactorily obtained.	× Appendix 6
3. p.m. do	114th Heavy Battery engaged 8a and 8b on account of a report from 20th Indian Infantry Brigade that hostile fire from direction of these hostile batteries was annoying the Gurkhas.*	× Appendix 6
4.30 p.m. do	114th Heavy Battery fired 20 Lyddite shells at LA HUE on account of message received from C.R.A. 3rd Division that his line was under shell fire which he supposed came from targets 10, 16 and A. C.R.A. ordered LA HUE to be engaged as its position so practically in same line with those mentioned, and it was doubtful that they could reach his line.	× Appendix 10
	12.50 p.m. Message (Appendix 11) received from Meerut Division that 19th Indian Infantry Brigade has been hard pressed, enemy building up firing line — asks for co-operation of artillery. Message (Appendix 12) to G.O.C. 20th Indian Infantry Bde and message (Appendix 13) to G.O.C. 21st Indian Infantry Brigade to ask for co-operation of the Field Artillery grouped with them.	Appendix 11 Appendix 12 Appendix 13
6.15 p.m. do	114th Battery fired on target 31 and between roads S.E. of 31.	
10.45 p.m. do	7th Battery co-operated in repulse of attacks on left front and centre. 114th Battery co-operated and shelled 31.* During the day Major PATERSON Commanding 2nd Battery reported that a form of Periscope adopted by his fitter from the battery helio mirrors has been used successfully by his observation officer in the Infantry trenches. 8th Battery kept up an intermittent fire all night on the German Sap against our trenches in the direction of LA QUINQUE RUE, in accordance with orders of C.L. Group.	Appendix 13(a)

Army Form C. 2118.

26

WAR DIARY (continued) VOL IV
or
INTELLIGENCE SUMMARY.
(Erase heading not required.)

Instructions regarding War Diaries and Intelligence Summaries are contained in F. S. Regs., Part II, and the Staff Manual respectively. Title pages will be prepared in manuscript.

Hour, Date, Place.	Summary of Events and Information.	Remarks and references to Appendices.
10.45 a.m. 8th November 1914 LOCON	Day commenced misty but dry. 114th Battery shelled German observing station. Lieut Pritchard very slightly wounded in the hand.	
11.30 a.m. do	19th Infantry Brigade heard [sound] during the morning and G.O.C. MEERUT DIVISION desired to concentrate fire of heavy guns on NEUVE CHAPPELLE at 11 A.M. and a gun at 11.30 a.m. 110k & 114th Heavy Batteries and 2nd Siege Battery were ordered to co-operate, and C.R.A. 3rd DIVISION also ordered his Heavy Battery to co-operate as well. Airman reported the high explosive shells bursting well in the village. 37ct Howitzer Battery also joined in the bombardment. O.C. 114th H. Battery reported he was trying a front battery [foundation] firing on NEUVE CHAPPELLE but [Battery] engaged German [trench?] where sapping was reported, position of sap being indicated by white shells on our opposing trenches.	X appendix 27
12.10 p.m. do	2nd Siege Battery fired on "The White House" sheet 142 H B13a. The roof and top storey of the house were lifted clean off.	
2. p.m. do	114th Heavy Battery engaged 32, 5, 6A and 17 in rotation.	
3.20 p.m. do	2nd Siege Battery engaged target 8a with aeroplane observation. Confusion caused by another aeroplane which appeared at 3.p.m. and Jena lights near the battery. Line and range accurately found. 65th Battery and 37th Battery shelled target No 26 with good effect. This was a house mound about which the airman had reported a good deal of trenching had taken place quite recently.	+ Appendix 6
5. p.m. do	Enemy were shelling GIVENCHY and 2nd Battery opened fire and silenced hostile guns.	
8. p.m. do	Very heavy firing heard to the North.	
10. p.m. do	Col. 13th Brigade R.J.A. (Lt Colonel TYLER) reports that he got in communication with the FRENCH Artillery Commander in order to employ his fire if necessary - but no necessity arose.	M.9.2

Army Form C. 2118

27

WAR DIARY (continued) Vol IV

Instructions regarding War Diaries and Intelligence Summaries are contained in F. S. Regs., Part II, and the Staff Manual respectively. Title pages will be prepared in manuscript.

INTELLIGENCE SUMMARY.

(Erase heading not required.)

Hour, Date, Place.	Summary of Events and Information.	Remarks and references to Appendices.
1 a.m. 9th November 1914 LOCON	2nd Battery fired 2 bursts of gun fire at request of our Infantry in order to catch the enemy out of the trenches.	Appendix 6
about 1 a.m. do	19th Battery opened on hostile Artillery fire from the direction of Target 7a*	
9 a.m. do	Weather thick and somewhat windy, observation by aircraft impossible. Information received from C.R.A. 3rd Division (telegram) that their trenches were being shelled, and asking for a few rounds to be fired in direction of groups of batteries near SALOME. Orders sent to O.C. 114th Heavy Battery to engage targets 16, 10 and then 34 (portion of big howitzer). At 9.30 am 114th Heavy Battery engaged these targets - firing 34 cyclitte.	*Appendix 14 *appendix 6
9.20 am do	Report from MEERUT Division that the 19th Indian Infantry Brigade that at 8.40 am the Seaforths and Jats trenches were being heavily shelled.	Ø Appendix 15
9.35 a.m. do	Orders sent to O.C. 110th Heavy Battery to engage Target 4†.- This was done at 9.40 a.m.	# appendix 6
10.40 a.m. do	Orders sent to O.C. 114th Heavy Battery to engage Targets 22, 18†, 18a† and 2†	
10.15 a.m. do	114th Battery engaged hostile batteries 18 + 18a.	
10.45 a.m. do	66th " Shelled trenches in front of 2/39th Garhwal Rifles.	
	7th " engaged hostile batteries 18 + 18a	
10.47 a.m. do	Orders sent to 110th Heavy Battery to engage targets 21 + 22.- This was done at 11.30 a.m.	
11 a.m. do	Orders to 2nd Siege Battery to engage Target 23.- This was engaged between 12.25 and 12.50 p.m. Hostile batteries in neighbourhood of BOIS du BIEZ which it was ordered that hostile batteries in neighbourhood of the 19th Infantry Bde.- Observation was most be the batteries that were annoying the 19th Infantry Bde.- Observation was impossible, shooting by map and bearings, which has hitherto always proved very accurate with the new square map. This seemed correct as at 11.40 am. H.Q Bde R.J Aetesports that the night trenches of the Seaforths and 2/39th Garhwal Rifles were being heavily shelled from direction of 18a and 2 or else from 21, 22, + 23. He further reports that the batteries of his Brigade have exhausted ⅓ their hostile batteries but owing to limit the expenditure of 18 pr. ammunition, he could not pay with what results.	ξ Appendix 16

Army Form C. 2118
28

WAR DIARY (continued) VOL IV
INTELLIGENCE SUMMARY.
(Erase heading not required.)

Hour, Date, Place.	Summary of Events and Information.	Remarks and references to Appendices.
11.10 a.m. 9th November 1914 LOCON	37th Battery engaged hostile batteries 18 + 18a.	
11.15 a.m. do	7th Battery shelled German infantry in front of Garhwalis.	Appendix 6
11.45 a.m. do	Detached section of 66th Battery shelled No 2.	
3 p.m. do	2nd Siege Battery fired 4 heavy lyddite at White House to check line and range.	Shot 1427. B13a. Skeleton Sq card m/p 1/20,000 appendix 27.
4.10 p.m. 6 do 4.15 p.m. do	114th Heavy Battery engaged target 18a and 18 simultaneously. 110 do " " 18a and 18 " In accordance with orders sent out to these batteries at 3-5 p.m.	
4.25 p.m. do	37th Battery ranged on new German trenches in front of the Leverbers	
4.35 p.m. do	110th Heavy Battery engaged target 22. } both these were engaged with a rapid rate of fire 114th " " " " 21. } Lieut M.M.M.GRATH 8th Battery & J.P moved in retiring from supply trench. 37th (How) Battery shelled trenches near target 26.	Appendix 6
5 p.m. do	" " " " "	
7.30 p.m. do	" " " " "	
8.15 p.m. do	37th (How) Battery " " " "	No. 89
9.45 a.m. 6 10th November 1914 LOCON	37th Battery fire at a slow rate on new German trench near 26.	65th Howitzer Battery with an officer observer from the Leverdes trench shelled bomb throwers in hostile trenches (appendices 16a + 16b)
10.2 a.m. do	Enemy shelled late position of 114th Heavy Battery apparently with field guns at extreme range	Col 9th Bgr. Q.H. reports enemy were busy shelling RUE du BOIS during the morning
10.35 a.m. do	Very heavy firing to N.E; late position of 114th Heavy Battery again shelled about this time.	
11.30 a.m. do	Col 2nd Siege Battery located smoke of hostile battery about middle of thick line joining squares B14tc and F2a firing N.W. This was engaged 32 rounds of heavy lyddite being fired.	
11.38-a.m do	8th Battery engaged an own opposite to the Black Watch trenches to stop sapping operations. Reports from trenches state fire effective.	Shrapnel Shot statistic. 20.000 appendix 27 142h. SEBI EPA
12. noon do	61st Battery also fired in direction of sap 55 already engaged by 8th Battery.	
12.30 p.m. do	7th Battery shelled trench in front of 2/39th Garhwal Rifles	
12.57 p.m. do		

WAR DIARY (continued) VOL IV
INTELLIGENCE SUMMARY
(Erase heading not required.)

Army Form C. 2118

Hour, Date, Place.	Summary of Events and Information.	Remarks and references to Appendices.
3. p.m. 10th November 1914 LOCON	In accordance with Operation Orders 69, 70 & 72 the 114th & 110th Heavy Batteries and 2nd Siege Battery opened fire simultaneously on NEUVE CHAPELLE, the two former with lyddite at the village itself, latter with shrapnel, which was directed at the large supporting trenches located by airman which is shown roughly in sketch (Appendix 20) by red chalk line "A".	Appendices 17, 18 & 19 Appendix 20
3.45 p.m. do	The above operation was repeated	
5.15 p.m. do	Meerut Division Operation Order No 2 received. C.R.A. sent for and personally explained situation and issued orders to O.C.'s 4th, 8th and 9th Brigades R.F.A. and O.C.'s 110th and 114th Heavy Batteries and 2nd Siege Battery. During the day description of Periscope used by 2nd Battery R.F.A. was received. Also a hint for Infantry use in provision from 18 pr. cartridge cases, at which the battery was still working. The day was very thick and misty and observation very difficult. Observation by aeroplane quite impossible.	✗ Appendix 21 ⊙ Appendix 13a No 2.
12.1.a.m 11th November 1914 LOCON	The bombardment in accordance with MEERUT Division Operation Order No 2 of 10.11.14 (Appendix 21) commenced. The 114th Heavy Battery fired 65 rounds lyddite between 12 and 12.42 a.m. The most Heavy Battery fired 65 rounds lyddite between same hours at a range of 7450* and then after 12.45 a.m. fired a further 12 rounds into the BOIS de BIEZ at 8650*. The 2nd Siege Battery fired 61 heavy lyddite shells into same area at same time, and afterwards 4 rounds heavy lyddite were fired into the BOIS de BIEZ.✗ O.C. 8th Bde R.F.A reports that in accordance with instructions received from C.R.A. he ordered the 28th Battery R.F.A. and 2 batteries of 13th Bde R.F.A. to shell the German trenches on maps ✗ Sheet 142(N) E44ª and E88 and ✗ Sheet 142(J) A47 and d, fire being kept up in bursts of six rounds at ten minutes interval between 12 midnight and 1. a.m. The 2 FRENCH Batteries also co-operated by shelling RUE DOUVERT and ✗ CHAPELLE STE ROCHE P.T.O	Appendix 6 ✳ Appendix 27

Army Form C. 2118.

30

WAR DIARY (continued) VOL IX

INTELLIGENCE SUMMARY.

(Erase heading not required.)

Instructions regarding War Diaries and Intelligence Summaries are contained in F. S. Regs., Part II, and the Staff Manual respectively. Title pages will be prepared in manuscript.

Hour, Date, Place.	Summary of Events and Information.	Remarks and references to Appendices.
8.30 a.m. 11th November 1914 LOCON	under the orders of O.C. 13th Brigade R.F.A. The tactical operation required by this bombardment was satisfactorily accomplished, several houses being knocked down. The continued fusilade along the line drew the German fire, they also disclosed a searchlight and used Star Shell.	
12.5 p.m.	28th Battery R.F.A. opened fire on battery at No 19 which was firing at the time, and made it stop firing.	× Appendix 6.
do	2nd Siege Battery accurately located from its observing station a hostile 6 gun battery in a position judged by him to be ×26; 56 rounds heavy lyddite were fired at this battery.	
12.30 p.m. 1.30 p.m.	Most of the above engaged hostile batteries at 18+18a Battery at 19 × opened fire, but at once ceased when 28th Battery fired a few more rounds at it. 7th Battery shelled new hostile battery recently located at No 40.	
2. P.M.	110th Heavy Battery engaged 2 batteries located at No 2 with 20 rounds lyddite – the 114th Heavy Battery also cooperated in this.	
3 P.M.	11th Heavy Battery turned a section each on to No 22 + 23 × the 110th turned on to 21, and the 2nd Siege Battery a section each on to No. 22 + 23 ×. Fire was opened simultaneously. Observation impossible.	
3.32 p.m.	2nd Siege Battery fired 10 time shrapnel at target No. 14 ×.	
3.45 p.m.	LA COUTURE shelled by hostile heavy artillery. The 110th Heavy Battery observing station in that village. During morning an officer of the Black Watch having reported that they were much molested by snipers and bombs from a house in orchard about ×E8 (142(M))– the O.C. Battery fired through the one & knocked the house about. O.C. 13th Bde R.F.A. reports that during the day the 2nd Battery was employed engaging gaps and trenches towards N end of RUE BOUVERT and the 8th and 61st Batteries were assisting our infantry near the front where our trenches cross LA QUINQUE RUE. A very high wind was blowing all day, which made it impossible for aircraft to	× Appendix 27

Army Form C. 2118

31

WAR DIARY (continued) VOL IV.

or

INTELLIGENCE SUMMARY.

(Erase heading not required.)

Instructions regarding War Diaries and Intelligence Summaries are contained in F. S. Regs., Part II, and the Staff Manual respectively. Title pages will be prepared in manuscript.

Hour, Date, Place.	Summary of Events and Information.	Remarks and references to Appendices.
12th November 1914 LOCON	The day opened much brighter and clearer and hopes were entertained that our aeroplanes would be able to carry out a reconnaissance of the enemy's positions which have probably changed a good deal during the last ten foggy days. A high wind, however, put up and work by aircraft rendered impossible.	
9.45 a.m.	28th Battery R.F.A. opened fire on hostile battery at 7a,* which was shelling RUE du BOIS.	* Appendix 6.
10.35 a.m.	2nd Siege Battery opened fire at target 25.* 28 rounds heavy lyddite being fired. During the month the situated section of the 114th Battery near GIVENCHY was shelled, 2 men being hit.	
11. a.m.	20th Battery R.F.A. shelled German trench near QUINQUE RUE from which loopholes reported trouble with bomb throwers.	
11.12 a.m.	20th Battery R.F.A. saw bomb burst on right of Black Watch trench so fired at house indicated as containing bomb thrower and brought down the roof.	
11.50 a.m.	114th Heavy Battery engaged targets No 10, 16 and 17, which is was thought might have been the batteries that were shelling FESTUBERT during the morning.	
12. noon	8th Battery R.F.A. attempted to engage hostile battery which had been shelling FESTUBERT believed to be in direction of 8a or 25.*	
	110th Heavy Battery was turned on to hostile gun emplacements at 4t.* 7a,* which had ceased firing on being shelled by 28th Battery earlier during the day, again opened fire and was promptly silenced again by 28th Battery.	
12.5 p.m.	2nd Siege Battery opened fire with lime shrapnel on flash of single gun located by its observing officer near old position of N°6a. Enemy's Battery at 25 then commenced firing and the left section of 2nd Siege Battery was switched on to it at 1.50 p.m. with lime shrapnel. After 6 rounds this battery stopped firing – probably 26.* — probably 26"	✗ Appendix 27
1.45 p.m.	65th Howitzer Battery shelled bomb thrower in E 4 a (11.12/h). — probably from A Battery at long range – fired at the old position of 114th Heavy Battery.	
2. p.m.	30 rounds – probably from A Battery at long range – fired at the old position of 114th Heavy Battery.	
3. p.m.	110th Heavy Battery engaged hostile battery at 21,* flashes of which were visible to their observation party. This battery stopped firing after the 63rd round had been fired at it.	
3.15 p.m.	Col. 9th Brigade R.F.A. reports flashes from N° 19 target plainly visible.	
4. p.m.	28th Battery again fired on 7a. Col.9th Bde R.F.A. reports hostile batteries at 40 & 7a apparently silent.	
4.45 p.m.	7a,* 114th + 65th Batteries shelled trenches in front of junction of 139R + 239R Garhwalis.	

Army Form C. 2118.

32

VOL IX.

WAR DIARY (continued)

INTELLIGENCE SUMMARY.

(Erase heading not required.)

Instructions regarding War Diaries and Intelligence Summaries are contained in F. S. Regs., Part II, and the Staff Manual respectively. Title pages will be prepared in manuscript.

Hour, Date, Place.	Summary of Events and Information.	Remarks and references to Appendices.
12th November 1914 LOCON	At 11.30 a.m. Field Marshal LORD ROBERTS inspected representatives of the INDIAN Expeditionary Force at LOCON.	
13th November 1914 LOCON	During the morning "N" Battery R.H.A. were ordered to a position near GIVENCHY by the Indian Corps to co-operate in defence of that locality, especially in conjunction with the FRENCH Batteries there. No available horses however being found for the horses in the vicinity, it was ordered into billet at ESSARS by the G.O.C. MEERUT Division.	
	In accordance with instructions orders by G.O.C. MEERUT DIVISION for a combined shelling of hostile entrenchments to E. of the LA BASSEE - ESTAIRES road near	MR82
8.a.m.	0142(h) B/40C the following batteries opened fire at 8.a.m.:-	⊙ Appendix 2)
	110th Heavy Battery, 114th Heavy Battery, 2nd Siege Battery; the 7th a.m 14th Field Batteries also co-operated.	
8.25 a.m.	28th Battery was ordered to detail a section to neutralize hostile guns at 7a, which yesterday had been shelling horses in the RUE du BOIS in the vicinity of which several of our battery observing stations are located.	× Appendix 6.
9.30 a.m.	61st Battery "searched" for hostile battery at 7t, which was thought to be the battery which shelled the detached GIVENCHY section of the 114th Battery yesterday. Line by the square map. ⊙	
10.30 a.m.	114th Heavy Battery registered trenches near LA BASSEE - ESTAIRES road - O.C. 2nd Siege Battery observing results for the battery from his observing station.	
11.a.m.	Enemy shelled environs of BETHUNE. Fire appeared to come from direction of 33.	
11.30 a.m.	The 110th Heavy Battery also registered this area in a similar manner. Range 6500'-6700'.	
11.35 a.m.	114th Heavy Battery & 2nd Siege Battery engaged targets 2 and 32* - firing 12 rounds at each.	
11.45 a.m.	28th Battery engaged 7a* on account of a hostile shell falling over RUE au BOIS.	

Army Form C. 2118
33

WAR DIARY (continued) VOL IV

INTELLIGENCE SUMMARY.

(Erase heading not required.)

Hour, Date, Place.	Summary of Events and Information.	Remarks and references to Appendices.
11.50 a.m. 13th November 1914 LOCON.	110th Heavy Battery searched for 6a - range 8600ˣ	ˣAppendix 6
12.15 p.m. do	110th Heavy Battery engaged 4.7 with 16 rounds lyddite - range 10,200ˣ Observation impossible	
2. p.m. do	110th Heavy Battery engaged target No 5 firing 20 rounds lyddite at 10,200ˣ 114th Heavy Battery engaged target 14ˣ firing 16 rounds. 2nd Siege Battery opened fire on hostile battery with shrapnel - observation very difficult. Hostile trenches at B114a (142h) were registered.	ˣAppendix 27
2.45 p.m. do	20th Battery fired 23 rounds at trench near 26ˣ said to contain a bomb-thrower, dropping 10 rounds in position indicated by the aeroplane as the spot	ˣAppendix 22
9.5. p.m. do	In accordance with Operation Order No 3 dated 13.11.1914, paragraph 6, the 110th and 114th Heavy Batteries and the 2nd Siege Battery opened fire on hostile trenches in LA BASSEE - ESTAIRES road. This fire was kept up until 12 midnight.	See 2
till 12 m.n. do	The day was misty and wet and it was impossible for aircraft to work. The three batteries of the 4th Brigade R.F.A together with the 65th Howitzer Battery cooperated with the Garhwal Bde in an attack on the German trenches. The Infantry assembly party started at 9 p.m. and at 9.5 p.m. was supported by rapid bursts of fire. From 9.15 p.m. till midnight desultory firing was kept up by three batteries over area containing German trenches.	

WAR DIARY
or
INTELLIGENCE SUMMARY.

Army Form C. 2118
34

Hour, Date, Place.	Summary of Events and Information.	Remarks and references to Appendices.
Midnight 13/14th November 1914 LOCON	The 3 batteries of the H.K. Bde R.F.A. and the 65th Howitzer Battery poured in heavy bursts of fire until 12.10.a.m in order to cover the retirement of working parties. Area for shelling had been pointed out by C.R.A. personally to O.C's Brigades.	+ Appendix 22.
12.15 a.m. 14th November 1914 LOCON	O.C. 4th Bde R.F.A. received information from G.O.C. GARHWAL Brigade that the working party had not effected its retirement and asking for further artillery support. Rate of fire doubled on receipt of a second message from G.O.C. GARHWAL Brigade; firing was kept up until 5 a.m. GARHWAL Brigade reported to C.R.A. that shells from our heavy guns were falling in our trenches. Fire should have stopped by then - no action taken.	
12.40 a.m.	do	Message received from GARHWAL Brigade asking for fire to be continued with lengthened range owing to difficulty in withdrawing.	
12.50 a.m.	do	Orders sent by telephone to O.C. 110th Heavy Battery to continue firing at an increased range. This was done and firing continued until 3.10.a.m	+ Appendix 23
4.10 a.m	do	Message received from MEERUT Division No. G.553 that prisoners captured stated that an attack had been planned at dawn.	
4.38 a.m	do	Informed O.C's 110th & 114th Heavy Battery, 2nd Siege Battery and O.C. 9th Brigade R.F.A. also 37th Battery which was resting in billets at LOCON.	
5.30 a.m.	do	13th Brigade batteries "searched and swept" Eastern half of square E 87 and a (142(h)) to catch enemy concentration.	Appendix 27
9.24 a.m } 10.3 a.m }	do	20th Battery fired at troops visible in N.E. corner of square E 87 (142(h)).	
9.43 a.m	do	The 3 batteries of 9th Bde R.F.A. fired two bursts of falling fire E of LA QUINQUE RUE where information stated enemy to be concentrating.	
10.27 a.m.	do	2nd Siege Battery opened fire with one gun on target 14 with lyddite.	

WAR DIARY (continued) VOL IV
INTELLIGENCE SUMMARY.

(Erase heading not required.)

Army Form C. 2118.

Hour, Date, Place.	Summary of Events and Information.	Remarks and references to Appendices.
11.15 a.m. 14th November 1914 LOCON	28th Battery had high dropping shell fired on its observing station, believed to be target 19A, which was engaged promptly when firing ceased.	+ Appendix 6.
11.30 a.m. do	2nd Siege Battery opened fire on hostile battery E of LE TILLEUT, observation difficult. Both the target & target 14 (Nde 10 37 a.m.) appeared to be just beyond the range of the 6" Howitzer.	
12.30 p.m. do	110th Heavy Battery fired at target 14* by map.	
1. p.m. do	The Pth Battery fired on targets 40* + 6a. Which it was thought had the shelling the detached section at GIVENCHY and 13th Brigade Hd Qrs respectively.	
1.30 p.m. do	114th Heavy Battery engaged target N° 34, while doing this their 2nd position was heavily shelled by enemy.	
3. p.m. do	110th Heavy Battery endeavoured to engage hostile battery at 4(b) with aircraft observation. Result not very satisfactory and work of airmen very difficult owing to the inclement weather. Range about 10,200*.	
3.30 p.m. do	Target N° 14 reported active.	
3.40 p.m. do	2nd Siege Battery shelled two houses on LA BASSEE – ESTAIRES road supposed to be occupied by hostile observing parties with heavy lyddite. 3 or 4 direct hits were obtained.	
3.45 p.m. do	110th Heavy Battery fired 12 rounds lyddite at range of 8160 at house "A" reported to contain hostile observing station. The 6th round reported no range by observing officer.	
4.15 p.m. do	Heavy shrapnel was dropped near 28th Battery.	

Army Form C. 2118.

36

WAR DIARY (continued)

VOL IV

INTELLIGENCE SUMMARY.

(Erase heading not required.)

Instructions regarding War Diaries and Intelligence Summaries are contained in F. S. Regs., Part II, and the Staff Manual respectively. Title pages will be prepared in manuscript.

Hour, Date, Place.	Summary of Events and Information.	Remarks and references to Appendices.
5 a.m. 15th November 1914 LOCON	In accordance with the orders of the G.O.C. MEERUT Division batteries opened fire at 5 a.m. and kept up an intermittent rate of slow fire till 6.30 a.m. in order to forestall any plan for an attack at dawn on the part of the enemy. 110th & 114th Heavy Batteries and 2nd Siege Battery each fired 30 rounds during this period, on areas including hostile trenches near the "White House", and on the LA BASSEE-ESTAIRES road as a searching fire on the BOIS du BIEZ. At the same time the 4th Brigade R.F.A. (7th, 14th & 65th (Howitzer) Batteries) opened fire on trenches to front of the 1st Sqdn and 2nd 39th Garhwalis. The 9th Brigade R.F.A. also opened fire at 5 a.m. on Square F5a and C and Southern half F1c (142(h) Skeleton squared map), in bursts of fire at intervals of from 5 to 10 minutes. The 13th Brigade R.F.A. and the three FRENCH batteries near this position were also ordered to open fire at 5 a.m. on squares E8 and C(142(h)) and A4+(142(J)).	× Appendix 6. ⊙ Appendix 2?
5:20 a.m. do	The 28th Battery R.F.A. was shelled with heavy shrapnel (estimated both), about 30 rounds fired in groups of 3 (3"minutes) at intervals of 5 minutes between groups. Shells all high, but immediately above guns; velocity low and angle of descent steep - impossible to locate direction from whence fired.	
5:30 a.m. do	One section of the 66th Battery in action 400× E of GARHWAL Brigade Headquarters was shelled by 3 German batteries - apparently 5" howitzer, estimated to be firing from near VIOLANES, as the range was judged over 5000×. one fuse picked up set at 22 (long set possible 26).	
9 a.m. do	19th Battery opened fire on target No. located by fire heard to its flanks from observing station (158g). fire also opened on them at 2 and 3 p.m. Observation difficult.	
10 a.m. do	2nd Battery fired on trench strongly occupied by enemy in Square A4a(142(J)) and observation from trenches. 110th and 114th Heavy Batteries simultaneously engaged battery I(c) newly located at LE TILLEUL- fired 30 rounds lyddite each. (10,400× for 110th Heavy Battery). Shooting	× Appendix 6.

Gulab Singh & Sons, Calcutta—No. 22 Army C.—5-8-14—1,07,000.

Army Form C. 2118.

37

WAR DIARY (continued) VOL IV

or

INTELLIGENCE SUMMARY.

(Erase heading not required.)

Instructions regarding War Diaries and Intelligence Summaries are contained in F. S. Regs., Part II, and the Staff Manual respectively. Title pages will be prepared in manuscript.

Hour, Date, Place.	Summary of Events and Information.	Remarks and references to Appendices.
12. noon 15th November 1914. LOCON	Both 110th and 114th Heavy Batteries were turned on to target No. 14 on its newly located position simultaneously with 16 rounds hyddite each. This target was active at commencement of series but ceased fire during series (Range for 110th Heavy Battery 10,800 to 10,800). O.C. 110th Heavy Battery observed line so correct, & it estimated that the battery was at a greater range than that at which shown on m.p.	×Appendix 6
12.27 p.m. do	2nd Siege Battery opened fire on RICHEBOURG Distillery, fired 29 heavy lyddite at it, the 2 large houses there being reduced to stelle.	
1. p.m. do	2nd Siege Battery observed two guns at target No. 25 firing, and switched one gun on to it with light lyddite, but 1 gun still firing at the Distillery. 36 rounds light lyddite fired at target ×25, which was silenced.	
1.58 p.m. do	2nd Siege Battery turned one gun on to target 19 (mortar).	
2.15 p.m. do	110th Heavy Battery engaged target 6(a) which was active - but stopped firing when engaged by 110th, reopened however at 3.15 p.m.	
2.45 p.m. do	2nd Siege Battery turned one gun on to hostile battery located on N.E corner Square F5-a (u×2/h), 5 heavy lyddite being fired and line not range, being obtained. Observation extremely difficult owing to O.P. being so far to a flank. This target has now been fixed by intersection of 3 bearings taken to it.	× Appendix 7
3.15 p.m. do	110th & 114th Heavy Batteries simultaneously opened fire on H(b) - latter firing 12 lyddite and 4 shrapnel; former 16 lyddite. This hostile battery has been fired at many times, but it is well concealed and appears to have head cover (probably howitzers)	
10. p.m. do	Searchlight located by re-section from bearings taken by 3rd Division and 110th Heavy Battery on LA BASSEE road. 110th Heavy Battery engaged it with Shrapnel.	

Army Form C. 2118.

38

WAR DIARY (continued) VOL IV
or
INTELLIGENCE SUMMARY.
(Erase heading not required.)

Instructions regarding War Diaries and Intelligence Summaries are contained in F. S. Regs., Part II, and the Staff Manual respectively. Title pages will be prepared in manuscript.

Hour, Date, Place.	Summary of Events and Information.	Remarks and references to Appendices.
11.30 a.m 16th November 1914 LOCON	Under orders from G.O.C. MEERUT DIVISION 110th & 114th Heavy Batteries and 2nd Siege Battery fired at slow rate till 6 a.m. to frustrate any German offensive.	
5. a.m. do	9th Brigade R.F.A., 13th Bde. R.F.A. & 14th Battery opened fire the same as at 5 a.m. 15th November.	
	37th Battery R.F.A. returned from 3 days rest and took up their former position during the night.	
8.30 a.m. do	8th Battery R.F.A. engaged enemys trenches.	
10.15 a.m. do	20th Battery R.F.A. shelled enemys trenches N.W. of LA QUINQUE RUE.	
10.30 a.m. do	37th Battery verified their lines. 19th Battery engaged 4 gun battery at N. end of 7t.	v appendix 6
11. a.m. do	7th Battery shelled enemys trenches in front of 139th Gurkurahs at request of G.O.C. Infantry Brigade.	
11.30 a.m. do	Information received from 8th Brigade R.F.A. that situation in front of RUE D'OUVERT indicated a general attack. Orders issued to 2nd Siege Battery & 110th Heavy Battery to be prepared to open fire in this direction.	
12. noon do	13th Brigade R.F.A. engaged enemy massing in front of QUINQUE RUE, and two FRENCH batteries searched RUE D'OUVERT. 65th Battery shot at ovens going up haystack.	
12.28 p.m. do	9th Brigade R.F.A. engaged enemy massing in front of QUINQUE RUE.	
12.35 p.m. do	110th Heavy Battery engaged hostile cavalry massing in front of LA QUINQUE RUE.	
12.45 p.m. do	114th Battery fired on Germans digging new observing station from trenches in front of 1st and 2nd 39th Garhwalis. 1 section 110th Heavy Battery engaged in counter battery search for 8a, 8b and 25.	x appendix 6

Gulab Singh & Sons, Calcutta—No. 22 Army C.—5.8.11—1,07,000
x 34. One section of same battery searched for 8a, 8b and 25.

Army Form C. 2118.

39

WAR DIARY
or
INTELLIGENCE SUMMARY.

(Erase heading not required.)

Instructions regarding War Diaries and Intelligence Summaries are contained in F. S. Regs., Part II, and the Staff Manual respectively. Title pages will be prepared in manuscript.

Hour, Date, Place.	Summary of Events and Information.	Remarks and references to Appendices.
16th November 1914 LOCON 1.16 p.m	65th Battery R.F.A engaged bomb throwers in front of Leicesters at request from Infantry.	
1.35 p.m	37th Battery engaged 7+ with lyddite.	
1.55 p.m	19th Battery engaged farm buildings containing snipers in front of left section BAREILLY Brigade.	
2. p.m	8th Battery R.F.A shelled enemys trenches near QUINQUE RUE. 1 gun 65th Battery engaged bomb throwers in front of Leicesters.	
2.40 p.m	20th Battery searched an area at neighbourhood of BAREILLY Brigade	
3. p.m	65th Battery engaged one gun 500×E of 26.	+Appendix 6.
3.30 a.m	Target 40 was observed to open fire.	
3.50 p.m	114th Battery R.F.A. shelled 8(c).×	
4. p.m	114th Heavy Battery commenced moving to new position at LES FACONS.	
4.30 p.m	7th Battery R.F.A shelled 8a.× 37th Battery + 114th Battery shelled 25, whole flankers were visible. One gun 110th Heavy Battery moved to new position about 500×S+ came into action and was ready to open fire in one hour.	
5.30 p.m	19th Battery again shelled battery at N. end of 7J.×	
	"L" "N" Battery R.H.A spent day with Oc 19th Battery R.F.A preparatory to relieving him. 61st Battery tried to fire down a house close in front of left section BAREILLY Brigade trenches but the house was empty. One gun of GIVENCHY Section of 111th Battery moved to new position. Bomb gun cast for 2nd Battery at BETHUNE. 66th Battery not engaged. Platforms given much trouble to Heavy Batteries. 114th Heavy Battery spent from 8 a.m to 6 p.m improving their platforms. 4th Brigade R.F.A instructed to make arrangements to locate search lights by reflection from magnetic bearings + to engage them at once when located. Flight lines for all heavy batteries on RUE D'OUVERT. One section 110th H.B on 44T and 2nd Liege Battery on 39.	

Army Form C. 2118.

Vol IV

WAR DIARY (continued)
INTELLIGENCE SUMMARY.
(Erase heading not required.)

Instructions regarding War Diaries and Intelligence Summaries are contained in F. S. Regs., Part II, and the Staff Manual respectively. Title pages will be prepared in manuscript.

Hour, Date, Place.	Summary of Events and Information.	Remarks and references to Appendices.
16th November 1914 LOCON		
9.p.m.	114th Battery R.F.A. opened slow rate of fire on trenches in front of left flank of GARHWAL Brigade.	
9.15.p.m.	9th Bde. R.F.A. and both Howitzer Battery fired bursts of rapid fire in allotted areas to cover local counter attacks - by 11.45.p.m. the movement was completed.	
9.40.p.m.	One section of 114th Battery turned on to enemys searchlight seen on the LA BASSEE - ROUGE CROIX road.	
11.30.p.m.	7th Battery on attack of Germans on flank of Garhwal Brigade supported by F.A.	MR 9
	During night 16th/17th the second gun of detached section of 44th Battery at GIVENCHY has moved to new position. During the 17th the position vacated by this section was shelled by the enemy.	+ Appendix 6.
6.a.m. 17th November 1914 LOCON	114th Heavy Battery in new position at LES FACONS, working at improving gun platforms.	
	19th Battery R.F.A. relieved by "N" Battery R.H.A. - 19th moved into billets at ESSARS for 3 days rest	
10.10.a.m.	One section of 20th Battery detailed to neutralize target 70.	
11.a.m.	110th Heavy Battery engaged No.14 which was active at the time 10,800 range it stopped firing	
12.30.p.m.	110th Heavy Battery took on House "A" fired 10 rounds lyddite - last round a direct hit	
1.p.m.	114th H.B. gun platform for second section ready.	
1.10.p.m.	110th H.B. engaged 40 (?25) no. gd. fire 6700. 2 lyddite 11 shrapnel	
3.17.p.m.	2nd large batton fired at target 40.	
3.30.p.m.	Target No.14 being active was engaged by 110th H.B. 3rd round fired at hit	
11.30.p.m.	114th Battery fired at a searchlight and fired no more, presumably	

Army Form C. 2118.

WAR DIARY (continued) VOL IV
or
INTELLIGENCE SUMMARY.
(Erase heading not required.)

Instructions regarding War Diaries and Intelligence Summaries are contained in F. S. Regs., Part II, and the Staff Manual respectively. Title pages will be prepared in manuscript.

Hour, Date, Place.	Summary of Events and Information.	Remarks and references to Appendices.
17th November 1914. LOCON		
4.5 p.m.	On arrival, the 2nd round opened to front east for the air ranges of 4000x 7th Battery fired at Kerriams digging.	
6.45 p.m.	13th Brigade R.F.A. only left 8th Battery in action — at 6.45 p.m. the Centre section of the defence reported that no more hostile fires on and the 8th Battery and French batteries were called on to cover its front with fire — this was done.	NB.8
11 p.m.	7th Battery fired at a searchlight reported in the front of the East Lancs.	
18th November 1914. LOCON	A sharp frost during night ad roads and puddles all frozen in the early morning.	
8.25 a.m.	7th Battery fired a few rounds at horses in B14c — 142(h) — likely observation stations.	Appendix 2
11 a.m.	110th Heavy Battery engaged hostile battery at 25°. Range by map 8750x — but range fired 9600x — possibly due to high wind.	
11.20 a.m.	9th Brigade R.F.A. received orders to engage enemies detached guns at F5a, F5b and F1c — 142(h). N Battery R.H.A., 20th Battery R.F.A., 28th Battery R.F.A. & 65th How Battery were allotted tasks accordingly.	Appendix 6
12.10 p.m.	114th Heavy Battery with aircraft observation, fired at 445-yards front, some confusion own aeroplane — 3 of our own up.	
1.45 to 2 p.m.	8th & 114th Batteries fired bursts of fire in connection with temporary withdrawal of our own infantry from their forward trenches to allow of a bombardment by the 23rd Howitzers of certain houses very nearby our own lines. This was repeated between 2.45 + 3/5 p.m. During this period the 61st Howitzer Battery bombarded the house mentioned and its surroundings. 110th Heavy Battery engaged hostile 6″ Howitzer (4gun) Battery at LE HUE who was active during the day, it stopped firing after 6 shots from the 110th — though latter estimated that its range was short of the enemy.	
2.10 p.m.	By request of Col Lancaster, 20th Battery	
2.25 p.m.	1st Hospital Battery opened fire on 2 guns near cross roads in F5a — 142(h) and Colonel Min.	

WAR DIARY (continued)
INTELLIGENCE SUMMARY.

Army Form C. 2118.
VOL IV
42

(Erase heading not required.)

Hour, Date, Place.	Summary of Events and Information.	Remarks and references to Appendices.
2.30 p.m 18th November 1914 LOCON	At request of Black Watch, German sap in front of left section fired on by 20th Battery	
3 p.m do	2nd Siege Battery noticed No. 25 in action - turned one gun on to it with slight hydrate and silenced it.	
3.45 p.m do	110th Heavy Battery engaged No. 22 with aircraft observation. Fire reported left and 400 yards short	*Appendix 6.
4 p.m do	7th Battery shelled enemy digging in trenches.	
8.30 p.m do	7th Battery shelled enemy searchlight near centre pt of square B10R.1142(h) on the road after 6 rounds the searchlight disappeared	
11.20 p.m do	114th Battery shelled enemy trenches to keep down their musketry fire. Infantry report this had the desired effect.	MR9
6 a.m. 19th November 1914 LOCON	Very quiet and hazy.	
9 a.m do	Airman over 114th Heavy Battery but reported too thick for observation.	
10.30 a.m do	110th Heavy Battery turned left section on to L E HVC (34*) which was reported active. Fire reported correct - range doubtful.	
11 a.m do	Airman (Lieut Barrett R.F.A.) again tried to range 114th Heavy Battery by observation but still too thick to observe.	
12 noon do	An attempt was made to correct line of 114th Heavy Battery by observing offices of 114th Heavy Battery - nothing the C.R.A's office as a transmitting station - 10 rounds were fired but snow falling observation became impossible	
12.15 p.m } 2.30 p.m } do	2d th Battery R.F.A. fired occasional rounds at German sap NW corner of E 87-142(h)	
12.30 p.m do	63rd Howitzer Battery engaged the "Wattle Sam" in square F1C-142(h) & obtained a direct hit. This single gun in hostile infantry trenches had caused considerable annoyance for 2 days.	⊙ Appendix 27

Army Form C. 2118

43

WAR DIARY (continued) VOL IV
INTELLIGENCE SUMMARY.

(Erase heading not required.)

Instructions regarding War Diaries and Intelligence Summaries are contained in F.S. Regs., Part II, and the Staff Manual respectively. Title pages will be prepared in manuscript.

Hour, Date, Place.	Summary of Events and Information.	Remarks and references to Appendices.
12.45 p.m. 19th November 1914. LOCON	110th Heavy Battery engaged hostile battery 2.5" which was active, with 30 rounds lyddite - bursts of fire being employed, this battery stopped firing - Range 9800".	
2.15 p.m. do	Owing to very thick mist and snow falling, 20th Battery unable to engage hostile battery shelling our infantry lines.	
	General 19.11.14	
	It was very unfortunate that snow fell during the day, and that misty conditions generally prevailed, as there were 3 aircraft temporarily at the disposal of the C.R.A.	
	During the day the 110th Battery R.F.A. was withdrawn for 3 days rest and proceeded to AVELETTES, being relieved by the 19th Battery, which had been resting for 3 days at ESSARS.	
	The 61st Howitzer Battery was also withdrawn and went into billets at LOISNE, for 3 days rest being relieved temporarily by one section of the 37th Howitzer Battery.	
	The position vacated by the detached section near GIVENCHY was shelled by the enemy during the day - this Section is now at BURBURE, S. of the canal.	
	The 61st Howitzer Battery moved to a new position about 800° further West.	
	The 114th Battery also occupied a new position about 300° N.W. of the former position.	
9 p.m. 19th November 1914. LOCON	19th Battery fired on enemy's trenches in front of 2/3rd Gurkhas. All batteries of 13th Brigade R.F.A. remained in action during the night with orders to cover squares A84 - 142(J) on account of a report that enemy were in numbers at WAVRIN and active near and N. of LA BASSEE.	Appendix 2)
20th November 1914. LOCON	Day opened very misty and thick. The light fall of snow all frozen hard. Chance of observation during the day poor. 19th Battery returned from "rest" to the 20th Battery position, registered Zones so far no light permitting.	
10 a.m. do	8th Battery located and fired on the gun which normally shells FESTUBERT - Target 7a, in centre of square F57-(142/H).	

Gulab Singh & Sons, Calcutta—No. 22 Army C.—5-8-14—1,07,000.

Army Form C. 2118.

44

WAR DIARY (continued)
or
INTELLIGENCE SUMMARY.

VOL IV

(Erase heading not required.)

Instructions regarding War Diaries and Intelligence Summaries are contained in F. S. Regs., Part II, and the Staff Manual respectively. Title pages will be prepared in manuscript.

Hour, Date, Place.	Summary of Events and Information.	Remarks and references to Appendices.
12.30.p.m. 20th November 1914. LOCON	34 reported active - by sound - So 2 Salvoes fired at it. 114th Heavy Battery engaged target 34ˣ firing 6 rounds by map bearing	ˣ Appendix 6
2.15.p.m. do	At request of O.C. 114th Gurkha Rifles some men seen N.W. of target 39 were shelled - 17 Heavy Lyddite fired, effect appeared good.	
2.30 p.m. do	114th Heavy Battery started to engage 42 with air-man, but owing to an aero hostile aeroplane had to descend.	
2.35.p.m. do	114th Heavy Battery endeavoured to engage 34ˣ using 110th Heavy Battery's observation officers, communication through C.R.A. only 6 rounds fired as unfortunately telephone communication broke down.	
3.30. P.M do	Airman arrived for 110th Heavy Battery and proceeded to direct fire on to target 25ˣ 14 rounds fired - Range 9800ˣ, as very high wind probably accounted for additional elevation required.	
	During the day fire of Major Paterson's 4 bomb guns were used in the trenches by an R.E. Officer; 31 rounds were fired, and the bombs and guns worked well.	
10. a.m 21st November 1914. LOCON do	Hard frosty morning. 37th Howitzer Battery fired on guns located on the dividing line F5a and J(142(h)); after a few rounds lyddite the battery stopped firing.	
" + onwards do	61st Howitzer Battery firing at an area containing houses and works between centre and left sections of Defence, in order to destroy these houses. Observing officer had our own Infantry trenches. One house was set on fire and another knocked about.	ⓒ Appendix 27
10.48 a.m do	2nd Siege Battery checked and registered line and shelled RICHEBOURG Distillery, Ledi.- Shelled house the horses in F17 (142(h)) where airman had located horses yesterday	
12. noon do	110th Heavy Battery fired 14 rounds at LE HUE (34ˣ) which was active and stopped the battery firing.	
12. noon +1.p.m do	37th Battery engaged German mechanical transfer which cover be seen thrown & into Trench G.2458/1-1.107.000 earth on N. side of LA QUINQUE RUE in N.E. corner of Square E.8t (142(h)).	ⓒ

Gulab Singh & Sons, Calcutta—No. 22

Army Form C. 2118

45

WAR DIARY (continued) Vol IV
or
INTELLIGENCE SUMMARY.

(Erase heading not required.)

Instructions regarding War Diaries and Intelligence Summaries are contained in F. S. Regs., Part II, and the Staff Manual respectively. Title pages will be prepared in manuscript.

Hour, Date, Place.	Summary of Events and Information.	Remarks and references to Appendices.
1 p.m. 21st November 1914 LOCON	110th Heavy Battery endeavoured to engage LE HUC (34) with observation from 110th Heavy Battery's O.P. in RUE du BOIS. 20 rounds were fired but owing to the extreme difficulty of observation the range was not found.	×Appendix 6
1.30 p.m. do	A German bi-plane was seen to fall near LE TOURET village, much men from several batteries were said to capture it. This was effected.	
2 p.m. do	LE HUC (34) Battery reopened fire, but 110th Heavy Battery fired 14 more rounds at it and it stopped.	
3.15 p.m. do	110th Heavy Battery engaged target 25 with aeroplane observation – range obtained.	
4.30 p.m. do	Some German howitzer shell fell on road running East and West just N of the 8th Battery position. 4 men of this battery were wounded – two severely.	
11.35 p.m. do	Information received that General JOUBERT expected an attack on GIVENCHY during the night. The 13th Brigade R.F.A, the French batteries at LE PLANTIN and the BURBURE section of 44th Battery were ordered to stand ready to cover the front of GIVENCHY. Orders were also given to the 110th & 111th Heavy Batteries and Siege Battery to be prepared to bring a cross fire in front of GIVENCHY and along the RUE DOUVERT should need arise.	
9.15 a.m. 22nd November 1914 LOCON	2nd Battery R.F.A. fired on German trenches at request of O.C. 58th Rifles	
9.40 a.m. do	110th Heavy Battery engaged hostile battery 25× with aeroplane observation – Operation delayed considerably by a German aeroplane overhead. Centre of effect reported slightly plus.	
10.30 a.m. do	Detached section of 44th Battery near BURBURE fired at German S.P.	
11.30 a.m. do	110th Heavy Battery fired 7 rounds at German opening station on large house at distillery cross roads. B147 (142/h), range 9,600×	O Appendix 27

Army Form C. 2118

46

WAR DIARY (continued) VOL. IV
or
INTELLIGENCE SUMMARY.

(Erase heading not required.)

Instructions regarding War Diaries and Intelligence Summaries are contained in F. S. Regs., Part II, and the Staff Manual respectively. Title pages will be prepared in manuscript.

Hour, Date, Place.	Summary of Events and Information.	Remarks and references to Appendices.
11.45 a.m. 22nd November 1914 LOCON	110th Heavy Battery engaged mobile batteries at 8a and 8b with aeroplane observation - range at the practically found - zero on 8a being reported slightly plus and left.	* Appendix 6.
12.25 p.m. do	37th Howitzer Battery fired at the White House (39).	
12.50 p.m. do	114th Heavy Battery engaged gun emplacements at 4t, fired 16 rounds by map and bearings. 2nd Siege Battery registered and re-checked various lines.	
1.15 p.m. do	37th Howitzer Battery engaged target 25*	
1.30 p.m. do	114th Heavy Battery engaged target 41* by map and bearings and then 42*	
3 p.m. do	110th Heavy Battery fired 2 rounds battery fire at target 25* at slightly reduced range. 114th Heavy Battery fired on targets 43 & 41, so they thought, with aeroplane observation, the airman flying over them and firing the normal lights. Unfortunately this was the aeroplane observing for the 2nd Siege Battery, the airman arranged for 110th Heavy Battery having been sent for a tactical reconnaissance by the Corps. It would seem advisable if practicable, when 2 or more aeroplanes are working for batteries in a confined area that some distinguishing flag or streamer should be flown or that aircraft of a very marked variety be employed when possible, observer mindful of this had are apt to err. In this case 114th Heavy Battery thinking their line and range observer correct fired a considerable number of rounds at those targets in order to destroy them. 2nd Siege Battery with aeroplane observation engaged in target 6x, airman gave line and range correct - one direct hit being recorded. CANTELEUX was then registered with airman observing, this latter with a view to bringing fire in front of GINENCHY by the end of a shoot attack there. Those were the two series, the results of which were to unfortunately

WAR DIARY (continued) VOL IX

Army Form C. 2118

42?

INTELLIGENCE SUMMARY.
(Erase heading not required.)

Hour, Date, Place.	Summary of Events and Information.	Remarks and references to Appendices.
3.50 p.m. 22nd November 1914 LOCON	Mistake as thrown by the 114th Heavy Battery. 110th Heavy Battery fired battery fire and salvos at 25ˣ with slight charge of elevation and range (27 rounds). The observer in aeroplane reported one direct hit on hostile gun emplacements at 25ˣ.	×Appendix 6
3.30 p.m.	During the day the batteries of the 9th Brigade R.G.A. shelled various houses containing snipers and observing stations, also sap-heads with food months - several of these houses been demolished.	
10. p.m.	114th Battery shelled two houses used as observation posts on the LA BASSÉE-ESTAIRES road near 6a and 6c.	
10. p.m.	7th Battery engaged same houses as above.	NR25
9 a.m. 23rd November 1914 LOCON	114th Heavy Battery fired 6 rounds at 42ˣ. 13th Brigade R.G.A. engaged enemy in front of left of left section BAREILLY Brigade — continued to 12.30 p.m.	
9.25 a.m.	Message received from Lt Colonel DUFFUS from GORRE that our white section were driven from our first trenches in the centre, and that the situation was reported as critical.	
9.30 a.m.	114th Heavy Battery engaged 21ˣ and 42ˣ.	
9.50 a.m.	37th Battery shelled 36ˣ.	
10 a.m.	110th Heavy Battery shelled RUE D'OUVERT.	
10.10 a.m.	37th Battery engaged 7.C	
10.40 a.m.	114th Battery engaged same observing posts as last night - Houses burnt & destroyed.	
10.45 a.m.	2nd Siege Battery engaged 6a with our gun and RUE D'OUVERT with a section.	
11.30 a.m.	114th Battery engaged flashes near 2.5ˣ observation difficult.	
12.5 p.m.	9th Bde R.G.A. with "N" Battery R.H.A. and 65th Battery shelled the area in front	

Army Form C. 2118

48

WAR DIARY (continued) VOL IV

or

INTELLIGENCE SUMMARY.

(Erase heading not required.)

Instructions regarding War Diaries and Intelligence Summaries are contained in F. S. Regs., Part II, and the Staff Manual respectively. Title pages will be prepared in manuscript.

Hour, Date, Place.	Summary of Events and Information.	Remarks and references to Appendices.
12.30 p.m. 23rd November 1914 LOCON	If the left and left centre of the BAREILLY Brigade 2nd and 110th Batteries shelled German infantry advancing against centre section of BAREILLY Brigade who had been forced back.	Appendix 6
1.25 p.m. do	110th Heavy Battery again shelled RUE D'OUVERT.	
1.40 p.m. do	110th Heavy Battery endeavoured to engage 34th but observation too difficult. 2nd Siege Battery shelled RUE D'OUVERT.	
2.10 p.m. do	110th Heavy Battery engaged RUE D'OUVERT with slow rate of fire.	
3 p.m. do	7th Battery engaged trenches on left front of battery. 2nd and 8th Batteries turned fire on Germans in front of BAREILLY Brigade centre, going to rapid rate of fire from 4.65 and increased range at 4.30. when counter attack was delivered. 110th Battery shelled trenches evacuated by BAREILLY BRIGADE and increased range at 4.30 p.m.	
3.30 p.m. do	9th Brigade R.F.A. "N" Battery R.H.A. and 65th Battery supported counter attack by BAREILLY Brigade. 65th Howitzer Battery shelling trenches evacuated by the centre section of the defence - fire rapid from 4.6 - 5 p.m.	
4.30 p.m. do	4th Brigade R.F.A. batteries supported counter attack by BAREILLY Brigade near QUINQUE RUE.	
4.35 p.m. do	114th Heavy Battery engaged 41.	
4.30 p.m. do	110th Heavy Battery shelled RUE D'OUVERT and searched ground behind it with alternate bursts of rapid and steady fire. 2nd Siege Battery searched RUE D'OUVERT with one gun and area round 26" as far as 39 with a section.	
4.45 p.m. do	114th stopped firing.	
5.25 p.m. do	110th " "	
5.40 p.m. do	13th Brigade R.F.A. ceased firing.	
6.5 p.m. do	2nd Siege Battery stopped firing	
6.29 p.m. do	9th Brigade R.F.A. stopped firing.	

Army Form C. 2118

WAR DIARY (continued) VOL IV
INTELLIGENCE SUMMARY.
(Erase heading not required.)

Instructions regarding War Diaries and Intelligence Summaries are contained in F. S. Regs., Part II, and the Staff Manual respectively. Title pages will be prepared in manuscript.

Hour, Date, Place.	Summary of Events and Information.	Remarks and references to Appendices.
8.10 P.M. 23rd November 1914. LOCON.	9th Brigade R.F.A. "N" Battery R.H.A. and 65th Battery engaged counter attack by Germans on centre of BAREILLY Brigade continuing to 8.30 P.M. when attack appeared to have ceased.	WBS
24th November 1914 LOCON	The MEERUT Division were to have been relieved by the LAHORE Division at 10 A.M., but owing to the situation in the centre of the Right Brigade, the change was ordered to stand fast by the Corps Commander until the normal situation had been established. About 11 A.M news were received that the whole of the trenches that had been taken by the Germans had been recaptured by us and were now occupied by our own troops. Orders were now given for the command to be handed over at 2 P.M and this was carried out. C.R.A of LAHORE Division takes over command from the C.R.A. MEERUT Division. The 110th Heavy Battery were relieved during the morning by the 109th Heavy Battery (LAHORE Division), and moved into billets at PACAUT, but the following units of the MEERUT Division were left temporarily under the command of the C.R.A. LAHORE Division:— 4th Brigade R.F.A. 9th Brigade R.F.A. 13th Brigade R.F.A. 8th (Howitzer) Brigade R.F.A. 110th Heavy Battery R.G.A. Divisional Ammunition Column. Arrangements were made for the relief of these units on arrival of others from INDIA. GENERAL About 100 German prisoners were captured when the trenches were retaken, also 3 maxim guns and a trench mortar. A certain amount of useful information was obtained from some of the prisoners. Complimentary message now received from Commander in Chief on the successful counter attack.	*Appendix 2 LL* WBS

Army Form C. 2118

50

WAR DIARY (corrected) VOL IX

of

INTELLIGENCE SUMMARY.

(Erase heading not required.)

Hour, Date, Place.	Summary of Events and Information.	Remarks and references to Appendices.
25th November 1914 LOCON	MEERUT Division notes. During the day the 9th Brigade R.F.A. was relieved by the 5th Brigade R.F.A of the LAHORE Division, the former then went into billets at ROBECQ.	NBS Appendix 25
26th November 1914 LOCON.	56th Howitzer Battery R.F.A joined the MEERUT Division (vide appendix 25) and went into billets at HARISOIS. 110th Heavy Battery moved into billets at CORAT MALO 500x W. of LOCON. 13th Brigade R.F.A was relieved by the 18th Brigade R.F.A of the LAHORE Division, the former proceeded to its billets at ROBECQ.	NBS
27th November 1914 LOCON.	8th Howitzer Brigade R.F.A. left to rejoin the II Corps, also the 37th Battery attached to the LAHORE Division, vide appendix 25	NBS
28th November 1914 LOCON.	MEERUT Division resting.	NBS
29th November 1914 LOCON	do.	NBS
30th November 1914	MEERUT Division notes. Operation Orders issued in connection with MEERUT Division R.A relieving the LAHORE Division R.A. The 4th Brigade R.F.A and MEERUT Divisional Ammunition Column remained in action with the LAHORE Division R.A. during the rest period.	*Appendix 26 NBS

W. Sepp Frank
Major R.A
for C.R.A. Meerut Division

30.11.14.

APPENDIX. 6(a)

To The
    Adjutant,
        4th Brigade R.F.A.

Sir,
    I have the honour to report that yesterday Captain L. DOUGLAS VERNON of the battery under my command laid a telephone wire to the forward trenches of the Leicester Regiment. Whilst observing for me he was hit by a shrapnel bullet in the forearm, the bullet breaking the bone. I understand he continued to observe for me throughout the day, and by his remaining at his post I was enabled to carefully and accurately range on about 700 yards extent of German trenches and also shell a house used by the enemy as a "collecting house". Captain VERNON did not report to me that he was wounded until all my ranging was completed. He had, I believe, lost a good deal of blood and was in severe pain, and his devotion to duty, I think, calls for special mention. The event above described occurred on the 1st November 1914.

                I have the honour to be,
                      Sir,
                Your obedient servant,

                (sd) E. Harding Newman, Major
2nd November 1914.   Commdg 37th Battery R.F.A.

To,
    The Brigade Major R.A.
        Meerut Division.

    I should like the attention of the C.R.A. drawn to this case, which shows a high degree of courage and devotion to duty.

                sd. L.A.C. GORDON. Lt Colonel
2nd November 1914.   Royal Field Artillery.

To,
    The D.A.A.G., Meerut Division.

    Forwarded for the information of the G.O.C. Meerut Division, and with a recommendation of Captain L. DOUGLAS VERNON's conduct being brought to the notice of the Field Marshal Commander-in-Chief.

                sd A.B. Scott, Brig:General.

3rd November 1914. Commanding Royal Artillery, Meerut Divn

MESSAGES & SIGNALS.

Appendix 7

Army Form C 2123.

(Duplicate.)

Rec 12.35 a.m.

Service Instructions. IHQ

Handed in at the .... Office at 11.55 P.M. Received here at 12.22 A.M.

TO: MEERUT Division

Sender's Number	Day of Month	In reply to Number	A. A. A.
54/6 K	30/10/14	—	

General Headquarters wires no 18 p[o]r ammunition available for issue your division at railhead tomorrow

To C.R.A. I.G.A. 16
Passed for information

12.45 a.m.

FROM: INDIAN Corps
PLACE:
TIME:

MESSAGES, SIGNALS AND FIELD TELEGRAPHS.

Army Form C. 2121. Modified for India.

No. of Message 43

Prefix **SG** Code **19A**
Office of Origin and Service Instructions. **ZIU**

Words **49** Charge **1**

Sent At ___ m. To ___ By ___

(X) For Stamps. **APPENDIX 8**

Recd. at **9.45** m.
Date ___
From **ZIU**
By **Pte Schofield A**

NOTHING TO BE WRITTEN BY THE ADDRESSER ABOVE THIS LINE.

To: CRA MEERUT DIVN LOCON

Sender's Number	Day of Month	In reply to number	AAA
9851	second		

19th Indian Infty Bde reports biggr guns and shrapnel have got onto their trenches AAA Artillery support urgently required AAA Enemy also advancing against Second Gurkhas AAA Can try if your batteries assist AAA if so open at once

FROM: GEN STAFF
Place ___
Time ___

(Y) The above may be forwarded as now corrected.
(Z) ___
Class of Message ___

Countersignature of Censor or Authorising Officer. Signature of addresser and his instructions, vide reverse.

* This line should be erased if not required.

A Schofield Pte

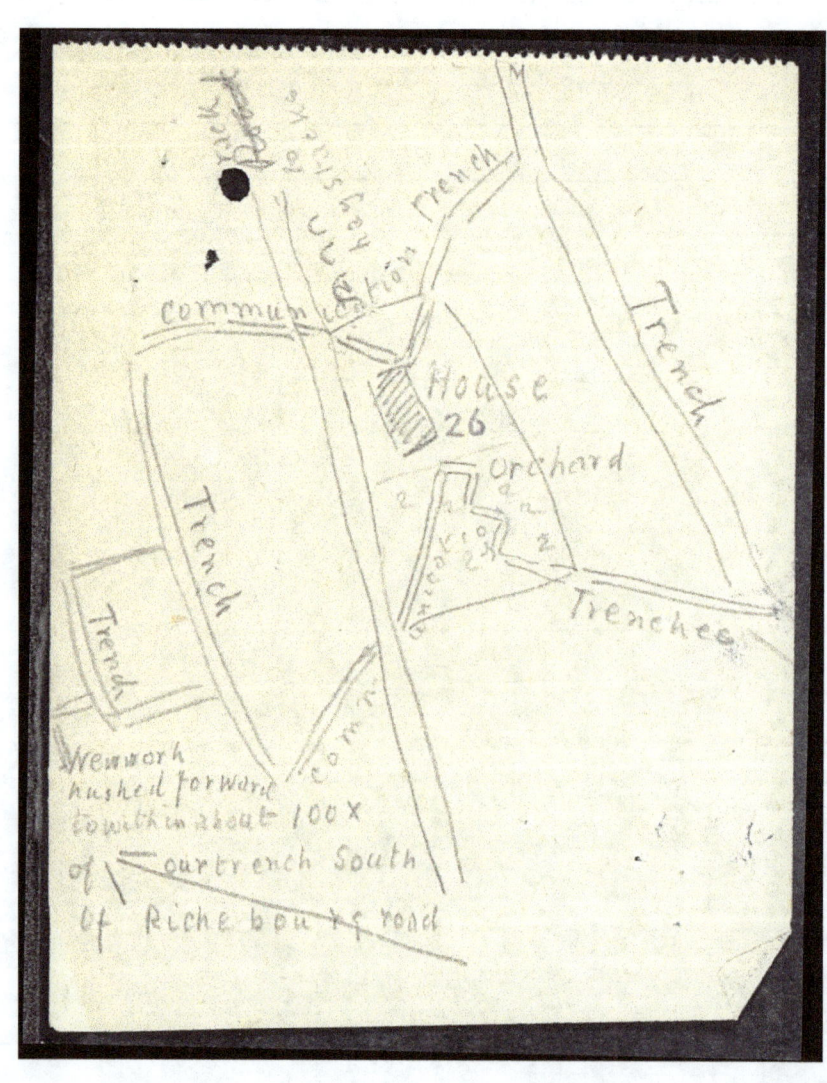

APPENDIX 8(a)

Small sketch
showing layout Nº 26
(with Lieut Macpherson)

MESSAGES, SIGNALS AND FIELD TELEGRAPHS.

Army Form C. 2121. Modified for India.   APPENDIX 8(i)

TO: G.O.C. 21st Infantry Brigade

Day of Month: 3rd Nov.

12 RA(2) Please instruct any spare batteries of ninth artillery brigade Infantry to co-operate with 19th cross fire brigade by bringing guns on to any hostile they locate shelling latter

FROM: CRA
Time: 7.30 a.m.

Appendices to Diary
2nd S
R.A. Division
from 1st - 11 14
to 30 July 14
Volume 6
Ap - 6 -

APPENDIX 28

MERVILLE — LA BASSÉE

Map to illustrate
WAR DIARY for
November 1915
of
Headquarters
Artillery
MEERUT
DIVISION

Indian Army Corps

Shewing
Battery Positions
& Regtl. Hd.Qrs.
Area of
MEERUT
DIVISION R.A.

MESSAGES, SIGNALS AND FIELD TELEGRAPHS.

Army Form C. 2121. Modified for India.

APPENDIX

TO: BRIGADE MAJOR

Infantry fire has died down but telephone comms broken and things appear quiet aaa Thank you for cooperation

July 4 / 6.30 pm

FROM: 20th BDE

Bde Major R.A.

INSTRUCTIONS.

1. Telegrams in the field are accepted under the rulings in chapter XVI, F. S. R. II (Indian Supplement)
2. The addressor will enter (a) any instructions re the delivery of this message (e.g., "to await arrival"), after the address in the space "Address TO," (b) the class of his message, following his signature, in space 7, e.g., "Clear line," "Urgent Railway," "Priority," "State," "Press Express," "Press," "Private Express," "Private."
3. If a receipt is required for the message it will be prepared by the addressor and signed by the Signaller in charge.

Gulab Singh & Sons, Calcutta—No. 11 Army C.–8-8-14–22,50,000.

MESSAGES, SIGNALS AND FIELD TELEGRAPHS.

Army Form C. 2121. Modified for India.

No. of Message 145

APPENDIX 9

Words: 20
Recd. at 2.45 m
Date 5-11-14
From 219
By Schofield

TO BDE MAJOR ROYAL ARTILLERY MEERUT DIVN

Can you open fire on RUE D'OUVERT with six inch howitzers

[circled annotation:] Is attacked all night? if so the man can go straight on to the Sig. Coy with it? Stks.

Stks 2.00 pm

mortar (19) is just where RUE d'OUVERT turns into RUE du MARAIS.

FROM LIEUT COL DUFFUS
Time 2—30 PM

MESSAGES, SIGNALS AND FIELD TELEGRAPHS.

Army Form C. 2121. Modified for India.

APPX g

TO	O	C	8th	Howitzer
	Bde	R.F.A.	GORRE	

Sender's Number: CRA M.14

AAA

6 inch howitzers are opening fire shortly on northern end of RUE d'OUVERT AAA Do you require them to knock RUE d'OUVERT down

about 3-10 pm

FROM: Bde Major R A

Signature of addressor: McFarlane Lieut RA for Bde RA

MESSAGES, SIGNALS AND FIELD TELEGRAPHS.

Army Form C. 2121. Modified for India.

APPX 9 No. of Message 203

Words 24

TO: BRIGADE MAJOR R A MEERUT DIVN

Day of Month: 5th M 14

Yes AAA Roark X down

FROM: O C 8TH BDE
Place: RFA
Time: 3.40 PM

MESSAGES, SIGNALS AND FIELD TELEGRAPHS.

APPENDIX 10

Army Form C. 2121. Modified for India.

No. of Message _____

Prefix ____ Code ____ m. Words 32 Charge ____ (X) For Stamps.

Recd. at 4.4 P m
Date 4/11/14
From ZU
By Pte Rawson W

Sent. At ____ m. To ____ By ____

NOTHING TO BE WRITTEN BY THE ADDRESSEE ABOVE THIS LINE.

TO	C	R	A	
	MEERUT	DIVISON		

Sender's Number	Day of Month	In reply to number	AAA
BM 49	4th		

our	line	under	shell	fire
we	expect	from	10	16
of	R A	can	you	engage
AAA				

FROM: C R A 3 RD DIVISION
Time: 3.50 PM

MESSAGES, SIGNALS AND FIELD TELEGRAPHS.

Army Form C. 2121. Modified for India.

No. of Message 131

APPENDIX 11

TO CRA Meerut Divn

Sender's Number: G 243
Day of Month: 7th

19th Ind. Infy Bde reports that enemy attacked right and right centre of Seaforths AAA This attack has been repulsed but not driven back completely and enemy trying to build up firing line AAA For information and any cooperation possible

FROM
Place: Meerut Divn
Time: 12.50 pm

MESSAGES, SIGNALS AND FIELD TELEGRAPHS.

Army Form C. 2121. Modified for India.

APPENDIX 14

NOTHING TO BE WRITTEN BY THE ADDRESSER ABOVE THIS LINE.

TO: G.O.C. 20th Indian Inf. Bde.

Sender's Number: Ra 44
Day of Month: 7th
AAA

19th Indian Inf. Bde reports enemy attacked right and right centre of Seaforths AAA attack repulsed but not driven back completely and enemy trying build up firing line AAA for information and cooperation of your artillery if possible AAA repeated 21st Indian Inf. Bde.

FROM Place: C R A MEERUT

MESSAGES, SIGNALS AND FIELD TELEGRAPHS.

Army Form C. 2121. *Modified for India.*

Appendix 13

TO GOC 21st Indian Inf. Bde.

Sender's Number	Day of Month	In reply to number	AAA
19th	Indian	Inf.	Bde	report
Enemy	attacked	right	and	right
centre	of	bn position	AAA	attack
repulsed	but	hot	driven	back
complete	and	enemy	trying	bombs
up	firing	line	AAA	for
information	and	cooperation	of	on
artillery	if	possible	AAA	repulsed
20th	Indian	infantry	Bde	

FROM
Place: C R A
Time: 1166

REPORT BY O.C. 2ND BATTERY ON PERISCOPE.

Herewith description of the instrument and report by Lieut. Buchan, who actually used the periscope in the trenches.

I have used it myself in advanced trenches for reconnoitring, observation stations, etc. In one instance German trenches were within 50 yards, in this case a good view of the situation was obtained and as far as I could make out the periscope did not attract particular attention. I think that in misty weather when nothing can be made out except in the most advanced positions, it is indispensible. Some experience in its use is necessary to obtain its full benefit.

Dated 10-11-14.

P. J. PATERSON, MAJOR, R.F.A.,
Commanding, 2nd Battery, R.F.A.

REPORT ON THE PERISCOPE, INVENTED BY MAJOR PATERSON, R.F.A.

The Instrument.—

The instrument consists of two mirrors one above the other, inclined to one another so as to give in the bottom mirror a view to the front as reflected in the top one. The mirrors are fitted into an oblong box, about 2 feet 6 inches long and about 3 inches square cross section. The box has openings (3 inches square) at either end on opposite sides. The long sides being vertical, the mirrors should be fixed at an angle of 45° to the vertical, facing the two openings, if it is desired to look horizontally into the bottom mirror (see Sketch A, below).

With the tools and materials available in the battery it was found impossible to set the mirrors accurately this can be counteracted by tilting the box and altering the position of the eye, (See Sketch B, below).

The instrument put together in the Battery was made from two 3 inch helio glasses in a box made from wood from an ordinary packing case. The field of view in this case is just over 6°.

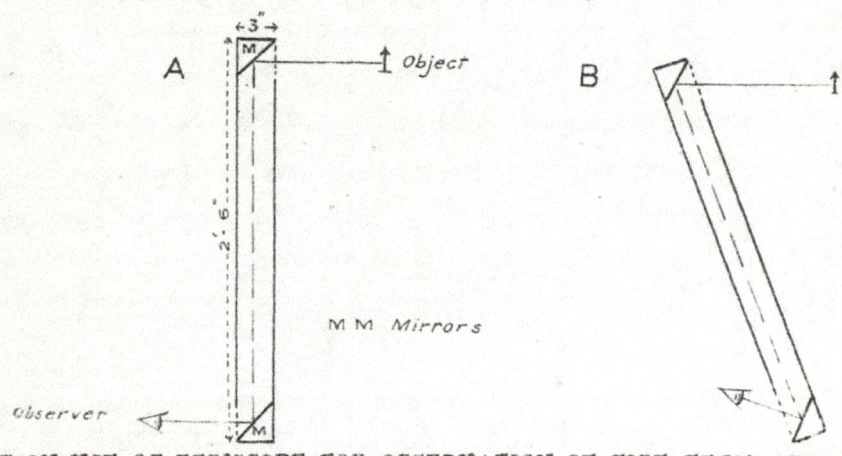

REPORT ON USE OF PERISCOPE FOR OBSERVATION OF FIRE FROM ADVANCED TRENCHES.

On the evening of 5th instant, the Officer Commanding Right Section of Defence, asked for an Artillery Officer to be sent into his trenches for next day. Accordingly I was sent down with his reliefs that evening. I took the Periscope with me.

The 6th November, 1914, was misty and the Officer Commanding Battery, 800 yards in rear of the trenches could see nothing to his front. During the morning the Infantry asked for fire to be brought to bear on a sap about 50 yards in front of their left trenches. Giving the Officer Commanding a compass bearing, by getting up with my glasses I was able to pick up his first rounds. From them I gave corrections and endeavoured to pick up the next rounds with the periscope. As long as my corrections were small I found no difficulty in this, as I could point the periscope where they should fall and get the actual burst in the field of view. I managed to bring the fire of the guns actually on to the sap into which they fired percussion shrapnel.

This operation was repeated against another sap 150 yards in front of the right trenches of this Section.

In each case it was necessary to find the first rounds by getting up with glasses but from them corrections could be made with the periscope. Care should be taken not to give corrections which take the shell outside the field of the instrument, as shells bursting outside this field are not very easily picked up. I found that if I put mud on the top of box and arranged so that the bottom third of my view was the parapet immediately in front, the periscope protruded less than 3 inches above the parapet and did not attract attention from the enemy.

Dated 10th November, 1914.

D. A. BUCHAN, LIEUT., R.F.A.

Operation Orders. APPX 17

by   Place LOCON

69 Brig-Genl. A.B. Scott   Date 10/11/14
    C.R.A. Meerut Divn.   Time 12-7 p.m.

---

*on 8/11/14

1. Be prepared to shell the same area* of NEUVE CHAPELLE as you bombarded before, at 3 p.m. precisely this afternoon.

2. 20 lyddite to be fired, and a fairly quick rate of fire maintained. —

3. Operation to be repeated at 3-45 p.m. —

4. Watch herewith will correct Hd. Qrs. time, which please return.

J.M. Lynch-Staunton
Major R.A.

T.O.O. 114¼ H.B.

By m.c. orderly.

Operation Orders. APPX 18

by   Place LOCON
Brig.-Genl. A.B. Scott   Date 10/11/14
C.R.A.   Time 12.17 pm
Meerut Divn.

1. Be prepared to shell the same area of NEUVE CHAPELLE as you bombarded on 8/11/14, at 3 p.m. to-day precisely. —

2. 20 Lyddite to be fired and a fairly quick rate of fire maintained until the 20 rds are expended.

3. Operation to be repeated at 3-45 p.m. precisely.

4. A watch herewith will correct Hd. Qrs. time, which please return.

R.W. Aylmer-Strumh
Major R.A.
Vice Major Rob.

To. O.C. 110th H.B.
By mtd. orderly.

Operation Orders. APPX 19

No. 72   by Brig-Gen: A.B. Scott   Place LOCON
     C.R.A. Meerut Div.   Date ~~12.35pm~~ 10.11.14.
        Time 12.35pm

To O.C. 2nd Siege Bty
Watchful Short. Night R.A.
2nd watchful

1. NEUVE CHAPELLE will be bombarded this afternoon at 3 p.m. exactly & again at 3.45 p.m. precisely by 110th & 114th Heavy Batteries.

2. At these times exactly, you are to engage the hostile trench to the East of NEUVE CHAPELLE with shrapnel fire. — 24 Rounds on each occasion. — Trench to be engaged is a long trench for "Supports", marked in Red on rough sketch attached.

3. Herewith watch will correct Hd Qrs time, please note & return watch.

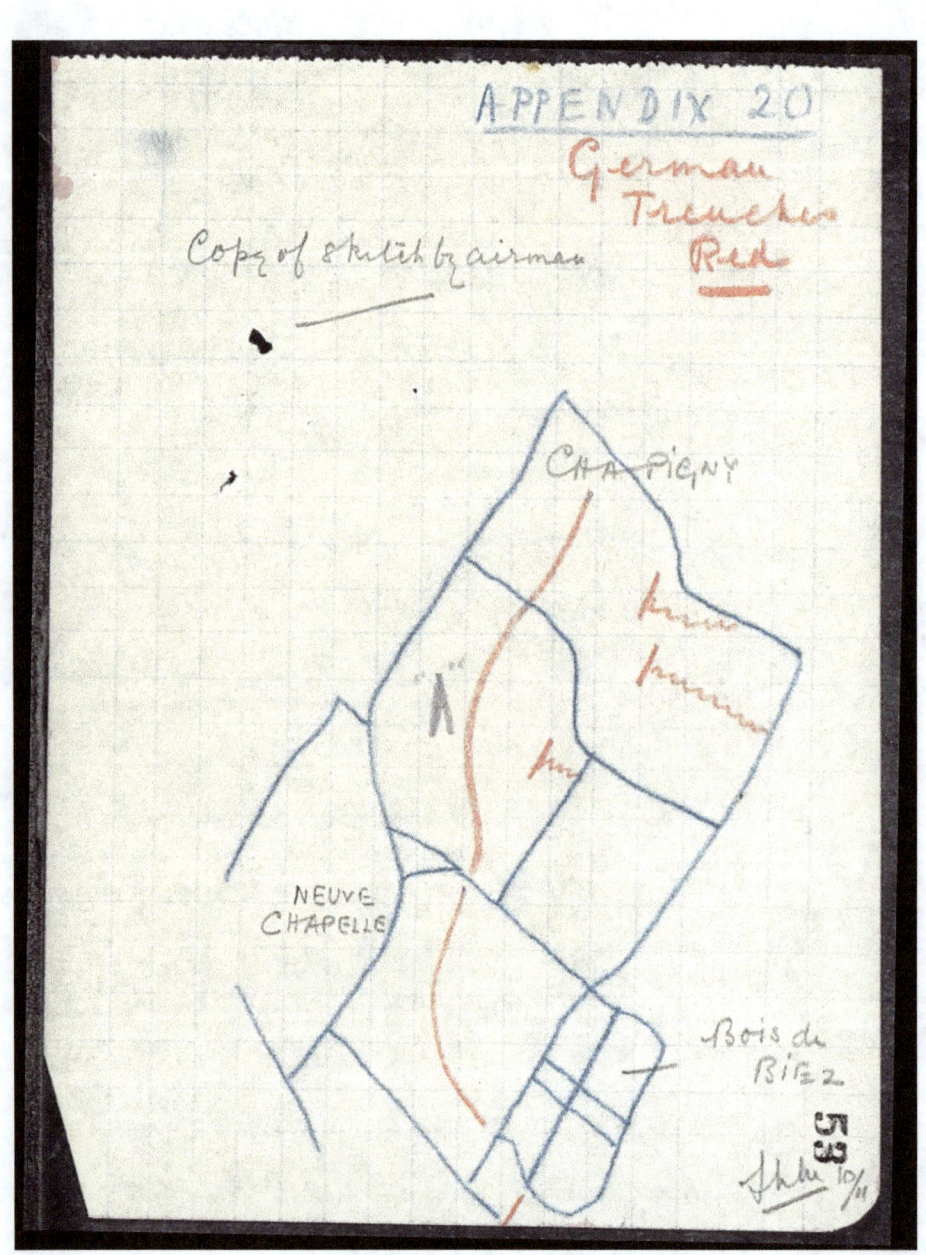

Army Form C. 2121. Modified for India.   APPX 16 B

TO O.C. g/t Ado R.A.

Please order out Battery ...
Aliabad for to ... ...
Captain ... A.A. ...
request ... left ...
Boyd AAA Nos later ...
to be take off ...
particular track around to
by to on Brigade
purpose

FROM Royal Arty 9.H.
Place
Time

R.M. R.A. Indian Dr.

MESSAGES, SIGNALS AND FIELD TELEGRAPHS.

Army Form C. 2121. Modified for India. APPX 16a

TO Meerut Divn

Sender's Number: 13
Day of Month: 10th

AAA

70th Bde wire begins Leicesters any Light Battn reports bomb thrower still in same position as yesterday AAA Capt Davidson of Howitzer Battery knows where he is AAA Could they try and out him AAA Capt Davidson is in 65th Howitzer Battery I understand ends CRA 3rd Divn now with my Bde regrets he has no guns to turn in this direction AAA Capt Davidson is in 65th How Battery working with Meerut Divn AAA Addressed Meerut Divn repeated 70th Bde

fm 19th Ind Inf Bde
11-45 AM

C.R.A.

FROM

In confirmation of conversation with GSO(1)

"A" Form.   APPENDIX 16   Army Form C. 2121.
MESSAGES AND SIGNALS.

TO BRIGADE MAJOR R A MEERUT DIVN.

AAA

The right trenches of the Seaforths and the left trenches of the 2/39th have been heavily shelled this morning either from direction of 18 A and 2 or from 21 22 and 23 my brigade has searched for them but with what success I cannot say and I cannot expend more ammunition on them could the heaviest fire be turned on them as they certainly annoy the trenches considerably

From O C FOURTH BRIGADE
Place R F A

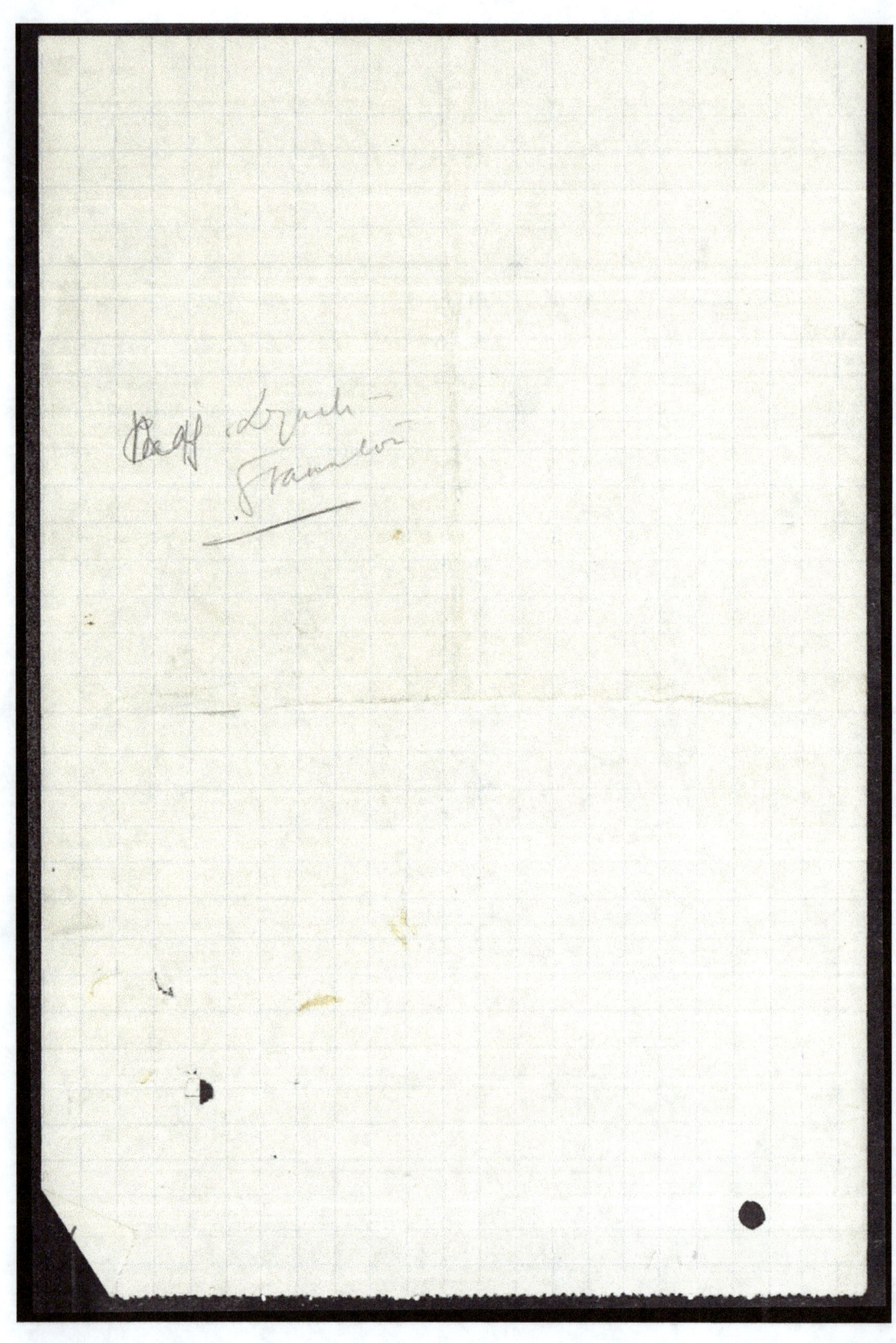

MESSAGES, SIGNALS AND FIELD TELEGRAPHS.

Army Form C. 2121. Modified for India.

APPENDIX 15

NOTHING TO BE WRITTEN BY THE ADDRESSER ABOVE THIS LINE.

TO: C.R.A.

Sender's Number: G 54/5 | Day of Month: 9th

AAA

19th Ind Inf Bde reports about 8.40 AM that Seaforths and Jats trenches were being heavily shelled.

9.20 a.m.

FROM
Place: Meerut Divn
Time: 9.0 AM

MESSAGES, SIGNALS AND FIELD TELEGRAPHS.

Army Form C. 2121. Modified for India.   No. of Message **26**

Prefix ___ Code ___ m. Words. **31** Charge. (X) For Stamps. **APPENDIX 14** Recd. at **8.40** m
Office of Origin and Service Instructions. Sent. At ___ m. To ___ By ___   Date ___ From **2...** By **R. Barnard(?)**

NOTHING TO BE WRITTEN BY THE ADDRESSOR ABOVE THIS LINE.

TO: **MEERUT DIV (THROUGH 19TH BDE)**

Sender's Number	Day of Month	In reply to number	AAA
BM L	9		

Our trenches being shelled AAA Can you fire a few rounds at enemys battys sea near SALOME

Ent. 9/11/14 / 8.42 am

CRA
Can you comply
Recvd (Sd)

FROM Place: **3RD DIV ARTY**
Time: **8.25 AM**

(Y) The above may be forwarded as now corrected. (Z)   Class of Message.

Countersignature of Censor or Authorising Officer.   Signature of addresser and his instructions, vide reverse.

* This line should be erased if not required.

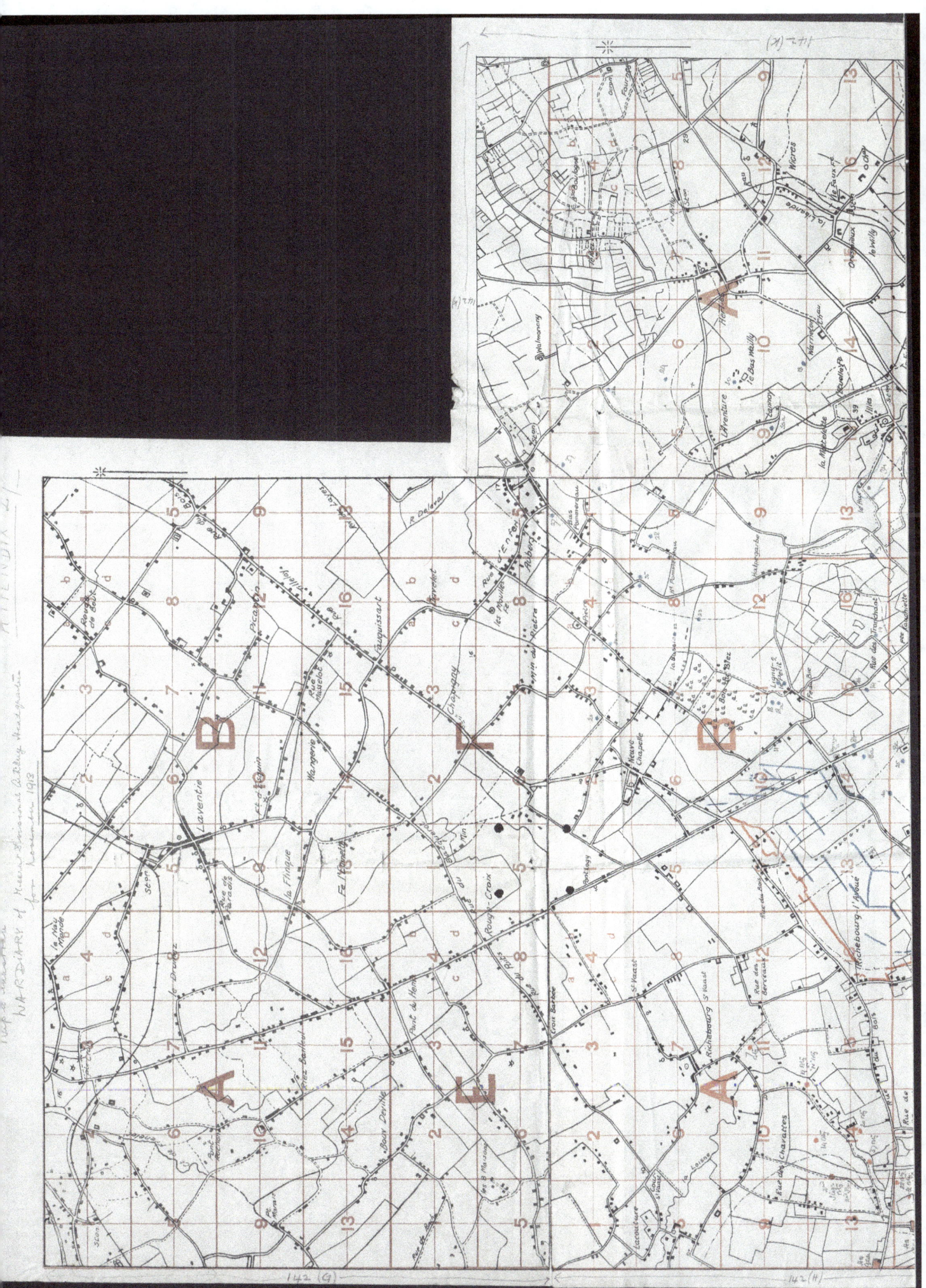

Map of Area LA BASSÉE - PONT DU HEM.

APPENDIX 21
Copy No. 6

Operation Order No. 2
by
Lieut. General C.A. Anderson, C.B.
Commanding Meerut Division

Reference Map:—
France 1/80,000 ARRAS, ST. OMER & LILLE Sheets.

LOCON 10th November 1914

Intention 1. With the intention of destroying buildings and German trenches to the N.E. and in front of the right of the trenches now held by the Seaforths a bombardment by all Artillery will commence at 12 midnight tonight and will be maintained till 12.45 A.M. 11-11-14.

Artillery 2. All Artillery which can be effectively brought to bear will bombard the N.E. half of the quadrilateral enclosed by the four roads immediately N.E. of the junction of the RUE du BOIS and the ROUGE CROIX – LA BASSEE Road, and which has been explained to C.R.A.s. The intention of this bombardment is to destroy houses and trenches in this area.

No gun is to fire on the area after 12.45 a.m.

All artillery not able to bear effectively on the above area will be directed on the terrain East of the above-mentioned area, toward and including the BOIS de BIEZ to check movement of German reserves.

After 12.45 A.M. 11th Novr. all Artillery fire along the front will be directed by C.R.A.s under normal conditions.

Seaforths 3. The Seaforths will retire on the supporting line of trenches which are now being prepared in rear of their present line of trenches, their right about 300 yards down the RUE du BOIS from the junction of that road with the ESTAIRES – LA BASSEE Road, their left remaining in their present trenches and well clear of the houses to their front. This supporting line of trenches is to be worked at hard from now onward and is to be completely occupied by 12 midnight. At midnight no man should remain in the present front line except to the left of the point where the new line of trenches commences.

After the shelling is over at 12.45 A.M. 11th Novr. the original line of trenches is to be at once re-occupied.

Genl. Bowes 4. The portion of the 8th British Brigade will be
8th Brit Inf Bde held in readiness in the vicinity of RICHEBOURG St
less 1½ Battns. VAAST at 9.30 p.m in support of, and reserve to, the 19th
& 4th D. Guards. Ind. Inf. Bde.

General Bowes will place himself in communication with General Johne in Commdg 19th Ind. Inf. Bde; and will detach the 7th. D.Gs to 19th Ind Inf Bde H Qrs to report to Lieut. Col. NORIE, 2/2nd Gurkha Rifles at 9.0. p.m.

Lt. Col NORIE
2/2nd G.R.
7H. D.Gs
2/2nd. G.R.s

5. The 7th. D.Gs, dismounted, and ½ of 2/2nd Gurkha Rifles under Lt. Col. NORIE, D.S.O. will be in direct support of the 1/9th Gurkha Rifles. Col NORIE will at first occupy the RUE de BACQUEROT N.E. of ROUGE CROIX and get into communication with Col WIDDICOMBE Commdg 1/9th Gurkha Rifles, and through him with the 6th JATS.

This detachment is responsible that the line of trenches now occupied by the 6th Jats and 9th Gurkhas is not broken, and will be in the position indicated above at 10.0 p.m.

20th I.I. Bde

6. The G.O.C. 20th I.I. Bde will ensure that the left flank of the 2/39th Garhwalis is withdrawn gradually commencing at 11.30 p.m. tonight, on to a line connecting with the right of the new trench of the Seaforths and that this operation is completed before the Artillery fire commences at midnight.

The present line is to be re-occupied as soon as the Artillery fire ceased at 12-45 A.M on 11th Novr.

No 3 Coy.
Sappers & Miners

7. No 3 Coy. S & M now with 19th I.I. Bde will commence work at dusk tonight on the trenches of the supporting line to be occupied by the Seaforths.

Rifle fire.

8. At 12 midnight when the Artillery commences the bombardment, all infantry, except the Seaforths, in the front line of trenches will open rifle fire on the enemy's trenches to their front. The fire action of the Seaforths is left to the discretion of the O.C. Battn.

9. All units in reserve are to parade with filled water bottles and food for the next day

10. Report to LOCON.

C.U. Jacob.
Colonel,
General Staff
Meerut Division

Issued at 5.0 p.m. by Staff Officers to:—
Indian Corps   Copy No 1 (by cyclist)
8th Brit. Inf Bde   2
7th Dragoon Guards   2
19th Ind Inf Bde   4 (Copy No 5 for C.R.A)
C.R.A. Meerut Divn   1
20th Ind Inf Bde   2
21st Ind Inf Bde   6 (Copy No 9 for Genl JOUBERT)
                        (Copy No 10 at GIVENCHY)
Lahore Divn Copy No 11 by cyclist.

SECRET

APPENDIX 22

OPERATION ORDER NO. 3. Copy No. ......
By Lieutenant-General G.A. ANDERSON, C.B.,
Commanding MEERUT Division.
LOCON, 13th November 1914.

INTENTION.	1. The trench recently made by the Germans and lying about 50 yards to the front of the line occupied by the 1st and 2nd 39th GARHWAL Rifles will be assaulted and destroyed tonight as follows :-
ASSAULTING PARTY - Half Battn. less tool-carrying party.	2. To be detailed by G.O.C. GARHWAL Brigade. This party will silently assault the trench at 9 p.m.
WORKING PARTY - Half No.4 Coy. S. & Ms. plus portion of Assaulting party.	3. This party will be of sufficient strength to provide 1 man per yard of the enemy's trench to be destroyed, and will follow the assaulting party under arrangements to be made by G.O.C. GARHWAL Brigade. After the trench has been carried the assaulting and working parties will fill in the trench, ramp the front to enable it to be fired into from our trenches, block the heads of the German communicating trenches, and open channels opposite them to enable our maxims to g fire down them if reopened, and generally render the trench untenable.
DETACHMENT 150 POONA HORSE.	4. The detachment POONA Horse to provide 150 men for dismounted work will report to a Staff Officer, GARHWAL Brigade at 5.30 p.m. today at the cross-roads on the RUE DU BOIS, half a mile east of the LE TOURET cross-roads, and will be utilised to fill up such portions of the firing trenches as may be required by G.O.C. GARHWAL Brigade. This party will carry 150 rounds S.A.A. per man and will have filled water-bottles and food for 1 day.
1/9th GURKHA RIFLES.	5. The 1/9th GURKHA Rifles will report to a Staff Officer, GARHWAL Brigade at 6.30 p.m. at the cross-roads specified in paragraph 4, for use as Brigade Reserve during the operations. To carry filled water bottles and food for 1 day.
ARTILLERY.	6. All available Artillery will open a bombardment on the main supporting German trenches as described to G.R.As. at 9.5 p.m. and fire will be continued with vigour to 9.15 p.m. Fire will then be directed on the trenches and area in rear of this trench and also on the trenches lying each side of the PONT LUGY LA BASSEE Road in front of the Seaforths and 2/39th GARHWAL Rifles. The fire will be increased in volume from 12 midnight to 12.10 a.m. 14th November, when it will cease. Detailed instructions for these bombardments will be issued by the G.R.As. MEERUT and 3rd Divisions
RETIREMENT.	7. The assaulting and working parties will retire punctually at 12 midnight. Supporting troops will be sent to billets as soon as they can be dispensed with by G.O.C. GARHWAL Brigade.
WATCHES.	8. All watches will be set by those of G.R.As. 3rd and MEERUT Divisions and G.O.C. GARHWAL Brigade, to whom correct time has been given.

Major,
General Staff, Meerut Divn.

Issued at 10 a.m.
Copy No. 1 to Ind. Corps.

(Continued)

Copy No. 2 to   C.R.A. MEERUT Division.
"   " 3 to   C.R.A. 3rd Division.
"   " 4 to G.O.C. GARHWAL Brigade
"   " 5 to   G.O.C. BAREILLY Brigade
"   " 6 to   G.O.C. DEHRA DUN BRIGADE (with Copy No.
                                 7 for 1/8th Gurkha-Rifles).
"   " 8 to   G.O.C. 8th British Infy. Bde.
"   " 9 to   G.O.C. Secunderabad Cavalry Brigade
                    (with Copy No. 10 for POONA Horse)
"   ..11 to   C.R.E. MEERUT Division.
"   12 to   WAR DIARY.
"   ..13 to   File

A. Form.   MESSAGES, SIGNALS AND FIELD TELEGR[APHS]   No. of Message _____

424 APPX 23

TO   C.R.A.

Sender's Number G.553   Day of Month 14   In reply to number.   AAA

Garhwal Bde reports as follows at 3 a.m. — Attack trench only partially successful owing searchlights and heavy fire not possible to tell aaa several officers and men wounded and missing trying to bring in aaa prisoners report attack was ordered for morning AAA am keeping 1/9th Gurkhas and Cavalry till situation clearer message ends — we should therefore be prepared for an attack at dawn

From: MEERUT DIVN.
Time: 4 a.m.

Class of Message: By hand

"A" Form. APPX 24 Army Form C. 2121.
MESSAGES AND SIGNALS.

This message is on a/c of: 218 Service.

TO CRA

Sender's Number: 891/16
Day of Month: 24th

Following wire received from Indian Corps begins G209 following received from G.H.Q. begins C in C congratulates Indian Corps on their successful counter attack and considers troops engaged have done splendidly inds addressed both Divns and attached Cavalry Bde ends for communication to troops

From Place: Meerut Divn
Time: 2/a.m.

APPX 25

Headquarters, MEERUT Division.
25th November 1914.

Copy of a letter from Headquarters, Indian Corps to LAHORE Division No.G.279, dated 25th November 1914. (Copy to Meerut Divn)
----

1. Under orders from G.H.Q. following transfer of 4.5 Howitzer batteries will take place as soon as possible:-

I Corps will send one battery to Indian Corps.

x   x   x   x

Howitzer Brigade now with Indian Corps will rejoin IInd Corps leaving one battery with Indian Corps.

x   x   x   x

Each battery will be accompanied by a due proportion of the Brigade Ammunition Column and by 4 G.S. Wagons containing 4.5" ammunition from the Divisional Ammunition Column.

2. Please direct VIII Howitzer Brigade (less one battery) and a due proportion of its Ammunition Column, together with the Howitzer Section of No 5 Divisional Ammunition Column (less 4 G.S. Wagons) now attached to Meerut Divisional Ammunition Column to rejoin II Corps and inform me by telegram which battery is to be retained.

3. FThe Battery of the VIII How Brigade retained will be attached to the 5th Brigade R.F.A. and the battery received from the 8 Corps will be attached to the 4th Brigade R.F.A.

No. 9/30 G.

For information. The Howitzer Battery from Ist Corps has been directed to join at LOCON. Hour and date of arrival will be communicated in due course.

R. Davies Major,
General Staff,
MEERUT Division.

To,
C.R.A. Meerut Division.

Copy to:- "Q", "A" & "M" Branches.

APPX 26   Copy No. 25

Operation Orders No 3.
by
Brigadier General A.B. Scott, C.B., D.S.O.
Commanding Royal Artillery, MEERUT Division.

LOCON 30th November 1914.

Reference - map MERVILLE - LA BASSÉE 1/40,000.

1. The MEERUT Division will take up the defensive line from GIVENCHY to cross-roads ¼ mile south-west of G in LES BAULOTS from 12 noon 1st December.

2. The following reliefs will take place:—

(a) 9th Brigade R.F.A. will relieve the 5th Brigade R.F.A. during day of 2nd instant.

(b) 13th Brigade R.F.A. will relieve the 11th Brigade R.F.A. during the night of 3rd – 4th December.

(c) 56th Battery R.F.A. will relieve the 37th Battery R.F.A.:— Headquarters and 2 sections during day of 3rd instant in Northern section of line; one section during night of 3rd – 4th instant in Southern section of line.

(d) 110th and 114th Heavy Batteries will relieve respectively the 113th and 109th Heavy Batteries during the day of 3rd inst.

In all cases the exact times of relief will be arranged by the Officers Commanding Brigades or Batteries concerned, and on completion of relief a report will be made to C.R.A., MEERUT Division.

3. The Artillery will be grouped as follows:—

4th Brigade R.F.A., 9th Brigade R.F.A., Headquarters and 2 Sections 56th Battery R.F.A. under Lt. Col. L.A.C. Gordon and grouped with GARHWAL Brigade, Headquarters at CHE DU ROUX.

18th Brigade R.F.A., 13th Brigade R.F.A., 1 Section 56th Battery R.F.A. under Lt. Col. A.G. Oasley D.S.O. and grouped with BAREILLY Brigade, Headquarters at GORRE.

The 110th, 114th Heavy Batteries and 2nd Siege Battery R.G.A. and Section of Anti-Aircraft guns under G.O.C., R.A. Meerut Division.

4. Each Brigade R.F.A. and Heavy Battery R.G.A. will furnish a mounted orderly who will report at the C.R.A.'s

Office in LOCON every morning and evening for orders.

5. Diaries of events will be furnished, as heretofore, every evening commencing December 4th. In addition, Officers Commanding R.A. of Troops will please furnish a "morning report", if any event of importance occurs during the night.

C.E. Bspdrs Chamber.

Major R.A,
Brigade Major R.A,
Meerut Division.

Copies Nos. 1 to 5 to O.C. 4th Brigade R.F.A.
"   "   6 to 10 to O.C. 9th Brigade R.F.A.
"   "   11 to 15 to O.C. 13th Brigade R.F.A.
Copy No. 16 to O.C. 56th Battery R.F.A.
"   "   17 to O.C. Section Anti-Aircraft guns.
"   "   18 to O.C. Meerut Divisional Ammunition Column.
"   "   19 to O.C. 2nd Siege Battery R.G.A.
"   "   20 to O.C. 110th Heavy Battery R.G.A.
"   "   21 to O.C. 114th Heavy Battery R.G.A.
"   "   22 to C.R.A. Lahore Division.
"   "   23 to Brigade Major, Bareilly Brigade
"   "   24 to Brigade Major, Dehradun Brigade
"   "   25 to War Diary.
"   "   26 to File.

War Diary
of
Headquarters Divisional Artillery
Meerut Division

From 1-12-14
to 31-12-14

Volume II
Pp 1 to 43

Army Form C. 2118.

Headquarters Divisional Artillery
Meerut Division

WAR DIARY VOLUME V.
of
INTELLIGENCE SUMMARY.

Instructions regarding War Diaries and Intelligence Summaries are contained in F. S. Regs., Part II, and the Staff Manual respectively. Title pages will be prepared in manuscript.

(Erase heading not required.)

Hour, Date, Place.	Summary of Events and Information.	Remarks and references to Appendices.
1st December 1914. LOCON	Meerut Division Resting.	
10.30 a.m. do	H.M. The KING inspected representatives of the Expeditionary Force. His Majesty presented the Victoria Cross to a Bomb. Corble and Driver Drain of the 37th Howitzer Battery R.F.A. His Majesty was also introduced to members of the Staff of the MEERUT Division.	No.9.
2nd December 1914. LOCON	Meerut Division resting. During the day the 9th Brigade R.F.A relieved the 5th Brigade R.F.A. vide operation Order (appendix 26)	No.9.
3rd December 1914. LOCON	During the day the following units were carried out, vide operation Order (Appx 26) :— 13th Brigade R.F.A (less 2nd Battery) and Brigade Am Col 56th Howitzer Battery R.F.A 110th Heavy Battery R.G.A. 114th Heavy Battery R.G.A relieved the 11th Brigade R.F.A " 37th How.Bty.R.F.A " 113th Heavy Battery " 109th Heavy Battery The 11th Brigade R.F.A. Amm Col. remained in action to supply the 13th Bde R.F.A with 18 pr. ammunition	No.3.

Army Form C. 2118

WAR DIARY VOLUME V
or
INTELLIGENCE SUMMARY.
(Erase heading not required.)

Hour, Date, Place.	Summary of Events and Information.	Remarks and references to Appendices.
4th December 1914 LOCON.	Day opened very boisterous indeed, work by aircraft impossible. Lieut Powell however, made an ascent, but his aircraft was eventually blown down. Positions of the Artillery on the resumption of command by C.R.A. MEERUT Division at 12 noon on December 4th 1914:- R.A. NORTHERN GROUP:- O.C. Lt-Colonel L.A.C. GORDON. R.F.A with GARHWAL Brigade. 4th Brigade R.F.A in its old positions about the RUE des CHEVATTES, Brigade Ammunition Column at LE CASSAN, and Brigade Headquarters at C⁰ RAUX. 9th Brigade R.F.A in former positions on RUE des CHEVATTES and RUE du BOIS, Brigade Ammunition Column at LE HAMEL, and Brigade Headquarters at LE TOURET. Headquarters and 2 Sections 56th Howitzer Battery at S. end of RUE de CHEVATTES, Battery Ammunition Column at LE HAMEL. R.A. SOUTHERN GROUP:- O.C. Lt-Colonel R.G. OUSELY, D.S.O with BAREILLY Brigade, Headquarters at GORRE. 18th Brigade R.F.A at LOISNE and GORRE wood, Brigade Ammunition Column at ECLUSE d' ESSARS, Brigade Headquarters at LOISNE. 13th Brigade R.F.A at LE PLANTIN and MARAIS (one Battery and Brigade Ammunition Column) resting at ROBECQ, some horses with Park Eye). One section ½ m. S.W of CUINCHY. Brigade Headquarters at RUE de BETHUNE. 11th Brigade R.F.A Ammunition Column at LA CROIX de FER supplying ammunition to 13th Brigade R.F.A. One section 56th Howitzer Battery ½ m. S.W of CUINCHY. 114th Heavy Battery R.G.A at LES FACONS, Ammunition Column at BETHUNE. 110th Heavy Battery R.G.A at LES LOBES, Ammunition Column at LOCON, North. 2nd Siege Battery R.G.A at RUE de CHEVATTE, Ammunition Column at BETHUNE Section 13 pr Anti Aircraft guns, 1 mile. N of LE TOURET. Divisional Ammunition Column, Headquarters at LOCON. Nos. 1 and 2 Sections at LES CHOQUAUX (West). No. 3rd (Howitzer) Section at Ferme ROI, N⁰ 4 (Heavy) Section at LES CHOQUAUX (East). C.R.A at LOCON in telephone communication with 110th & 114th Heavy Batteries.	

Army Form C. 2118.

3

WAR DIARY

VOLUME V.
(Continued)

or

INTELLIGENCE SUMMARY.

(Erase heading not required.)

Instructions regarding War Diaries and Intelligence Summaries are contained in F. S. Regs., Part II, and the Staff Manual respectively. Title pages will be prepared in manuscript.

Hour, Date, Place.	Summary of Events and Information.	Remarks and references to Appendices.
4th December 1914 LOCON.	According to Operation Order No 6, the C.R.A. MEERUT Division took over command of the Artillery from C.R.A. LAHORE Division at 12 noon. The whole of the MEERUT Divisional Staff moved billets to the South side of the Cross roads in LOCON, this making the 3rd lot of billets occupied in LOCON since the arrival of the MEERUT Division on 30th October; much inconvenience cannot through these constant moves.	✕ Appendix 29
6.30. a.m. do.	✕	
about 6.35 a.m. do.	66th Battery R.F.A engaged hostile battery at 25 and silenced it. 2nd Siege Battery fired a few rounds into German trenches B13c and d (142h) as the enemy had been working on them a good deal.	
10. a.m. do.	93rd Battery fired at 8.30 a.m at request of the Infantry.	
10.10. a.m. do.	7th Battery fired on German machine guns opposite No 3 Section of GARHWAL Infantry Brigade.	
11.45. a.m. do.	110th Heavy Battery registered with 7 rounds Lyddite on trenches behind "White" House (39✕) range found at 8950✕ - 450✕ over map range	✕ Appendix 6
12.30 p.m. do.	19th Battery registered a farm, position F2c-142(h) not marked on this map.	
2.30. P.M. do.	By permission arrangement with the O.C Seaforths, who vacated his trenches for this purpose, a heavy fire was poured into the enemy's trenches opposite next sapo by the 93rd Battery R.F.A 110th Heavy Battery fired 16 shrapnel at the "White house (39) - fuses bursting most erratically varying from very high "ten to Graze - No. 83 or 62 fuses available only, they the Su fuzes. As the daily allowance of Lyddite has been restricted to practically Nil the employment of 4.7 guns is for the time very nearly impossible.	
2. 40. P.M. do.	7th Battery fired on enemy's machine guns opposite No 3 Section of GARHWAL Brigade.	
3. 20. P.M. do.	7th Battery fired on hostile battery at 25✕ which had opened fire.	
3. 45. P.M. do.	19th Battery observed flashes of a hostile battery firing towards FESTUBERT; this was engaged and located 100✕ E of figure 6 of square F6-142(h) just N. of the line dividing F6t and F6a-142(h). (Note: There might be guns	

Gulab Singh & Sons, Calcutta—No. 22 Army C.—5-8-14—1,07,000.

Army Form C. 2118.

WAR DIARY VOL V
(continued)
INTELLIGENCE SUMMARY.
(Erase heading not required.)

Hour, Date, Place.	Summary of Events and Information.	Remarks and references to Appendices.
	men down from Target 6a, or flashes of At might have been mistaken from the observing station of 19th Battery in the RUE du BOIS.	*Appendix 6
	During the day the 9th and 13th Brigades R.F.A. registered their lines of fire after re-occupation of their old positions. The 2nd Siege Battery fired a few rounds into LA BASSEE from one gun run forward to RUE des BERCEAUX. A few rounds were also fired at Battalion Headquarters No 6* or prisoners sketch.	*Appendix 30. MRS
5th December 1914. LOCON		
9.30.a.m. do	Day opened very squally and unsuitable for aeroplane work.	
10.30 a.m. do	Hostile field battery shelled neighbourhood of RUE de BETHUNE and MARAIS, possibly 6a or guns detached from that battery.	
11.40 a.m. do	RICHEBOURG ST VAAST shelled by hostile heavy howitzers for about 20 minutes from a S.E. direction, after this the RUE du BOIS was also shelled. Target 25 opened fire, 110 Heavy Battery fired 12 rounds lyddite at it.	
11.50 a.m. do	114th Heavy Battery fired 8 rounds shrapnel at 34 (LE HUE) which had been active. Firing by map and compass bearing.	
12. noon do	7th Battery shelled target No 25 and afterwards 66th Battery at Vikenrie.	
1.45 p.m. do	110th Heavy Battery fired 6 lyddite shell at 34 (LE HUE) which had been active at intervals all day. Firing by map and compass bearing.	
2.30.p.m. do	Section of 56th How Battery (detached yesterday to Cse Zn RAUK) registered with a few rounds.	
3.30 p.m. do	114th Heavy Battery fired 6 rounds lyddite at 34*	
3.35 p.m. do	2nd Siege Battery bombarded hostile trenches and demolished a house much frequented by snipers close to front trenches of left section of the BAREILLY Brigade.	MRS

Army Form C. 2118.

WAR DIARY (continued) VOL V.
or
INTELLIGENCE SUMMARY.
(Erase heading not required.)

Instructions regarding War Diaries and Intelligence Summaries are contained in F. S. Regs., Part II, and the Staff Manual respectively. Title pages will be prepared in manuscript.

Hour, Date, Place.	Summary of Events and Information.	Remarks and references to Appendices.
6th December 1914 LOCON	Light frost in early morning, wind had died down and atmosphere fairly clear. Several aeroplanes up early doing reconnaissance work.	
7.30.a.m. to 8.15.a.m.	BURBURE Section of 114th Battery R.F.A. shelled german trenches East of Right section of BAREILLY Brigade	× Appendix 6.
8.a.m.	7th Battery fired a few rounds at enemy sharpshooters in White House (39).	
9.10.a.m.	Airman dropped message to inform the 110th Heavy Battery that hostile emplacements at 8a× were occupied.	
9.30.a.m.	110th Heavy Battery engaged this battery (8a) with observation from aeroplane. Results, however, were not satisfactory. Airman appeared over 114th Heavy Battery which engaged target 33, weather rather thick and observation difficult. 7 Shrapnel and 5 lyddite were fired.	
11.a.m.	No 11 Anti Aircraft Section sighted an ALBATROSS, which, however, circled away out of range.	
11.15 a.m.	66th Battery fired at the "White Horse" (39).	×
12.30.p.m.	Airman over 114 Heavy Battery which engaged enemy battery at 4B, only 5 rounds lyddite fired.	
1.p.m.	Left Gun Section of 56th Battery fired at the White Horse (39).	×
1.55.p.m.	Airman again over 110 H.B. which fired 6 more rounds at 8(a), but no fresh results were obtained.	×
1.50 p.m.	2nd Siege Battery fired on target 6a and obtained direct hits on two of the six gun emplacements there.	

Army Form C. 2118.

WAR DIARY (continued) VOL V.
or
INTELLIGENCE SUMMARY.
(Erase heading not required.)

Instructions regarding War Diaries and Intelligence Summaries are contained in F. S. Regs., Part II, and the Staff Manual respectively. Title pages will be prepared in manuscript.

Hour, Date, Place.	Summary of Events and Information.	Remarks and references to Appendices.
2 P.M. 6th December 1914. LOCON	114th Heavy Battery started to engage 34 (LE HUE) but unfortunately confusion re causes between aeroplane observing for 114th Heavy Battery and 2nd Siege Battery. Very thick and hazy.	
2.15 P.M. do	20th Battery R.F.A fired 12 rounds at house N.E. corner of square E 14.a - 142(h) as some Germans were seen going into it.	
2.30 P.M. do	20th Battery R.F.A fired 12 rounds at house in N.W. corner of F12 - 142(h), which appeared as likely observing station.	
2.30 P.M. to 3 P.M. do	Section of 56th Howitzer Battery near Cse du RUIX fired on Sapo and trenches between left and centre sections of BAREILLY Brigade, their fire being observed by 59th Battery R.F.A. Detonation of lyddite shell reported poor.	× Appendix 6
2.15 P.M. to 3.15 P.M. do	2nd Siege Battery no pre arranged bombarded German trenches in front of 9th Gurkhas and Black Watch. Effect reported good and no rounds short of our own front trench, or casualties through our own fire.	
3 P.M. do	59th Battery fired over left section of BAREILLY Brigade, leaving heavy firing there.	
3.30 P.M. do	8th Battery R.F.A. shelled hostile trenches in front of Centre Section of BAREILLY Brigade, in conjunction with O.C. that section.	
5.30 P.M. do	There being a certain amount of musketry fire opposite No 1 Section of the GARHWAL Brigade, the 28th Battery fired rapid bursts of fire at intervals while firing continued.	

Army Form C. 2118.

WAR DIARY (continued) VOL V
or
INTELLIGENCE SUMMARY.
(Erase heading not required.)

Instructions regarding War Diaries and Intelligence Summaries are contained in F. S. Regs., Part II, and the Staff Manual respectively. Title pages will be prepared in manuscript.

Hour, Date, Place.	Summary of Events and Information.	Remarks and references to Appendices.
6th December 1914 LOCON	This was the first day for some considerable time that work by aeroplane observation was possible. A good deal of information was brought in by them, but it was most unfortunate that there should again have been confusion as to which aeroplanes were observing for which batteries. A great advance will be made when wireless installations are provided on aeroplanes.	MRS
7th December 1914 LOCON	High wind blowing, aerial work impossible. Little note worthy from artillery point of view.	
10.30 a.m.	Section of 4·7" Battery at BURBURE shelled house marked on sketch as containing a German Headquarters and obtained 2 direct hits on it.	+Appendix 30
11 a.m.	4·7" Battery fired into the RUE D'OUVERT.	
12 noon	59th Battery detached section at BURBURE shelled a house in square F5a-142(2)	+Appendix 27
12 noon	As previously arranged the 2nd Siege Battery bombarded enemy in front of Black Watch trenches - 24 rounds.	
2.30 p.m. 2.30 p.m.	One Siege turret at shell no bombing emplacement in corner of 349,3a,9 opposite in front of 9th Gurkhas.	
3.40 p.m.	Section of 56th Hov. Battery at C.Ste. Au RUIX opened fire on sap opposite left and centre section of BAREILLY Brigade. Observation obtained from observing officer of the 59th Battery R.F.A. in forward trenches. Observations transmitted by "buzzer" twice. telephone working badly and results poor.	
2.45 p.m.	9·A· and 4th Brigade R.F.A. nothing to report all day. 110th & 114th Heavy Batteries did not open fire.	
	No hostile aircraft seen all day.	
9.30 p.m.	Very Lights showed fine up enemys trenches, as venting supported 2 rockets of very high trajectory going up from Right Section BAREILLY Brigade do. in artillery again fired at our Centre Section trenched, heavy 11 p.m. rifle fire from that direction.	

Army Form C. 2118.

WAR DIARY (continued) Vol. V

or

INTELLIGENCE SUMMARY.

(Erase heading not required.)

Instructions regarding War Diaries and Intelligence Summaries are contained in F. S. Regs., Part II, and the Staff Manual respectively. Title pages will be prepared in manuscript.

Hour, Date, Place.	Summary of Events and Information.	Remarks and references to Appendices.
8th December 1914. LOCON	Strong wind blowing and clouds very low, aeroplane work extremely hazardous, one hostile aeroplane completely broken up during morning. Colt gun shot down Lieut Birg battery was attached to the RUE-DES-BERCEAUX under Capt BURKE	
7.30 a.m.	BURBURE section of 44th Battery shelled trenches in front of right section of BAREILLY Brigade.	
10.30 a.m.	BURBURE section of 44th Battery shelled enemys trenches in front of right section of BAREILLY Brigade.	
10.50 a.m.	2nd Siege Battery with Lieut BARRETT (R.A.) Royal Flying Corps took charge of military aeroplane with gun emplacement 5.6 x (N.10.S.W.2.S.) one round fired, range and line partly correct, enemys battery shelled enemys working parties.	x Appendix 6
11.30 a.m.		
11. p.m.	BURBURE section of 56th Amn for Battery shelled trenches from which much rifle fire being followed.	
11-3.5 a.m.	One round fired by 2nd Siege Battery at German relief forming up in VIOLAINES church tower the observer riding at the "Brewery" S.405.1.14.2. (K)	
11.40 a.m.	0 Lieutenant Anderson O.C. report of 110th Heavy Battery from his hat in RUE DES-BOIS reported that the Battery at S.10.80 was invisible, that the detachments were there and had a line of fire.	
12. noon.	110 Heavy Battery fired 10 rounds of lyddite at no. 10 at intervals during night. explosive shells fell into the village of 7th battery R.A. at Neuve Chapelle, where one Charming Officer of its group went into battle, heard to date 12.00. in F.2, F.14.2 (K) 20 x bearing of 1500 bearing officer fired fine on hostile these billets, no hostility thus is the battery which wheeled these billets, but met so fate at the hands of the 2nd siege, 110th Heavy battery 7th 66th Field batteries.	
1. p.m.	7th Battery fired on hostile battery in F.2a (14.2.6) and 40 x 66 x battery also engaged this battery.	
1.30. p.m.	7.0 th Heavy Battery finish aeroplane observation fired 12 rounds at 5 x, only four rounds registered, aeroplane gave ? but line & sight not.	
2 p.m.	110 th Heavy Battery fired 10 rounds at target, shell burst partly been stopped, enemys snipers shelled Cne le RAILY fired on house on the 2nd brother. Two hits. Battery at Cne le RAILY fired on house in E.8 a.	

Retained section of 5th Howitzer L.P.R. = 1.07.000.
E.P.R. = S.14.2 (K) and Siphon on Cinema in E.8 a.

Army Form C. 2118.

WAR DIARY
or
INTELLIGENCE SUMMARY. (continued) Vol. I.
(Erase heading not required.)

Instructions regarding War Diaries and Intelligence Summaries are contained in F. S. Regs., Part II, and the Staff Manual respectively. Title pages will be prepared in manuscript.

Hour, Date, Place.	Summary of Events and Information.	Remarks and references to Appendices.
8th December 1914 LOCON		
2.25 p.m.	2.25 p.m. Single Howitzer of 2nd Siege Battery engaged hostile battery 750 yds located 750 yds N.W. of left hand top corner of letter F in squared map 143 (b). Gun in emplacement(?) was destroyed.	× appendix 6
3 p.m. do	One section of 114 Heavy Battery moved to new position about 1000 yds S.W. of LA COUTURE.	
3.30 p.m. do	110 H. Battery fired 7 rounds at No. 40 × two unimportant range.	
5.20 p.m. do	66th Battery R.F.A. fired salvos at enemy who were endeavouring to remove the debris of 40 ×	
	During the day the 2nd Siege Battery reported that they located the tramline running in front of the Gurkha trenches about 25 yds W. of SNIPERS HOUSE in square E.6.a.-14.2 (b). The 110th Heavy Battery reported working of steam on one neigh- bourhood of ULLIES windmill. The 8th Battery made some excellent practice, a heavy of 3 trojan in two cases obtaining direct hits with 2nd round fired. This fire can be observed accuracy of the map, and shews what results can be obtained working but by careful — anything by the from large, but definite angles. Map angles only differed by 25 yds reported excellent results from the Gun at 3659 yds — land battery against buildings.	
61st Battery opened fire on enemy trenches on ground running immediately in front of marching machine. Later fired at LIGHTNING... weather very thick and foggy all day, all observation Im- ... really impossible.	
5.30 p.m. do		
9th December 1914 LOCON	During the morning, a German battery EAST of 30.65-05.81.52 and 2nd Siege Battery opened fire on hostile trenches South of LA QUINQUE RUE 710. Left of hour, also enemy who came suddenly to shown.	
12.40 p.m. do		

Gulab Singh & Sons, Calcutta—No. 22 Army C.—5-8-14—1,07,000.

Army Form C. 2118.

WAR DIARY
or
INTELLIGENCE SUMMARY. (continued) Vol II

(Erase heading not required.)

Instructions regarding War Diaries and Intelligence Summaries are contained in F. S. Regs., Part II, and the Staff Manual respectively. Title pages will be prepared in manuscript.

Hour, Date, Place.	Summary of Events and Information.	Remarks and references to Appendices.
9th November 1914 LOCON	fired a few rounds at a German man shaft located just inside well on VIOLAINES. by map.	
1.15 p.m .. do .. 10th December 1914. LOCON	6th Battery fired high explosive shell on VIOLAINES. by map. All quiet during the night. Weather very hazy all day with drizzling rain at times. One of our airmen was taken to the steering station of his aeroplane to see the ground prior to two going up during the bombardment from 12.45 to 2 to observe the effect O.C. northern group R.A. was ordered to keep up steady fire on German trenches in the vicinity to prevent German shooting at the aeroplane which would probably have to come down rather low. The mist and wind however prevented a flight being made.	No 28 8.30 p.m. 6th Battery fired enemy's trenches in E & t. at starts and likely fire was then in this direction. A searchlight near 8.a was also engaged about this time.
6.15 a.m .. do ..	66th Battery fired a few rounds at airmen in trenches in E.4.t.	
7 a.m .. do ..	Both sections 114th Heavy Battery laid out on 4t for shooting with airmen, but weather too thick for flying.	
8.30 a.m .. do ..	7th Battery shelled observation house in B.14.t. and a German working party in the vicinity with good effect. In accordance with request from 2nd and 3rd GURKHAS, 20 th Battery at 9.25 stopped school house and stopped the enemy's snipers firing (No 39) much shrapnel. some more sniping from the white house.	× Appendix 6
10.30 a.m .. do ..	7th Battery reopened fire on their first objective scoring several direct hits.	⑨
11 a.m .. do ..	114th Heavy Battery ordered to return to LES·FACONS from LACOUTURE.	
11.30 a.m .. do ..	7th Battery shelled a barn near the white house. (39).	
11 a.m. to 11.30 a.m .. do ..	German Field Battery fired a few rounds of shrapnel at howitzer observing station in FESTUBERT and a few field howitzer high explosive shells fell near the 61t 4 6th Battery	
12.45 p.m. to 2 p.m .. do ..	bombardment of trench in front of willow trench S. of	

Army Form C. 2118.

WAR DIARY
or
INTELLIGENCE SUMMARY. (continued) Vol I

(Erase heading not required.)

Instructions regarding War Diaries and Intelligence Summaries are contained in F. S. Regs., Part II, and the Staff Manual respectively. Title pages will be prepared in manuscript.

Hour, Date, Place.	Summary of Events and Information.	Remarks and references to Appendices.
10th December 1914 LOCON.	Rigid hand at QUINQUE-RUE carried out by 2nd Siege Battery firing with three guns from RUE-de-CHAVATTER and one from RUE-de-BERGEAUX and 16th Howitzer Battery (one section) near G^{se} DU-RUIEX) Our infantry cleared their front trench under cover of fire from 2nd Siege and 59th Battery from 1pm to 1:45pm during which time the trenches and gaps in their immediate front were effectively bombarded by the section 56th Battery. 2nd Siege fired on the German support trenches about 150 yds further out all the time from 12:45pm to 2pm. Each Howitzer Battery fired 30 rounds of lyddite. Lyddens in white house (cp) again shelled by 20th Battery. During the morning the 54th Battery obtained notice 0:18. rounds from LACOUTURE obtained two direct hits on a. house in A+B C+42 (b) out of 3 rounds fired and 3 direct hits out of 4 rounds fired on 86:00 and the shooting was observed by OC 14th Battery. Range about 120 yds south of the great cope who was charged by OC 4.th.H. Battery from PESTUBERT. Great cope was taken as making all cal-culations, laying out the lines and preparing the platform which although under the remarkable accuracy in hearts, although the only protractor available was a wooden one! The 4th H Battery fired some shrapnel at the RUE-de OUVERT. The section 4:46 and 56th Howitzer Batteries near BURBURE shelled German trenches of GIVENCHY during the morning and also during the bombardment. Appdx 6 ×	
1.15 p.m. do do. 5 p.m. do do.	From 12:45 to 2 p.m. QUINQUE-RUE. A.O. 59th Battery also fired on the trenches near during the day the regiment of O.C. right sector RE BRIGADE their line on the trenches NORTH of GIVENCHY	

Army Form C. 2118.

WAR DIARY
or
INTELLIGENCE SUMMARY. (Continued) Vol V.
(Erase heading not required.)

12

Hour, Date, Place.	Summary of Events and Information.	Remarks and references to Appendices.
10th December 1914. LOCON.	O.C. 2nd Siege Battery reports considerable work still going on near the SNIPER'S HOUSE.	
6.13.p.m. do	28th Battery took bearing to hostile searchlight. O.C. 9th Brigade telephoned to O.C. 4th Brigade R.F.A. for a bearing to be taken from one of his batteries; this was done and position fixed by intersection on the road in B10c at 8.50.p.m.	
9.15.p.m. do	8th Battery fired 4 H.E. shell into large house in square F17-142(?), and at area in F57. Also 4 H.E. shell at VIOLANES.	※ appendix 31
9.30.p.m. do	Operation Order No 8 issued in conference with MEERUT Division Operation Order No 8.	※ appendix 32 M.O.9.
10.p.m. do	20th Battery opened fire on the searchlight, after 7th round it disappeared and did not re-appear during the night.	
11.a.m. 11th December 1914 LOCON	66th Battery shelled the White House barn.	
12.noon do	44th Battery fired at houses in RUE DOUVERT and got some direct hits with H.E. Shell. 44th Battery's detached Section at BURBURE shelled area in front of and E of Right Section of BAREILLY Brigade.	
1.30.p.m. do	1 Section of 110th Heavy Battery marched to new positions 500 yards E of last T in LE VERT LANNET (MERVILLE-LABASSEE map 40,000).	
2.p.m. do	110th Heavy Battery fired 10 rounds Lyddite at White House (39) from which our trenches were being sniped.	※ appendix 6

Army Form C. 2118.

WAR DIARY (continued) VOL V

INTELLIGENCE SUMMARY.

(Erase heading not required.)

Instructions regarding War Diaries and Intelligence Summaries are contained in F. S. Regs., Part II, and the Staff Manual respectively. Title pages will be prepared in manuscript.

/3

Hour, Date, Place.	Summary of Events and Information.	Remarks and references to Appendices.
2.20 p.m. 11th December 1914	Advanced gun of 2nd Siege Battery at RUE des BERCEAUX engaged gun or limber visible at 25x. It was shortly shelled and timber was shown up, indicating possible hit on "junk pit". 20th Battery shelled front of hostile entrenchment reported to contain a maxim.	
2.15 p.m. do	2nd Siege Battery fired a few rounds at traverse in zig zag approach 100x E of "Piquet House."	
2.30 p.m. do	Orders sent to R.A. Group Commander that as detached section of 56th Howitzer Battery at Csse du RAULX had accomplished the task for which it was temporarily formed to BAREILLY Brigade, it would now come back under the R.A. Group Commander of the GARHWAL Brigade.	✱ Appendix 33
	⊕ In accordance with wire from Indian Corps, changing time of Artillery relief to 12 noon on 12.12.14, orders sent to withdraw 13th Brigade R.F.A. at dusk this evening. This was done, with the exception of the detached BURBURE Section of the 41th Battery, which was not relieved by the LAHORE Divisional Artillery.	⊕ Appendix 34 
	During the day the Ol. 1st Siege Battery reports much timber and planking carried into enemy's trenches, probably to improve head cover of support trenches after our recent shelling with 6" howitzers.	

Army Form C. 2118.

WAR DIARY (Continued) VOL V

INTELLIGENCE SUMMARY.

(Erase heading not required.)

Instructions regarding War Diaries and Intelligence Summaries are contained in F. S. Regs., Part II, and the Staff Manual respectively. Title pages will be prepared in manuscript.

Hour, Date, Place.	Summary of Events and Information.	Remarks and references to Appendices.
11. a.m. 12th December 1914 LOCON	Airman arrived over 114th Heavy Battery, but clouds prevented observation. 114th and 110th Heavy Batteries and 2nd Siege Battery fired on target 25* which was reported active by 4th Brigade R.F.A., 7th & 10th and 7th Batteries standing by with shrapnel to catch any fugitives. The operation who not a success however.	* Appendix 6.
12 noon. do.	Shewing stations of 19th and 20th Batteries at RICHEBOURG L'AVOUE heavily shelled by enemy, about 40 "Little Willies" dropped in this own direction of BOIS du BIEZ. The 2nd/3rd Goorkhas also reported that their trenches were being shelled with heavy German shell at 12.4. p.m.	
1.15. p.m. do.	Signs of activity at "Distillery" cross roads in B147-142(h). 34 fired on our trenches. 110th Heavy Battery fired 10 rounds at Distillery and hit at 3 times possible observing station of 34.	
afternoon do.	Hostile flashes reported by 110 Heavy Battery in direction of LES 3 MAISONS, but afternoon it was decided they were N. of LE TILLEUL (?). 110 Heavy Battery fired 11 rounds and obtained correct line, but darkness coming on observation became impossible.	
1.40. p.m. do.	114th Heavy Battery fired on LE HUE. German battery replied by shelling 114th "D" Left position near LOISNE	
3.20. p.m. do.	114th Sound "artificial moon" at 47*	
4. p.m. do.	114th Heavy Battery fired on 1t. During the day the Right Section of the 110th Heavy Battery moved its position from W of the road to LA COUTURE to a position E of same road, prepared as a secondary position for 7th Battery R.F.A. A large round or "Redoubt" who located just N of road in B14C-142(h) which should signs of activity; it appeared to be used as a place for making CHEVAUX de FRISES for the forward trenches, as several were seen lying on the ground near it. The great height of some of the German parapets in front of the "PICKET House Trenches" suggested that they have got to "water". In spite of the day was the renewed activity of the hostile artillery which shelled our trenches both in RUE des BOIS and SE of FESTUBERT, aswell as the neighbourhood of FESTUBERT, both Shrapnel + H.E. Shell were used.

Army C - 5-8-14 - 1,07,000. Gulab Singh & Sons, Calcutta—No. 22

Army Form C. 2118.

WAR DIARY (continued.) VOL V
or
INTELLIGENCE SUMMARY.
(Erase heading not required.)

Instructions regarding War Diaries and Intelligence Summaries are contained in F. S. Regs., Part II, and the Staff Manual respectively. Title pages will be prepared in manuscript.

Hour, Date, Place.	Summary of Events and Information.	Remarks and references to Appendices.
13th December 1914 LoCoN 8.15 a.m.	66th Battery engaged No 25* which had opened fire at 8 a.m on a horse near their observing station; later fired at 12 mounted men seen in F37 — 19th Battery also fired at probably the same party, and which they located as a "battery staff" going towards haystacks about 1000* behind the solort house in square F1a - 142(h). Party dispersed and disappeared — The guns were observed by Lieut Ruddle, from top of tall chimney in A12a -142(h), to be begin very deeply. Same officer observed 2 bombs fired by our infantry into enemy's trenches to be most effective.	Appendix 6
10.45 a.m do.	56th How Battery fired 12 lyddite at a sap-head in Square A16a - 142(h), which appeared effective.	
11.30 a.m do.	Same battery fired 7 lyddite and 6 shrapnel into the "white house" (39*) endorme	
1.40 p.m do.	56th How Battery fired 15 rounds lyddite at the Distillery (cross roads B147 - 142(h)) but no direct hits on building were obtained. During the afternoon 110th Heavy Battery fired 14 rounds at target 25* guns of which were visible, but strong windy made shooting very flinky. The section of 110 Heavy Battery in new position overshoot yesterday registered on DISTILLERY and found range and line accurately.	
3. p.m do.	Germans shelled old position of 114th Heavy Battery near LOISNE with shrapnel and a few rounds of supposed Heavy Shell. During the day the 2nd Siege Battery engaged enemy's battery at 25*, 4 guns of which were visible, but high winds made shooting with extreme accuracy impossible. Same battery also observed that there were still 4 hostile guns remaining at 40. 2nd Lieut HAWES of 2nd Siege Battery severely wounded at observing station of battery by a sniper.	
6. p.m do.	66th and 7th Batteries fired a few rounds on German support trenches in front of GARHWAL Brigade.	

Army Form C. 2118.

WAR DIARY (continued) VOL V
or
INTELLIGENCE SUMMARY.
(Erase heading not required.)

Instructions regarding War Diaries and Intelligence Summaries are contained in F. S. Regs., Part II, and the Staff Manual respectively. Title pages will be prepared in manuscript.

/6

Hour, Date, Place.	Summary of Events and Information.	Remarks and references to Appendices.
7 a.m. 14th December 1914 LOCON	114th Heavy Battery laid out lines on 17 and 47 for shooting with aerial observation but the weather did not permit of it.	×Appendix 6.
7.30 a.m. do	7th Battery R.F.A. fired salvos at German support trenches in front of GARHWAL Brigade where cooking was going on.	
8 a.m. do	7th Battery shelled German O.P. in B14b - 142(h)	
9 a.m. do	7th Battery shelled parties of men and wagons on NEUVE-CHAPELLE - LORGIES Road. The observing officer at a chimney exposed himself very recklessly and this caused the enemy to shell it. 66th Battery engaged 25× which was thought to be shelling the observation post.	
9 a.m. to 3 p.m. do	66th Battery shelled the German trenches on their front at irregular intervals.	
8.40 a.m. to 3 p.m. do	56H Howitzer Battery shelled the following places at intervals. 39 and trenches in the vicinity. Suspected in B.13C - 142(h). Trenches in B10 a, c and d - 142(h) and trenches in A4b and B1c.	
9 a.m. to 4 p.m. do	9th Brigade R.F.A. kept up a steady rate of fire on German trenches on their front searching and sweeping, in the battery zones.	
9.30 a.m. do	Germans have 110th Heavy Battery, 2nd Siege and other batteries in RUE du BOIS shelled by 8× observing parties were driven out for a time. As soon as they could return 8t was shelled by both sections of 110th Heavy Battery and was silenced.	
11am to 11.15am do	2nd Siege Battery supported Right of MEERUT Division and Left of LAHORE Division in a breakengagement. Fired some very effective shell on enemy trenches at Rifle and silenced the German fire.	
11.10 a.m. do	114th Heavy Battery fired on RUE DOUVERT. 2nd Siege Battery shelled RUE DOUVERT.	
12.30 pm to 3 p.m. do	2nd Siege Battery engaged 40 inch gun at RUE des BERCEAUX	
do	7th Battery shelled German support trenches.	
12.45 p.m. do	114th shelled 8a and 8b. 2nd Siege Battery put a few rounds into remains of Snipers House at request of O.C. 19th Gurkhas. One corner completely laid bare	

Army Form C. 2118.

17

WAR DIARY (continued) VOL V
or
INTELLIGENCE SUMMARY.
(Erase heading not required.)

Instructions regarding War Diaries and Intelligence Summaries are contained in F. S. Regs., Part II, and the Staff Manual respectively. Title pages will be prepared in manuscript.

Hour, Date, Place.	Summary of Events and Information.	Remarks and references to Appendices.
3.p.m. 14th December 1914 LOCON	110th Heavy Battery shelled redoubt in B14C-142(h) where there was much activity.	
	GENERAL	
	Weather rather bright but no good for aeroplane observation and no hostile aircraft were sighted. During the afternoon flashes of guns were seen in an orchard south of and close to BEAU PUITS. Germans were noticed to be trotting out their trenches. About 60 horsemen were seen near LORGIES. 7rd Siege Battery commenced to lay down their platforms. 14th Battery changed position to 4400× N. W. of crossroads at ST VAAST. Shelled of RUE DOUVERT at 11 a.m. was in accordance with request from C.R.A. LAHORE Division and general shelling of German trenches by field artillery brigades and Howitzer Battery was in accordance with directions to keep enemy worried all day from G.O.C. MEERUT Division. Remaining section of 110th Heavy Battery joined the other section in new position. Orders were issued during the afternoon at the request of the GARHWAL Brigade that no Artillery should fire between 4 P.M. and 7.30.P.M. and midnight and 7.A.M. Orders were also issued to 2nd Siege Battery to fire star shell in front of GARHWAL Brigade between 9.15.P.m and 10.30.P.M. and to field Artillery Brigades to engage any searchlights which might appear during this operation.	
9.15.p.m. .. 10.30pm .. ..do.....	2nd Siege Bty. with one howitzer advanced to RUE de BERCEAUX experimented with star shell. Some of these gave good results, as many as 15 stars falling from same on the other hand a few interrupt from a few lyddite shells were also fired into enemy trenches from battery position in the RUE de BERCEAUX.	
9.50.p.m. .. .. do	66th Battery fired at enemy planting wine entanglements	
10.35.p.m. .. .. do	66th Battery fired to stop musketry fire on trenches to left front.	

Army Form C. 2118.

– 18

WAR DIARY (continued) Vol V

INTELLIGENCE SUMMARY.

(Erase heading not required.)

Instructions regarding War Diaries and Intelligence Summaries are contained in F. S. Regs., Part II, and the Staff Manual respectively. Title pages will be prepared in manuscript.

Hour, Date, Place.	Summary of Events and Information.	Remarks and references to Appendices.
15th December 1914 LOCON		
8 a.m.	7th Battery observed No. 25* active and promptly shelled it.	*Appendix 6
8.20 a.m.	20th Battery saw column of 50 men marching S.W. along track F2a-142(R), fired on them and they often't ink and went to ground near 7a. Enemy collected in Red House F27-142(R) which was then shelled by 7th Battery.	
9.15 a.m.	66th Battery fired on occupied houses F4c and observed 4 direct hits.	
9.45 a.m.	114th Heavy Battery fired on 4T and houses in VIOLAINES village	
9.30 a.m.	V10th Heavy Battery fired 10 rounds at 17.	
10.15 a.m.	Hostile Battery No. 40* was in action, 66th Battery shelled it, put one piece in and later got one H.E. into an emplacement.	
10.30 a.m.	7th Battery also fired on No. 40*. Sharped with an emplacement, and later got one H.E. into an emplacement.	
10.35 a.m.	110th Heavy Battery fired 8 rounds at the "Redoubt".	
11.10 a.m.	110th Heavy Battery fired 14 rounds at 25*.	
11.30 a.m.	2nd Siege Battery with aeroplane observation engaged which was supposed to be 87, but by a mistake was 25*.	
12 noon	19th Battery reported to Brigade Headquarters that hostile trenches were visible from their O.P. bearing 126°. This was reported to C.R.A. Information sent to O.C. 2nd Siege Battery which fired a few rounds at 6a during afternoon. Orders sent to O.C. 110th Heavy Battery no it was though it might be the BEAU PUITS (5) battery to shell BEAU PUITS.	
11.50 a.m.	2nd Siege Battery fired on 40* - 20 rounds were utilised. 110th Heavy Battery fired 15 rounds at battery near BEAU PUITS, line and range reported correct by O.P. in RUE du BOIS. Same battery fired 12 rounds at 87 by map.	
2.10 p.m.	110th Heavy Battery fired 12 rounds at 17* which its own observation.	
2.30 p.m.	2nd Siege Battery fired 4 rounds at VIOLAINES.	
3 p.m.	2nd Siege Battery fired 24 rounds at BEAU PUITS and LORGIES villages - one horse seen. 114th H.B. fired 20 rounds percussion shrapnel at VIOLAINES and LORGIES village.	

Army Form C. 2118.

WAR DIARY (continued) VOL V
or
INTELLIGENCE SUMMARY.

(Erase heading not required.)

Instructions regarding War Diaries and Intelligence Summaries are contained in F. S. Regs., Part II, and the Staff Manual respectively. Title pages will be prepared in manuscript.

Hour, Date, Place.	Summary of Events and Information.	Remarks and references to Appendices.
3.30 p.m. 15th December 1914 LOCON	2nd Siege Battery fired 4 rounds at 6A.	× Appendix 6.
3.40 p.m. do	2nd Siege Battery fired 5 rounds at VIOLAINES.	
16th December 1914 LOCON	On night of 15th December 1914, LAHORE Divisional Artillery Operation Order No 15 was received and MEERUT Divisional Artillery Operation Order No 5 was issued. The rôle to be played by the Heavy Batteries of the MEERUT Division being to keep all hostile Artillery under observation and open fire at once should they become active during the day. In the event of none being noticed to fire to the southward, fire was ordered to be opened on certain batteries at 6.45 a.m - a quarter of an hour after the attack by the LAHORE Division was timed for.	ø Appendix 35. ×Appendix 36.
6.30 a.m. do	The 56th Howitzer Battery ready to open fire with the object of co-operating with the LAHORE Division.	MM29
6.45 a.m. do	7th + 16th Batteries opened an irregular fire on enemy trenches in front of GARHWAL R⁴. In accordance with Operation Order No 5× following batteries opened fire. 110th Heavy Battery on { ×5 (BEAU PUITS) { 17 (LORGIES battery) 114th Heavy Battery on { 47 + 17 { +7 - (VIOLAINES) 2nd Siege Battery on { 6A. { 40.	
6.50 a.m. do	19th, 20th + 28th Batteries acting on orders received at midnight from DEHRA DUN Brigade, opened fire on hostile trenches in their zone of fire. A hostile battery was active E of (BOIS au BIEZ - not located. So far as could be seen no German battery opened fire on our troops during the actual attack from GIVENCHY (vide Appendix 35) nor was any information of any reported by LAHORE Divisional Artillery.	
9.5 a.m. 9.20 a.m. 9.45 a.m. do	Enemy fired 10 rounds shrapnel at FESTUBERT and 20 rounds H.E and shrapnel from high angle gun of big calibre and long range on centre of square E6a -142(7x)	

Army Form C. 2118.

WAR DIARY (continued) Vol V
or
INTELLIGENCE SUMMARY.

(Erase heading not required.)

Instructions regarding War Diaries and Intelligence Summaries are contained in F. S. Regs., Part II, and the Staff Manual respectively. Title pages will be prepared in manuscript.

— 20

Hour, Date, Place.	Summary of Events and Information.	Remarks and references to Appendices.
9.45 a.m. 16th December 1914 LOCON.	Captive "Sausage" Balloon seen over ILLIES. Some little delay in obtaining bearings from batteries to obtain a reaction, but this was eventually done.	Appendix 37.
10.15 a.m. do	7 more rounds fired by same gun, that fired at 2 p.m.	
10.30 a.m. do	114th Heavy Battery attempted to engage 47 with aeroplane observation, but aeroplane unable to observe. Aeroplane remained in touch with battery till 3 p.m. but weather too thick for further observation.	× appendix 6.
11.15 a.m. do	110th Heavy Battery fired 10 rounds at 5 - BEAU PUITS - observation difficult.	
11.30 a.m. do	110th Heavy Battery fired 20 rounds at 40°, about 10 or 12 rounds reported line and range.	
	Bn. report from 2nd Gurkhas the O.C. 9th Brigade turned fire of 20th & 26th Batteries on to horse lines at No1 A in E4 A - 142 (h). 66th Battery shelled LORGIES which showed signs of occupation.	
12.10 p.m. do	114th Heavy Battery fired 12 rounds time shrapnel at road near ILLIES windmill where "Sausage" Balloon and its wagon were expected to be, from reaction of bearings by their O.P. being shelled.	
1.30 p.m. do	2nd Battery commenced registering some enemy trenches, but were interrupted by their O.P. being shelled.	
2 p.m. do	About 20 feet of FACTORY chimney in RUE du BOIS (near the O.P of several batteries) was knocked down. Enemy fired about 40 rounds field howitzer at slow rate - from direction of 47 or 46. 5 more large howitzer shells fired into E.6.a - 142(h) - possibly from VIOLAINES - three fell 150° short of there fired at 10.15 a.m. 110th Heavy Battery fired 35 rounds at 86° and DISTILLERY.	
2.10 p.m. do	Rapid shrapnel fired against FESTUBERT.	
	During the day the GARHWAL Brigade asked for H.E. shell fire to be employed to destroy "Obstacles" on their front. On investigation these were found to be CHEVAUX de FRISES. They were not engaged. 2nd Siege brought accurate fire with its alternate gun at RUE de BERCEAUX on trenches in rear of PICQUET House. This was combined with a joint fire from howitzers on the main position in RUE des CHEVATTES.	

Army Form C. 2118.

WAR DIARY (continued) VOL V
or
INTELLIGENCE SUMMARY.

(Erase heading not required.)

Instructions regarding War Diaries and Intelligence Summaries are contained in F. S. Regs., Part II, and the Staff Manual respectively. Title pages will be prepared in manuscript.

Hour, Date, Place.	Summary of Events and Information.	Remarks and references to Appendices.
16th December 1914 LOCON	The enemy appeared fairly quiet all day, very little bombing or sniping. 2nd Siege got two of its platforms down during the day. Orders were given that so far as possible the enemy were to be kept busy and had to their positions during the day.	MR3
9.a.m to 17th December 1914 3.p.m	111th Heavy Battery registered targets 4T, 5 and 7T, with observation by aeroplane.	+ Appendix 6
10.30. a.m. — do —	20th Battery shelled house No. 26 in E4a-142-(h) N.E. of d. with H.E. shell. Effect reported good and house gutted.	
11.30. a.m. — do —	110th Heavy Battery noticed activity at the "Redoubt" and fired 12 rounds at it.	
1.5. p.m. — do —	2nd Siege Battery shelled hostile battery located by them near BEAU PUITS, and fired at 200× N.N.E of figure 7 in F7a-142(h).	
1.10. p.m. — do —	110th Heavy Battery observing officer saw a section of field guns firing from near BEAU PUITS - 21 rounds of "common pointed" shell were fired at it and range appeared correctly found. Section was fired near 32× in an orchard round an Estaminet at end of village.	
2.45. p.m. — do —	German "Saussage" Balloon up again near ILLIES. It was reported moving about until nearly 4 p.m when it became stationary.	
3.15 p.m — do —	Holtie Artillery shelled the H.L.I Trenches and 2nd Siege Battery retaliated on German Trenches.	
4. p.m — do —	111th Heavy Battery fired 3 rounds time shrapnel at balloon, but too dark for observation. 110th H.B. also fired 5 rounds at it. During the day the Germans shelled farm lying between RUE du BOIS and RUE du CAILLOUX. Some shrapnel and some universal shell were employed. During the day the 56th How. Bn Battery continued registering on enemys trenches + buildings. Information was received that Indian Corps had ordered 2 howitzers from the 2nd Siege Battery to form the LAHORE Division. During the day the 1st Bde R.F.A. was relieved by the 8th Brigade R.F.A. and proceeded to ROBECQ to rest.	MR3

Army Form C. 2118.

WAR DIARY (continued) VOL V

INTELLIGENCE SUMMARY.

(Erase heading not required.)

— 22

Hour, Date, Place.	Summary of Events and Information.	Remarks and references to Appendices.
3 a.m. 18th December 1914 LOCON	Orders received from MEERUT Division that batteries were not to fire at all before 10 a.m. without there being absolute necessity for doing so.	
3.30 a.m. do	Orders sent to O.C.'s 56th Howitzer Battery, 2nd Siege Battery, 110th and 114th Heavy Batteries accordingly by motor cyclist.	
8 a.m. do	Conference of General Staff and Brigadiers of the Division at Divisional Headquarters at which it was explained that a demonstration in force was to be made in the evening by the MEERUT Division, and various soft-hats and trenches were if possible to be taken. The Artillery were ordered to harass their ammunition during the day as far as possible, and only fire a few registering rounds on the trenches and zones which they would be ordered to fire on during this demonstration, the object of their fire being to stop the enemy's supports and reserves coming up to leave LA BASSÉE.	
11.30 a.m. do	O.C. 110th Heavy Battery reported a railway train who seen to leave LA BASSÉE.	
1.30 p.m. do	The Batteries of the 13th Brigade R.F.A. which had relieved the 11th Brigade in action registered their zones.	
	No Divisional Operation Orders had not yet been received. "Advance Orders" were sent to O.C.'s 56th Howitzer Battery and 2nd Siege Battery, there were also telephoned to 110th and 114th Heavy Batteries. They were informed of trenches and zones which they would be required to fire at and that Artillery fire would commence with a sharp burst at 5 p.m. A Staff Officer (Lieut. Fnr. Macfarlane, R.A.) was placed and no made temporarily alongside O/C Divisions more fully. Orders were also to move up 20 Batteries sent by motor cyclist to O.C. 13th Bde. R.F.A at ROBECQ to move up 20 cartes of S.A.A to position 3/4 mile S.W of ESSARS for the Corps Reserve if required.	✻ Appendix 6.
1.40 p.m. do		
2 p.m. do	110th Heavy Battery fired a few registering rounds at WHITE horse (39) and its cross roads in B148.	
3 p.m. do	114th Heavy Battery fired 4 registering rounds	
2.25 p.m. do	MEERUT Division Operation Order No 9 received, and Operation Order No 6 by C.R.A was drafted accordingly.	✻ Appendix 38. ⊕ Appendix 39. ⊗ Appendix 40.
3.30 p.m. do	Orders received from MEERUT Division postponing time of operation 1 hour.	
3.35 p.m. do	Operation Order No 6 by C.R.A MEERUT Division was issued by motor cyclist.	

Army Form C. 2118.

WAR DIARY (continued) VOL V

INTELLIGENCE SUMMARY.

(Erase heading not required.)

Instructions regarding War Diaries and Intelligence Summaries are contained in F. S. Regs., Part II, and the Staff Manual respectively. Title pages will be prepared in manuscript.

Hour, Date, Place.	Summary of Events and Information.	Remarks and references to Appendices.
10.45 p.m. 18th December 1914 LOCON.	*Order received from MEERUT Division that amount of ammunition allotted by G.H.Q. for the morning's bombardment would be the same as sanctioned for today. No action taken on this.	*Appendix 44
19th December 1914.	During the day one complete section of 2nd Siege Battery under Captain BURKE was despatched to LAHORE Division and took up a position in A14-142 (J). * In accordance with Operation Order No 6. all batteries opened fire at 4 a.m in support of the GARHWAL Brigade attack and materially assisted in the success of the attack which gained 300* of the trench in the N.W corner of E47-142 (h). Heavy fire was kept up for half an hour and a fairly rapid rate was continued by all batteries till about 6.30 am when news of the completion of the attack was received. Reactions of teams to a German Searchlight were taken by the No 11 Anti Aircraft guns 26th Battery and 110th Heavy Battery which placed the searchlight at the cross roads in B10 z - 142 (h). The 28th Battery fired on it at 4.5.a.r. but it was out of range so presumably the reaction was minimum.	*Appendix 39 MS. *Appendix 6
do	The 28th Battery shelled German Infantry on the VIOLAINES - LA BASSEE Road inflicting visible losses.	
do	The Anti Aircraft guns engaged 2 German "Albatros" machines, but they were only in their arc of fire for a very short time and no visible effect was obtained.	
11.10.a.r.	2nd Siege shelled trenches in F1C and eastern halves of E44 and E52.	
11.15.a.m	110th Heavy Battery engaged in with aeroplane observation.	
11.30.a.r.	Some German shrapnel fell near the 20th Battery and 2nd Siege Battery but no damage was done.	
11.40.a.r.	9th Brigade shelled trenches S.E of 25 reported to be full of Germans by the aircraft.	

Army Form C. 2118.

WAR DIARY (continued) VOL V

INTELLIGENCE SUMMARY.

(Erase heading not required.)

Instructions regarding War Diaries and Intelligence Summaries are contained in F. S. Regs., Part II, and the Staff Manual respectively. Title pages will be prepared in manuscript.

Hour, Date, Place.	Summary of Events and Information.	Remarks and references to Appendices.
12 noon 19th December 1914 LOCON	2nd and 8th Batteries fired at the German trenches S.E. of 26˟	Appendix 6
12.30 p.m.	114th Heavy Battery registered 4 B with airman. 110th Heavy Battery fired at trenches near 8C where considerable activity was noticed.	
1 p.m.	A German Howitzer Battery was noticed moving on the ILLIES- LA BASSEE Road.	
2 p.m.	114th Heavy Battery engaged 4B. 20th Battery engaged flashes of enemy's howitzer battery near BEAU-PUITS. These had been shelling centre of DEHRA DUN Brigade heavily, but were quickly silenced.	
2.5 p.m.	2nd Siege Battery engaged 8b with airman, with good effect. 6" gun still went west. In response to a request from G.O.C. GARHWAL Brigade guns were brought to bear on Germans in part of the trenches captured by the GARHWAL Brigade which the Germans had not evacuated. Observation and communications were very difficult, but effect was continually obtained.	
2.30 p.m.	114th Heavy Battery engaged 33˟	
3.20 p.m.	114th Heavy Battery registered trenches in F1c.	
3.30 p.m.	2nd Battery shelled the houses at 26˟ with lyddite - followed by shrapnel.	
3.50 p.m.	19th Battery silenced a Maxim Gun, which was enfilading the right of the GARHWAL Brigade.	
4 p.m.	114th Heavy Battery engaged F1c and 39˟. 110th Heavy Battery shelled 7a˟ which was active.	
	˟ During the day the 56th Howitzer Battery fired with effect on the Distillery, houses at cross roads in B14 z, trench in B14a and at N˚ 26 and the trenches in its vicinity. 4 guns of this battery were forged with the DEHRA DUN Brigade under Lieut Colonel POTTS, Commanding 9th Brigade R.F.A. to facilitate rapid	

WAR DIARY (continued) Vol V.
INTELLIGENCE SUMMARY.
(Erase heading not required.)

Army Form C. 2118.

25

Co-operation.

The German observation Balloon made several ascents between 11 a.m. and 2 p.m. from near ILLIES. The 114th Heavy Battery fired 3 rounds at it but it was just out of range.

During the afternoon the portion of the Leicesters Regt holding the trenches captured in the early morning by the GARHWAL Brigade became untenable owing to very heavy enfilade maxim gun fire and to the fact that the Germans brought up a very powerful Bomb Gun, which could not be located.

A further attack was planned for 6 p.m. but it had to be cancelled and the Leicesters withdrawn at dusk, covered by heavy fire from all batteries. The fact that they managed to carry out this difficult manoeuvre with very little loss was undoubtedly due to the very effective support of the field guns.

The great delay in sending back the news that the retirement had been successfully accomplished entailed a great waste of ammunition. The C.R.A. was only informed at 9.5 p.m., whereas the retirement was all over at 7 p.m.

At 6.10 p.m the enemy attacked to right of the centre section of the Dehra Dun Brigade heavily and a heavy fire was brought to bear on them by the 20th, 26th Batteries and the 2 Sections of howitzers grouped with the Brigade.

With the exception of the right centre of the DEHRA DUN Brigade which had pushed back slightly, the situation was exactly as it had been before the H.a.R. attack, and all batteries were laid out on their respective zones to repel any possible counter attack

Army Form C. 2118.

WAR DIARY (continued) VOLUME V

INTELLIGENCE SUMMARY.

(Erase heading not required.)

Instructions regarding War Diaries and Intelligence Summaries are contained in F. S. Regs., Part II, and the Staff Manual respectively. Title pages will be prepared in manuscript.

Hour, Date, Place.	Summary of Events and Information.	Remarks and references to Appendices.
9.0.a.m. 20th December 1914 LOCON	Heavy firing all along the front, musketry and machine guns, and RICHEBOURG was shelled also FESTUBERT.	
9.10 a.m. do.	O.C. "N" Battery R.H.A. reports to C.R.A. and was ordered to join the Artillery grouped with the DEHRA DUN Brigade, under the command of Lt Colonel POTTS R.F.A. O.C. 9th Brigade R.F.A.	
9.15 a.m. do	2 German "Albatros" aeroplanes approached LA COUTURE from E.S.E. at an altitude of 6000 feet. On approaching within 5,500 yards of No 11 Anti Aircraft Section one turned S. and the other turned N.W. and crossed the arc of fire at 4000 yards. This section fired 25 rounds, two bursting very near. The aeroplane turned N. and then E., increasing its height. Owing to the construction of the mounts of these guns the arc of fire is very limited, vide sketch*, only targets above 30° altitude and below 60° altitude can be engaged.	* Appendix 42
9.30 a.m. do	VIoK Heavy Battery fired 10 rounds at No 116 which was active, using their own O.P.	* Appendix 6
9.50 a.m. do	DEHRA DUN Brigade reported 2nd Gurkhas heavily attacked. 19th, 20th and 58th Batteries ordered by O.C. 9th Brigade R.F.A. to engage this attack. 28th Battery observed officers reported enemy's mines apparently all along the ridge from FESTUBERT road, continued towards GIVENCHY, and then men following immediately by the enemy quitting the trenches and rushing to the attack. The Garhwalis asked for support especially in direction of PICQUET House (E8c - 1142(n)). Good effect obtained on the enemy by 28th Battery the enemy being in force and fully exposed. Above information sent to DEHRA DUN Brigade.	
10.20.a.m. do	Garhwalis asked for fire support opposite their left; this was supplied by 12th & 15th Batteries.	

Army Form C. 2118.

WAR DIARY (continued) VOL V
or
INTELLIGENCE SUMMARY.
(Erase heading not required.)

Instructions regarding War Diaries and Intelligence Summaries are contained in F. S. Regs., Part II, and the Staff Manual respectively. Title pages will be prepared in manuscript.

Hour, Date, Place.	Summary of Events and Information.	Remarks and references to Appendices.
10.43.a.m. 20th December 1914 LOCON	The advanced observing station of the 28th Battery (now Infantry Trenches) reported the H.L.I. had lost trench right of Brigade and 2nd Seaforths on left of Seaforths. O.C. 9th Brigade R.F.A. forwarded this information to DEHRA DUN Brigade, and ordered the other batteries + 6th Howitzers to open heavy fire over area already allotted.	
10.57.a.m. do	29th Battery reported "Germans believed to have taken PICQUET-House."	
11.1.a.m. do	2nd Battery reported urgent call from Seaforths for fire in vicinity of L.7 LA QUINQUE RUE, as enemy in strong numbers there. Support given to both right and left of Seaforths.	
11.30.a.m. do	Aeroplane over 114th Heavy Battery which engaged it with two observers. Range correctly found. G.O.C. GARHWAL Brigade asked for fire of 13th Brigade R.F.A. along the front, especially on the right front as general attack was reported. This fire was kept up the whole hour at a slow rate.	† appendix 6.
11.32.a.m. do	DEHRA DUN Brigade reported to O.C. 9th Brigade R.F.A. that the enemy had broken through both sections of SIRHIND Brigade, also left of Seaforths, into front also attacked. The 19th Battery was ordered to support gap.	
12.15.p.m. do	"Albatross" approached from the N. N°.11 Section Anti-Aircraft fired 28 rounds. Altitude was 7,000 ft. It retired E. at once.	
12.37.p.m. do	28th Battery observer in infantry trench reported Seaforths front, on the right, now parallel to FESTUBERT road, their left steady and that the 2nd Gurkhas had rallied.	
12.39.p.m. do	20th Battery shelled with H.E. shell for about one hour probably by N°.5. Aeroplane approached from the S. 12 rounds fired at it, appeared very close; it turned E. at once.	

Army Form C. 2118.

WAR DIARY (continued) VOL V

INTELLIGENCE SUMMARY.

(Erase heading not required.)

Instructions regarding War Diaries and Intelligence Summaries are contained in F. S. Regs., Part II, and the Staff Manual respectively. Title pages will be prepared in manuscript.

Hour, Date, Place.	Summary of Events and Information.	Remarks and references to Appendices.
12.45 p.m. 20th December 1914 LOCON	Owing to the indistinct situation it was deemed advisable to withdraw the advanced gun of the 2nd Siege Battery from the RUE DE BERGEAUX to its secondary position near LA COUTURE. Orders sent accordingly. German airmen over 110th Heavy Battery which fired 2 rounds at it*, which were reported just over & just left. The airman must have seen something as the ground for T came down.	*Appendix 6.
1.3 p.m.	do. Col. 9th Brigade R.F.A ordered 20th Battery and the 56th Howitzer Battery to fire on vacated trenches of 2nd Gurkhas reported as full of Germans —	
1.20 p.m.	do. 114th Heavy Battery shelled hostile trenches in the neighbourhood of RUE d'OUVERT in F1c-1442 (?).	
1.45 p.m.	do. "Saucisse" balloon up in direction of LA BASSEE.	
2. p.m.	do. FESTUBERT heavily shelled by the enemy.	
2.30 p.m.	do. 110th Heavy Battery with airman again engaged L16 – 16 rounds fired – 3 hits reported.	
2.45 p.m.	do. DEHRA DUN Brigade informed O.C. 9th Brigade R.F.A that the 9th Gurkhas were hard pressed up to the vicinity of Jats trenches.	
2.50 to 3 p.m.	do. 110th Heavy Battery kept up a dropping fire on the WHITE House (39) trenches, one round observed to fall right in a trench.	
3.15 p.m.	do. 114th Heavy Battery with airman engaged 7a. Range correctly found.	
3.30 p.m.	do. German "Saucisse" balloon up in direction of ILLIES.	
4.15 p.m.	do. "Saucisse" balloon up in the neighbourhood of MANAVILLES.	
5.30 p.m.	do. Request from DEHRA DUN Brigade to warn heavy battery and others to stop firing on 2nd Gurkhas vacated trenches on receipt of information re time of delivery of counter attack.	*Appendix 43
5.46 p.m.	do. O.C. 9th Brigade R.F.A ord the 4th How. Battery to come to slow intermittent fire close in front of our trenches 3.11–1.05.000 supporting trenches, and their allotted zones.	

Army Form C. 2118.

WAR DIARY (continued) Vol V

INTELLIGENCE SUMMARY.

(Erase heading not required.)

Instructions regarding War Diaries and Intelligence Summaries are contained in F. S. Regs., Part II, and the Staff Manual respectively. Title pages will be prepared in manuscript.

Hour, Date, Place.	Summary of Events and Information.	Remarks and references to Appendices.
7.5.p.m. 20th December 1914 LOCON	Report from DEHRA DUN Brigade to stop firing on 2nd Gurkhas vacated trenches but to continue firing beyond. 28th Battery officer in Infantry trenches reported Dunford the front as follows "Wire was in unknown quantity except that it sloped back from front about 150 yards from road to front about 300 yards down road. There if possible reserve trench which H.L.I. held.	✗ Appendix 44.
8.5.p.m. do	During the day the 16th How Battery co-operated in the operations by shelling trenches in the neighbourhood of QUINQUE RUE & also trench from which the Gurkhas had been driven in E48. The 2nd Siege Battery during the day fired on trenches in front of GARHWAL Brigade with good effect - hostile fire from these became very small. Later same battery turned on to trenches across RUE du CAILLOUX in front of our late position. The O.C. from the "Brewery" was able to see that our trenches near QUINQUE RUE were empty, that Indians were retiring down support trench, and he acted accordingly, proceeding at once to green fill. The two how platforms of this battery were taken up and withdrawn during the day, and the advanced gun moved back to LA COUTURE in accordance with orders sent at 12.45 P.M. During the day the O.C. 4th Brigade (recent at ROBECQ) was sent for and given verbal orders by the C.R.A. as to his dispositions, should his Brigade be sent for to reinforce. 8th Battery opened fire on enemy's trenches fired rounds of fire from 9.20 p.m. till 11.45 p.m. Same battery fired at enemy's searchlight.	
9.16.p.m. do		
9.16 p.m. do		
11 p.m. to 6 a.m. do	Heavy fire all night in front of LAHORE Division.	

Army Form C. 2118.

WAR DIARY (continued) VOL V
INTELLIGENCE SUMMARY.
(Erase heading not required.)

Instructions regarding War Diaries and Intelligence Summaries are contained in F. S. Regs., Part II, and the Staff Manual respectively. Title pages will be prepared in manuscript.

30

Hour, Date, Place.	Summary of Events and Information.	Remarks and references to Appendices.
20th December 1914 LOCON	The statement of a Corporal of the 9th Brigade R.F.A. is attached; this aeroplane which he claims to have seen fall may have been the one fired at 12.17 p.m by N°11 Anti Aircraft.	Appendix 41 W2 2
1.10.a.m. 21st December 1914 LOCON.	O.C. 9th Brigade R.F.A. received news that 58th Rifles had regained part of 2nd Gurkhas trenches.	
7.30.a.m. do	The morning opened very misty, too thick to observe. O.C. 9th Brigade R.F.A. was requested by G.O.C. DEHRA DUN Brigade at an interview to bring fire on orchard in vicinity northern road junction in E8a-142(h). The situation was also described to him.	
7.40.a.m. do	O.C. 2nd Gurkhas asked 20 th Battery observing officer to fire on the orchard.	
8.a.m. do	O.C. 9th Brigade received following report from 28th Battery observing officer :- "Enemy trenches situation immediately right unchanged. A.L.I. still in Maine trench, enemy have maxim gun in Inforthe original trench, and another suspected in house on north 100 yards of PICQUET House. Germans working on road present trenches almost untenable owing to water.	
9.30.a.m. do	44th Battery fired on treades of hostile battery in S.E corner of F.3.2.-142(h). This battery then ceased fire. O.C. 2nd Siege Battery having ascertained from G.O.C. DEHRA DUN Bde that fire was especially needed on trench 150° N. of orchard, there own old line crossed the RUE du CAILLOUX and having selected new observing station in a tree near a mine exit for Battery and shelter this trench with effect.	
9.45.a.m. do	N° Battery R.H.A. fired on a german maxim. 56th Howitzer Battery fired on orchard and horses N. of cross roads in E.H.C and a.-142(h).	

Army Form C. 2118.

— 31

WAR DIARY (continued) Vol V
or
INTELLIGENCE SUMMARY.
(Erase heading not required.)

Instructions regarding War Diaries and Intelligence Summaries are contained in F. S. Regs., Part II, and the Staff Manual respectively. Title pages will be prepared in manuscript.

Hour, Date, Place.	Summary of Events and Information.	Remarks and references to Appendices.
10.22.a.m. 21st December 1914 LOCON	Bearing of Sausage balloon from 28th Battery reported as 69° "true."	Appendix 6.
10.30 a.m.	Target 43 reported active so was promptly engaged by 114th Heavy Battery and made to cease fire.	
10.33. a.m.	Infantry sent urgent call to 9th Brigade R.F.A. for Howitzer fire on PICQUET House. This was arranged for.	
10.45. a.m.	Infantry asked for more fire in 4 of E4 – 142(h) – so O.C. 9th Bde R.F.A. ordered batteries having this zone in their allotted task to increase their rate of fire. G.O.C. DEHRA DUN Bde informed O.C. 9th Bde R.F.A. that a British Brigade was arriving soon in support, with probable intention of counter attack.	
do.	Infantry noticed fire on a house 200 yards S. of a in E4 – containing a machine gun. Fire shelled by howitzers of 58th How. Battery here gave. This took and obtained good effect.	
11.26. a.m.	110th Heavy Battery with aeroplane observation engaged targets 82 and 46* – Range of both correctly found – wait shoots and gusty, adverse conditions the shooting.	
do.	114th Heavy Battery shelled enemy's trenches in F1c & F1a – 142(h).	
11.30. a.m.	O.C. 9th Bde R.F.A. interviewed G.O.C. Dehra Dun and met G.O.C. 2nd Brigade (2nd Division).	
11.35. a.m.	19th Battery reported it was carrying on the request of 6th Jats to slow continuous fire on their front.	
11.40. a.m.	2nd Battery fired H.E. shell at enemy's machine gun – results apparent good.	
11.45.a.m.	114th Battery fired on enemy's trenches and obtained several direct hits (with percussion at range of 1850 yards – a length of CHEVRUX de FRISES being broken up.	
12. noon		

WAR DIARY (continued) Vol V

INTELLIGENCE SUMMARY.

(Erase heading not required.)

Army Form C. 2118.

— 32 —

Hour, Date, Place.	Summary of Events and Information.	Remarks and references to Appendices.
12.10 p.m. 21st December 1914 LOCON	O.C. 2nd Siege Battery hears there were indications that the Germans intended resuming the offensive by enveloping both flanks of the Seaforths and that a German machine gun and many men were at PICQUET House, turned fire on to the den-ch-house on the third of PICQUET House at the fourth round, getting several front rounds into info & trenches there, throwing up what appeared to be clothes or bodies.	
12.35 p.m. do	56th How: Battery engaged house with machine gun in it in E4c-142(h) N.E. also PICQUET House in E8C N.E. at request of Seaforths with observing officers in trenches.	Appendix 6.
1.45 p.m. do	110th Heavy Battery fired at trenches & Squares B13c and a-142(h). Also fired at field guns which were located N.E. of 40ˣ. Several rounds at 8,700ˣ seemed to go into them.	
	111th Heavy Battery engaged target 43ˣ reported active by observing officers of 110 Heavy Battery.	
2. p.m. do	O.C. 19th Battery reported gun and fragments of home in M— RUE du MARAIS and smoke coming from chimney. Battery shelled it with H.E. for one gun shyt. set it on fire and bolted 8 or 10 Germans on which shrapnel fire on the remaining guns was opened.	
	56th How! Battery fired again on house at E4C N.E. at request of S.F.R. Rifles - fire very effective	
	16th How: Battery fired on PICQUET House — until informed	
2.30 p.m. do	2nd Siege Battery fired on trenches near orchard with co-operation that SF Rifles were close up	
2.55 p.m. do	O.C. 9th Bngde R.F.A. attended conference at Infantry Bde Headquarters	
3. p.m. do	W/24th Brigade in support of counter-attack and Artillery support consisted forth the Request for immediate fire on rectangle S.E. of E4 – 142(h) also for heavy fire on it. for ½ / an hour when the counter attack	

Army Form C. 2118.

33

WAR DIARY (continued)
or
INTELLIGENCE SUMMARY.

(Erase heading not required.)

Vol V

Instructions regarding War Diaries and Intelligence Summaries are contained in F. S. Regs., Part II, and the Staff Manual respectively. Title pages will be prepared in manuscript.

Hour, Date, Place.	Summary of Events and Information.	Remarks and references to Appendices.
3.30 p.m. 21st December 1915 LOOS	commenced from + point 500ˣ to 600ˣ W of there, and then for the 0f increased range - this result known.	
4.45 p.m. do	36th Howitzer Battery fired on "Snipers" House just N of PICQUET House fire effective.	
4.55 p.m. do	114th Heavy Battery fired 30 rounds at enemy's trenches.	
	Orders received by 9th Bde R.F.A. that attack would commence at 5.15 p.m. necessary orders issued to batteries accordingly. Attack was however delayed from 5.15 to 5.45 p.m. and then to 7.15 p.m. but unfortunately this information not received by 9th Bde R.F.A. till too late to avoid very large expenditure of ammunition needlessly. Eventually at 8.15 p.m. information received that attack was this latter place and assistance in best manner possible was asked for.	Appendix 6.
5. p.m. do	110th Heavy Battery fired 30 rounds on enemy trenches and the 10 rounds at No. 5.	Nil
5.30 p.m. do	114th Heavy Battery engaged 7aˣ.	

WAR DIARY (continued) VOL V

INTELLIGENCE SUMMARY.

(Erase heading not required.)

Army Form C. 2118.

34

Hour, Date, Place.	Summary of Events and Information.	Remarks and references to Appendices.
6.15 PM to 21st December 1914 LOCON	Enemy batteries No 5, 7a and 8b active	*Appendix 6.
6.45 PM		
7. P.M.	114th Heavy Battery engaged 8a and 8b. * Shells seen from near No 32.	
9.25 PM	In support of the attack being received, the O.C. 9th Brigade R.F.A. ordered slow intermittent fire to be continued by no 9 gun.	
9.42 PM	28th Battery officer phoned from Enforth's trenches "news just received that left counter attack have taken support trenches and that attack on fire trenches is believed to be going to be made immediately."	
10.30.h 11.15 PM	Shells seen from No 5.	
2.25 a.m. 22nd December 1914 LOCON	2nd Brigade phoned to O.L. 9th Brigade R.F.A. "Counter attack got into orchard and further no suitable trenches witheher to abandoned communication trench just in rear - has been ordered to gain original line of trenches and either hold them or get a line through orchard - Germans bolted before we got there."	
7.45 a.m.	Report received from LAHORE Divisional Artillery that they were suffering from Heavy Artillery fire from 41*, 42 and battery at SALOME - Orders issued to Heavy Batteries to engage those targets. - Reply sent	*Appendix 46 ⊙ Appendix 47
8.20. a.m.	114th Heavy Battery engaged 43 reported active by 110th Heavy Battery's observing officer.	
8.38 a.m.	Enforth's requested fire of howitzers on house on road 150× W of PICQUET House - 56th Battery complied with this.	*Appendix 47(a)
8.40 a.m.	Informed c.a.t LAHORE Divisional Artillery that owing to low temperature of cordite today the 114th Heavy Battery was unable to engage hostile battery at SALOME - out of range.	
8.50 a.m.	110th Heavy Battery fire to 4b + 4c.	
8.57. a.m.	114th Heavy Battery engaged 4c. 28th Battery officer in Infantry trench reported to Col. 9th Brigade R.F.A.	

Army Form C. 2118.

WAR DIARY (continued) Vol LV

Instructions regarding War Diaries and Intelligence Summaries are contained in F. S. Regs., Part II, and the Staff Manual respectively. Title pages will be prepared in manuscript.

INTELLIGENCE SUMMARY.

(Erase heading not required.)

Hour, Date, Place.	Summary of Events and Information.	Remarks and references to Appendices.
9.9 a.m. 22nd December 1914 LOCON	Infantry line as yesterday, unable to regain their right flank to the old position. Connected on right with South Wilts Borderers who had relieved H.L.I. Reserve Trench. Sussex Regt taking over from Bedfords. 2nd Infantry Brigade asked O.C. 9th Brigade if he could supply them any information - above was sent.	
9.10 a.m. do	19th Battery officer in fire trench reported their situation:- Same as yesterday - extending by yards S. of SALIENT.	
9.40 a.m. do	GARHWAL Brigade informed O.C. 13th Brigade that aviator at 6 a.m. had seen 6 battalions of Germans in a state of readiness at BAS POMMEREAU. The 6th and 11th Batteries shelled this locality and information was sent to O.C. 33rd Brigade R.F.A. 8th Division through the 8th Battery. He also acted on it.	
10.9 a.m. do	Infantry line requested fire on orchard through 25th Battery French officer. this was passed on to 16th Hvy Battery which acted on it. 20th Battery position shelled for a quarter of an hour.	
10.15 a.m. (approx) do	Soon after 10 a.m. report received from O.C. 2nd Siege Battery from his O.P. at the Brewery that white handkerchief was waving in orchard by them in the trenches.	X Appendix 48.
about 10.30 a.m. (approx) do	Second report received from 2nd Siege - both these were at once telephoned up to the General Staff MEERUT Division.	⊙ Appendix 49
10.50 a.m. do	*1. received from O.C. 2nd Siege Battery that men were running back from trench to trench, mention of Germans or own men, that he was firing on orchard (telephoned up to General Staff MEERUT Division. Message received from G.O.C. Divn. from the DEHRA DUN Brigade Headquarters to turn heavy fire on orchard.	* Appendix 50
11 a.m. do	Officer in fire trenches reported Germans entering orchard in two streams - 9th Brigade R.F.A. ordered to shell the vicinity. (114th Heavy) Battery were ordered to fire on Trenches in squares F1c F1a - 142(h).	⊘ Appendix 51

Army Form C. 2118.

WAR DIARY (continued) VOL V

INTELLIGENCE SUMMARY.

(Erase heading not required.)

Instructions regarding War Diaries and Intelligence Summaries are contained in F. S. Regs., Part II, and the Staff Manual respectively. Title pages will be prepared in manuscript.

Hour, Date, Place.	Summary of Events and Information.	Remarks and references to Appendices.
11.30 a.m. 22nd December 1914 LOCON	Message from G.O.C. Division that situation at orchard was not clear, and ordering fire to be directed to the East of it and not on it. This was reported to 2nd Siege under C.R.A.M. 98.	✻ Appendix 52
11.50 a.m. do	Message from O.C. 2nd Siege Battery confirming the fact that Germans had advanced up to the orchard and were holding our trenches — Informed General Staff & informed of this by telephone.	✻ Appendix 53
	Message from O.C. 2nd Siege Battery that our troops not N. of Brewery were being withdrawn from S.E. with Shrapnel. Orders sent to 114th Heavy Battery to engage 41 + 42 and to 110th Heavy Battery to engage &c and then to resume fire on trenches E of orchard. These all by telephone. 114th Heavy Battery again shelled above trenches, also hostile batteries at 42.	g Appendix 54 † appendix 6.
12 noon do	O.C. 13th Brigade R.J.A. received a report from GARHWAL Brigade that enemy had again captured the orchard in front of the DEHRA DUN Brigade. All 3 batteries of this Brigade were then ordered to turn their fire on to square E41 and E42 - 142(h) to prevent enemy supports coming up. Sussex Regt. noted through 28th Battery for horses in orchard to be destroyed. 56th How. Battery were ordered to put a section on to this task.	@ Appendix 55.
12.40 p.m. do	O.C. 110th Heavy Battery reported that Company of Infantry had retired S.E. behind the WHITE House (39⁴). Message from 2nd Siege Battery that only one man visible in trench in front of orchard. General Staff informed.	£ Appendix 56
12.45 p.m. do	Orders sent to 13th Brigade R.J.A. to engage 6a reported active by 110th Heavy Battery's observing officer, by telephone. 110th Heavy Battery fired on WHITE House.	⊘ Appendix 57
12.47 p.m. do	9th Gurkhas through 19th Battery officer reported that they had no one on the right. 3 of ft. 1.0.1000. North Lanes had surrendered in a body and the northern flank the second line. This information was forwarded to the	

Army Form C. 2118.

WAR DIARY (continued) VOL V

INTELLIGENCE SUMMARY.

(Erase heading not required.)

37

Hour, Date, Place.	Summary of Events and Information.	Remarks and references to Appendices.
12.50 p.m. 22nd December 1914 LOCON	G.O.C 2nd Infantry Brigade. 2nd & 44th Batteries engaged 6th reported active by 110th Heavy Battery to C.R.A. and by him to O.C. 13th Brigade R.H.A. 114th Heavy Battery fired on target 43x. 10 rounds of common pointed shell.	*Appendix 6.
1 P.M.	Information received for O.C. 110th Heavy Battery that German battery from near Distillery was shelling our trenches. 110th Heavy Battery was ordered to engage target 45b.	*Appendix 57-8
1.5 P.M.	56th Hoz. Battery complied with orders to fire on houses in orchard, 7 or 8 direct hits being obtained.	
1.10 P.M.	56th Hoz. Battery turned one section on to E edge of orchard, including trench along same - fire apparently effective. 110th Heavy Battery engaged target 45b.	
1.15 P.M.	O.C. 44th Battery and Lutz. O.C. 2nd Battery reported enemy's infantry returning towards houses in F.I.a.-14.2(?). These were engaged by 44th Battery. (It is conceivable these may have been our prisoners being taken to the rear).	
1.30 P.M.	28th Battery reported:- "Germans holding Western hedge of orchard - our right our line enemy reported moving near PICQUET House into an earthwork. O.C. Anwer Regt regards destruction of houses in orchard and the one directly N. of it as most important - Both loopholed and both contain machine gun." This reported to infantry Brigadier and to C.R.A. The 56th Hoz. Battery was ordered to engage houses and trench W of orchard.	Ø Appendix 59 ⊗ Appendix 60
2 P.M.	Report on situation received from O.C. 2nd Siege and further report from him that he intended shelling trenches this side of orchard and also one other battery's dug out likewise.	*: Appendix 61.
2.10 P.M.	This information (Appendix 60) forwarded to O.C. 9th Brigade by priority message.	
2.25 P.M.	20th Battery ordered to shell Eastern half of orchard and "search". 28th Western half & N Battery RHA to engage movements near PICQUET House.	

Army Form C. 2118.

— 38

WAR DIARY (Continued) Vol V
or
INTELLIGENCE SUMMARY.
(Erase heading not required.)

Hour, Date, Place.	Summary of Events and Information.	Remarks and references to Appendices.
2.57 p.m. 22nd December 1914 LOCON	56th How! Battery turned one Section's fire on house & orchard EHC-1142(h). obtaining 3 direct hits with lyddite.	*Appendix 62
3. p.m. do	Report from 9th Brigade R.F.A. that Infantry anxious for certain houses to be shelled with H.E.	¤ Appendix 63
3.8. p.m. do	Report from 2nd Siege that several Germans were seen in trenches & north of orchard. L formation 22.x to 2nd Siege that Infantry wanted Earthwork shelled	* Appendix 64
3.10 p.m. do	Report from 2nd Siege that Germans coming from South RUE du CAILLOUX were now in Second trenches N of orchard. — Reported to General Staff	¤ Appendix 65
3.52 p.m. do	19th Battery Officers in Jack trenches reported to O.C. 9th Bde R.F.A. that their salient on the W edge of EHb-142(h) was being bombed from a point 100 x to East and that light Battery were firing on it. and he no observing on it.	
	The day was too misty for good observation. During the day information was very scantily obtained from the Infantry, nearly all the information obtained from O.C 2nd Siege Battery, from No 6, O.P. on the Brewery or from the O.C. of the Rue R.F.A. through his officers on the Infantry trenches, or — from the 110th Heavy Battery officers in their observing station. These items were immediately communicated to the General Staff of the Division by through telephone from the C.R.A.'s office. Enemy's batteries were a good deal more active during the day than they had been lately, notably 62 & 43 who were shelling the neighbourhood of FESTUBERT, a battery near the Distillery 8 or 4b which shelled the Gurkha trenches, and a battery near VIOLAINES which shelled the 20th Battery (4t or 4c).	¤ Appendix 6. M.J.G.

Army Form C. 2118.

— 39

WAR DIARY (continued) VOL V
or
INTELLIGENCE SUMMARY.
(Erase heading not required.)

Hour, Date, Place.	Summary of Events and Information.	Remarks and references to Appendices.
23rd December 1914. LOCON.	During the night 22nd/23rd December 1914 the 9th Brigade R.F.A. and 56th How: Battery kept up a slow rate of fire on the trenches and ground that had been lost by the DEHRA DUN Bde. During the day information was received that the 1st Division would take over from the LAHORE Division and not for the MEERUT Division. C.R.A. 2nd Division who are now Brevet MEERUT Division visited C.R.A. MEERUT Division. O.C. 9th Brigade R.F.A. who have been providing NCOs for helping with the improvised trench mortars reported that the general opinion was that they could be most profitably employed in groups of two or three and that there was no doubt that the size of the german trench mortars had been much exaggerated by the infantry. 3rd Siege Battery put down their platforms again — The whole night and day passed off very quietly and the germans seemed to do very little. Made consolidating their position on the front they had won. 2nd Siege Battery fired a few rounds in the vicinity of the orchard and SNIPERS and PICQUET Houses to stop some work at the willow trenches. He from a E of the orchard and E of the left of the DEHRA DUN Brigade (19th Battery) the orchard and ground W of it (20th + 80th Batteries) and the vicinity of the PICQUET House (N Battery) were all shelled during the day.	
12 noon	4th Battery fired two bursts at a point where the germans were reported to be advancing.	Appendix 6.
1.30 p.m.	114th Heavy Battery shelled 47 and 47c which were shelling the FESTUBERT BREWERY road and silenced them.	
2.45 p.m.	56th How: Battery shelled houses in the orchard.	
3 p.m.	19th Battery shelled an M.G. emplacement which was being constructed opposite the salient in our line in E43-142(h). Good effect was obtained with percussion shrapnel.	

Army Form C. 2118.

WAR DIARY (continued) VOL V

or

INTELLIGENCE SUMMARY.

(Erase heading not required.)

Instructions regarding War Diaries and Intelligence Summaries are contained in F. S. Regs., Part II, and the Staff Manual respectively. Title pages will be prepared in manuscript.

Hour, Date, Place.	Summary of Events and Information.	Remarks and references to Appendices.
24th December 1914 LOCON	All was quiet during the night 23rd/24th December, although a certain amount of rifle fire took place all along the line. N. Battery and the 26th Battery fired a few rounds in the vicinity of the PICQUET House to stop sniping. In every case the Germans ceased firing after one burst of fire. Some Afridi Scouts went over the ground & then the orchard and found it packed with dead Germans.	
8 a.m.	A report was received from the GARHWAL Brigade that the enemy were pumping water into the left trenches of the Brigade by means of a pump on the ESTAIRES-LA BASSEE road and it was requested that this pump should be shelled. 16th How. Battery were ordered to carry this out but found their telephone arrangements did not admit of it. It was then arranged that 2nd Siege should place a howitzer at 56th Howitzer Battery's dropout near then and then 2/3rd Gurkha Rifles were with an officer in the trenches to observe. However owing to the activity of the MINENWERFERS during the day the Siege Howitzers were brought occupied with them all day and the pump no never not be shot at, although all arrangements were made to carry out the operation next day. Foggy weather prevailed all day.	*Appendix 6
6.30 a.m.	2nd Battery fired a few rounds in front of centre section GARHWAL Brigade.	
9.30 a.m.	110th Heavy Battery shelled N°5.×	
10.30 a.m.	43 + 5 of which fire and were engaged by 114th Heavy Battery.	
11.45 to 12.30 p.m.	2nd Siege Battery engaged 2 MINENWERFERS which were causing much trouble near the SNIPERS House and behind a house in the orchard. Both were soon silenced.	
12 noon	114th Heavy Battery shelled 43 + 34 which were active. The latter shoots by N. of NEUVE CHAPELLE. 2nd Battery engaged Howitzer gun NE of 39× with good effect.	
12.45 p.m.	16th How. Battery engaged MINENWERFER prob. S. of the orchard.	
1.45 p.m.	2nd Siege Battery shelled PICQUET House and SNIPERS House at request of Infantry, who suspected sniping operations being carried out there.	

Army Form C. 2118.

41

WAR DIARY (continued) VOL V

INTELLIGENCE SUMMARY.

(Erase heading not required.)

Instructions regarding War Diaries and Intelligence Summaries are contained in F. S. Regs., Part II, and the Staff Manual respectively. Title pages will be prepared in manuscript.

Hour, Date, Place.	Summary of Events and Information.	Remarks and references to Appendices.
2.10. p.m 24th December 1914 LOCON	"N" Battery shelled some germans who worked a trench near the PICQUET House.	
2.15 p.m do	2nd Siege Battery shelled trench W. of SNIPER'S House into which the Germans were seen to advance. Good effect was obtained.	*Appendix 6.
2.30 p.m do	114th Heavy Battery engaged 4+ and 4c	
2.45 p.m do	13th Brigade endeavoured to engage 32a with aeroplane observation, owing to the foggy weather only 8th Battery were enabled to see the aeroplane signals some of which were missed and no round was fired. *During the day the 111th Battery fired bursts of fire at a house in Flamertinghe [?] 142(h) near which germans were seen to collect from time to time. Another house near it which germans made round the trenches was also hit 3 times with H.E. C.R.A. and diviors made round the trenches very thick all day and difficult to observe - there was practically a lull in the proceedings - very little firing on either side. The MINENWERFERS did not fire all day, and few bombs were thrown. 19th Battery fired on enemy snipers i.e. E4B-142(h).	QM & Q
8 A.M. 25th December 1914 LOCON		
8.37 A.M. do	Officer in Grenadier trench phoned that they wished houses in neighbourhood of PICQUET House demolished as enemy used same for machine guns – owing to shoot 16th How. Battery did not engage these until 10.25 a.m., and continued till 12.10 p.m hand with good effect.	
9.36 A.M. do	20th Battery officer in trench Grenadiers reported that a new trench [?] was being dug by them across a re-entrant connect up with the Colet streams and that the Germans were digging another parallel to it and about 300× from it.	
10.57 A.M. do	58th How. Battery opened fire on enemy bomb in front of 39th Garhwali in B10a-142(h) which had been pumping water into their trenches. Fire reported effective.	
11.13 A.M. do	12th Battery fired a few rounds at PICQUET House at urgent request of Grenadiers.	
12 noon do	115th Battery fired occasional rounds at trps in E4b-142(h) and continued doing so until dark, no digging was perceptible.	

Army Form C. 2118.

42

WAR DIARY (continued) Vol V

INTELLIGENCE SUMMARY.

(Erase heading not required.)

Instructions regarding War Diaries and Intelligence Summaries are contained in F. S. Regs., Part II, and the Staff Manual respectively. Title pages will be prepared in manuscript.

Hour, Date, Place.	Summary of Events and Information.	Remarks and references to Appendices.
25th December 1914 12 noon	Col. 2nd Regt. at request of O.C. Grenadiers shelled houses in front of two lines from which persistent sniping had taken place, the roof of one important one was blown clear off.	
1.40.p.m. do	Shot Grads through 20th Battery officers in trenches requested 9th Brigade R.F.A. to demolish houses in orchard. This was passed to Col. 56th How. Battery.	
2.30.p.m. do	56th How. Battery shelled most northerly house in orchard E 47-142(h)	
3.p.m. do	20th Battery fired on snipers in orchard, and effectively stopped the sniping. 44th Battery fired a few rounds at request of O.C. 39th Garhwal.	
3.54 p.m. do	56th How Battery fired on Sap head in E47-142(h) at request of Kent Forks — 19th Battery officer in trenches observing fire.	
5 p.m. to 6 p.m. do	"N" Battery R.H.A. by request fired a few rounds "gun fire" every quarter of an hour while Coldstreams replaced the Grenadiers in the trenches.	
	✕ Lieut. S. GIFFARD R.F.A. wounded by a rifle bullet in the arm while returning along a road from observing.	✕ Appendix 66
	It was unfortunate that the day was so misty, an arrangement had been made for both 9th & 13th Brigades R.F.A. to attempt firing with aeroplane at unknown targets.	⊙ Appendix 67 No 3
	Officers of 4th Bde R.F.A. (reading at ROBECQ) to be prepared to watch the experiment. They had not yet been attached to the R.F.A. of this Division.	⊗ Appendix 67(b)
	Operation Order No 7 issued in accordance with MEERUT Division Operation Order No 10 dated 24.12.1914 for the withdrawal of the Artillery of the Division to new billeting area — See also Meerut Division Operation Order No 11 ⊗	
26th December 1914 HAM	The roll of the 4th Bde R.F.A. Gen. No 7 the role of the MEERUT Divisional Artillery was withdrawn during the day and moved to billets in the area of LILLERS, except the 9th Bde R.F.A. 19th Col and 13th Brigade R.F.A. 6th Col which was arranged should continue the supply of ammunition to the 2d Division until tomorrow. The 2nd Divisional Artillery having taken over.	

Army Form C. 2118.

WAR DIARY (continued) Vol V

or

INTELLIGENCE SUMMARY.

(Erase heading not required.)

Instructions regarding War Diaries and Intelligence Summaries are contained in F. S. Regs., Part II, and the Staff Manual respectively. Title pages will be prepared in manuscript.

Hour, Date, Place.	Summary of Events and Information.	Remarks and references to Appendices
27th December 1914. 11 A.M.	The C.R.A. MEERUT Division with his Staff proceeded into billets at HAM.	NP.2
28th December 1914. 11 A.M.	9th Brigade R.F.A. Am Col and 13th Brigade R.F.A. Am Col withdrawn to billets near LILLERS. Remainder MEERUT Divisional Artillery resting.	NP.2
29th December 1914. 11 A.M.	Meerut Divisional Artillery resting. 3 new guns arrived for 110th Heavy Battery to replace 3 badly scored ones.	NP.2
30th December 1914. 11 A.M.	MEERUT Divisional Artillery resting.	NP.2
	MEERUT Division resting in billets in neighbourhood of LILLERS *Copy of result of map shooting of Hanif by B.M. Battery R.F.A. on 10/12/14 attached. Also copy of circular memorandum No 12.9 R.A. (L) dated 15.12.14 issued to all R.A. units in MEERUT Division. Summary of information received to all R.A. units when forthcoming— *Copies of these are attached hereto	*Appendix 68. & Appendix 69. NP.29. *Appendix 70
31st December 1914. H.A.M.	MEERUT Division resting. The various references quoted in this volume will be found at Appendices 71 + 72.	The Appendices 71 + 72

Lieut R.A.

for C.R.A. Meerut Division

Appendix 29.

OPERATION ORDER No. 5
by
LIEUTENANT-GENERAL C.A. ANDERSON, C.B.,
COMMANDING MEERUT DIVISION

APPENDIX 29

Reference Map - France 1/80,000   LOCON, 1st December 1914.
Sheets Arras, Stomer & LILLE.

Intention. 1. The front now held by the LAHORE Division will be taken over by the MEERUT Division during the nights 2nd/3rd and 3rd/4th December 1914.

Dehra Dun Brigade. 2. The G.O.C. Dehra Dun Brigade will place the Seaforth Hrs, 6th Jats and 1/9th Gurkha R. at the disposal of G.O.C. Bareilly Bde, and the 2/2nd Gurkha R. at the disposal of the G.O.C. Garhwal Bde with effect from the afternoon of 2nd Decr in the case of the 1/9th G.R. and from afternoon of 3rd Decr in the case of the other battalions.

The G.O.C. Dehra Dun Brigade will himself, with his Staff, report to G.O.C. Bareilly Brigade at GORRE on the afternoon of 3rd Decr to act as reserve commander.

Garhwal Bde. 3. The Garhwal Brigade plus 41st Dogras, 2/2nd Gurkha R. and
41st Dogras machine gun detachments of 4th Cavalry, will take over the front
2/2nd G.R. now held by the Jullundur Brigade, the 2/39th Garhwalis and
M.G. Det 4th 1/39th Garhwalis taking over the left and left centre respect-
Ind. Cav. -ively on the night 2/3rd Decr and the 2/2nd G.R. and Leicesters taking over the right centre and right respectively on the night 3/4th Decr. The machine gun section 4th Cav. will accompany the battalions taking over trenches on night 2/3rd Decr.

The Brigade Reserve will be moved into position on the afternoon of 3rd Decr.

Further details of the relief will be arranged by Brigadiers concerned direct.

Bareilly Bde 4. The Bareilly Brigade less the 41st Dogras and plus the Sea-
(less 41st forth Hrs, 6th Jats and 1/9th Gurkha R. will take over the front
Dogras) now held by the Ferozepore Brigade, the 1/9th G.R. taking over
Sea. Hrs the left and the Black Watch & 2/8th G.R. taking over the left
6th Jats centre sections on night 2/3rd Decr. 260 Sea. Hrs will also take
1/9th G.R. over the extreme right of the line relieving an equal number of the Connaught Rangers on the night 2/3rd Decr.

The 58th Rifles and balance of Seaforth Hrs will take over the right centre and right respectively on night 3/4th Decr.

The Brigade Reserve will be moved into position on the afternoon of 3rd Decr.

Further details of the relief will be arranged by Brigadiers concerned direct.

Artillery. 5. "N" Battery R.H.A., the 4th & 9th Brigades R.F.A. & 56th How Battery R.F.A., under Lieut. Col. L.A.C. Gordon, R.F.A. will be in action in the Garhwal Brigade area.

N. & 1 Section The 5th & 11th Brigades R.F.A. & 1 Section 56th How Battery R.F.A., under Lieut. Col. L.G.F. Gordon, R.F.A., will be in action in the Bareilly Brigade area.

Nos 110 & 114 Heavy Batteries R.F.A. will be directly controlled by the C.R.A. Meerut Divn.

All details for the above reliefs will be made by the C.R.A. Meerut Divn in communication with the C.R.A. Lahore Divn, the relief to be completed by 6.0 a.m. on the 4th Decr.

6.
4th Ind. Cav. The 4th Ind. Cav. less Machine gun section, will move into billets in LOCON on the morning of 4th Decr, taking over the billets now occupied by the 15th Lancers, in direct communication with the O.C. that regiment. The regiment will be in Divisional Reserve.

The M.G. section will proceed to the trenches on the night 2/3rd Decr under orders to be issued by G.O.C. Garhwal Bde.

S. & M.	7.	No. 3 Coy S. & M. will retain its present billets and will be employed with the Bareilly Brigade. No. 4 Coy S. & M. will move into its former billets near LE TOURET on the afternoon of 3rd Decr and will be employed with the Garhwal Brigade.
107th Pioneers	8.	Retain their present billets in GORRE and form part of the Divisional Reserve.
Div. Amm Column.	9.	The Meerut Divisional Ammunition Column will continue in its present billets and supply all units in the Meerut Division Area.
Fd. Ambs.	10.	Field Ambulances will be distributed as follows:-

½ No. 19 B.F.A.
128 I.F.A. — LES GLATIGNIES — In reserve.

½ No. 19 B.F.A.
129 I.F.A. — MESPLAUX.

½ No. 20 B.F.A.
130 I.F.A. — CHATEAU de GORRE.

½ No. 20 B.F.A. — LOCON.

Details will be arranged by A.D.M.S. Meerut Division in direct communication with A.D.M.S. Lahore Divn.

Signals.	11.	Existing signal arrangements will be taken over by the O.C. MEERUT Signal Coy, to the extent necessary, in direct communication with the O.C. Lahore Signal Coy. The exchange to be effected by 10.0 a.m. on 4th Decr.
Divisional Reserve.	12.	The Divisional Reserve will consist of the 4th Cavalry, 107th Pioneers and two Battalions from Lahore Division, i.e. Connaught Rangers at LE TOURET & 129th Baluchis at LE HAMEL.
Billets.	13.	With the exceptions mentioned in these orders the Meerut Division will will exchange billeting areas with the Lahore Division; the exchange to be completed on or before the morning of 4th Decr.
Train.	14.	Infantry Units will return their baggage wagons to the Train on the afternoon prior to moves in relief, informing O.s C. Train Coys as to date and hour at which horses are required to be sent up. Vehicles of the Train will not use the BETHUNE - ESTAIRES Road for north & south movements during the period of relief. The Train will exchange billets with the Lahore Divn Train on the afternoon of Decr 4th; details of the move being arranged with the O.C. Lahore Divn Train.
Supplies.	15.	Refilling will continue as at present up to Decr 4th inclusive. From Decr 5th the Division will refill at 9.30 a.m. at the cross roads ½ mile North of the "V" in VENDIN.
Command.	16.	The G.O.C. Meerut Divn will assume command at 12 noon on 4th Decr, the Divnl Hdqrs being established in the buildings now occupied by those of the Lahore Divn. Brigadiers will assume command of sections when relief by their troops has been completed, reporting on night 3/4th Decr, reporting to Divnl Hdqrs that they have assumed command.

Of Meerut Division P. Davies
Major,
General Staff, MEERUT DIVISION.

Issued by orderly at 10.30 a.m.

Copy No. 1 to Indian Corps.
    2 Lahore Division,
    3 & 4 do (For Ferozepore & Jullundur Bdes)
    5 Bareilly Brigade
    6 Garhwal Brigade.
    7 Dehra Dun Brigade.
    8 C.R.A. Meerut Divn,
    9 C.R.E. Meerut Divn,
    10 4th Ind Cavalry,
    11 107th Pioneers,
    12 A.Q.M.G. Meerut Divn,
    13 A.D.M.S. ,, ,,
    14 O.C. Train,
    15 Meerut Signal Company,
    16 War Diary,
    17 File.

APPENDIX 24

No. G.97/4446

Headquarters, MEERUT Division,
1st December 1914.

Memorandum.

In paragraph 16 of OPERATION ORDER No. 8 of 1/12/1914, the time of assuming command should now read 12 noon, and not as therein stated.

Major,
General Staff, MEERUT Division.

"A" Form.
Army F
MESSAGES AND SIGNALS.

Prefix	Code	m.	Words	Charge	This message is on a/c of:	Recd. at
Office of Origin and Service Instructions			Sent			Date 24
			At m.		Service.	From
			To			
			By		(Signature of "Franking Officer.")	By

TO — CRA Meerut Divn

Sender's Number	Day of Month	In reply to Number	AAA
G97/8	1st		

The following correction is made to Meerut Divn Operation Order number six of date AAA Paragraph three line four for 1/39th Garhwalis read 2/2nd GR AAA line five for ~~----~~ 2/2nd read 2/3rd Addressed all concerned

From — Meerut Divn
Place
Time — 6-45 pm

The above may be forwarded as now corrected. (Z) Davis Major

Censor. Signature of Addressor or person authorised to telegraph in his n

*This line should be erased if not required.

M. & Co. Ltd. Wt. W929/549—100,000. 6/14. Forms C2121/10.

Appendix 30

Section of German Trenches opposite FESTUBERT

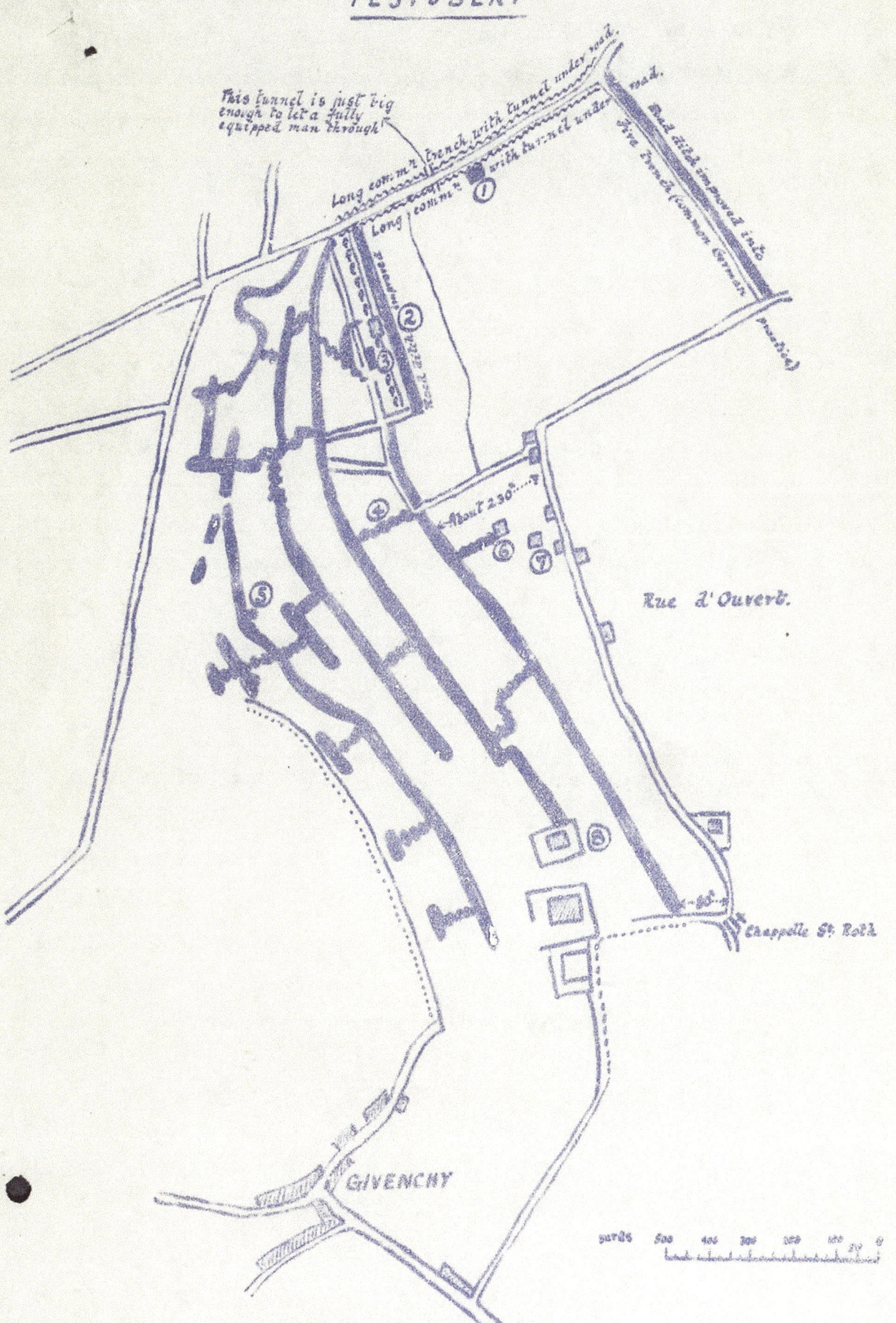

APPENDIX 30

The attached sketch map has been prepared according to information supplied by a German prisoner. The German trenches are shown by thick black lines. The method of advance is always the same, namely, pushing of saps, which are linked up by the lateral trenches until the line is continuous. Saps are driven by pioneers who are escorted by a party of 8 men under a N.C.O. Bombs thrown into saps would, therefore, do useful execution.

Trenches vary according to the ideas of the company commanders. In prisoner's company there was a traverse between every two men, for the neighbouring company there were six men between traverses, with the result that their losses were much heavier than those suffered by his company.

When a trench is captured saps are immediately pushed out, provided with head cover, and generally defended by a machine gun, which enfilades the whole length of the trench captured.

As regards the reference numbers on the sketch map:-

(1) is a dug-out, furnishing bomb-proof headquarters for a battalion
(2)   do.   do.   do.
viewed from FESTUBERT it should appear as a big mound of earth on right of 3 willow trees standing very close together.
(3) is an observation post, 10-15 yards loophole.
(4) is a communication trench, much used.
(5) is an observation post.
(6) is a battalion headquarters; damaged house.
(7) is a damaged farm, possibly occupied by some medical staff.

Reference MERVILLE-LA BASSEE map $\frac{1}{40,000}$.

The field kitchens are in DOUVRIN, where also is the heavy baggage. These kitchens come every evening through LA BASSEE and take up a position just left of road junction W of the CHAPELLE ST. ROTH, behind some stacks. They also sometimes go to RUE DE MARAIS. They arrive at these destinations between 6.30 and 7.p.m.

Copy No. 3 Dehra Dun Bde

Garhwal Brigade.	Copy No 4.
Lahore Division.	Copy No 5.
C.R.A.	Copy No 6.
C.R.A.	Copy No 7.
4th Ind. Cavalry.	Copy No 8.
107th Pioneers.	Copy No 9.
A.Q.M.G.	Copies No 10 & 11.
A.D.M.S.	Copy No 12.
War Diary.	Copy No 13.
File.	Copy No 14.

OPERATION ORDER NO. 7.
By
Lieutenant-General C.A. ANDERSON, C.B.
Commanding MEERUT Division.

Copy No. 6
APPENDIX 31

Reference Map –

MERVILLE - LA BASSEE 1/40,000   LOCON, 10th December 1914.

INTENTION. 1. The MEERUT Division will hold the line of trenches from the cross roads at the junction of the RUE DU BOIS and ESTAIRES - LA BASSEE Road exclusive, to the cross roads one quarter mile east of the X in RUE de CAILLOUX, including the road but excluding the Picquet House. This line will be divided into two portions :-
(1) The Right Front, and (2) The Left Front.

LEFT FRONT. 2. The GARHWAL Brigade will hold the Left Front from the cross roads at the junction of the RUE DU BOIS and the LA BASSEE - ESTAIRES Road exclusive, to the Machine Gun post two hundred yards south of the junction of the RUE DU BOIS and LA QUINQUE RUE - RICHEBOURG d'AVOUE road, inclusive.
Headquarters of the Brigade will be established at LA COUTURE by seven p.m. on 11th December.
The G.O.C. GARHWAL Brigade will withdraw the 2nd Bn. LEICESTERSHIRE Regiment on the nights 10th/11th and 11th/12th into Brigade Reserve at RICHEBOURG St. VAAST.

RIGHT FRONT. 3. The DEHRA DUN Brigade will hold the Right Front - from the Machine Gun post, mentioned in paragraph 2, exclusive, to the cross roads one quarter mile east of the X in RUE de CAILLOUX, including the road but excluding the Picquet House.
Brigade Headquarters will be established at CSE. du RAUX by seven p.m. on 11th December.
The 1/9th GURKHA Rifles will retain its present position in the trenches.
The 2/2nd GURKHA Rifles will, on the night 10th/11th, under the orders of G.O.C. GARHWAL Brigade, occupy a portion of the trenches now held by the right half-battalion, 2nd Bn. LEICESTERSHIRE Regiment.
The 6th JATS will report to G.O.C. GARHWAL Brigade at CSE. du RAUX, at four p.m. on the 11th, and will occupy the trenches held by the left half battalion, 2nd Bn. LEICESTERSHIRE Regiment.
The 1st Bn. SEAFORTH HIGHLANDERS will, on relief, move direct into Brigade Reserve of the Right Front, at RUE de l'EPINETTE.

CORPS RESERVE. 4. The BAREILLY Brigade, less 41st DOGRAS, will, on relief, become Corps Reserve, and will billet about VENDIN and OBLINGHEM, west of the LA BASSEE Canal.
Brigade Headquarters to be established at VENDIN.
The SIRHIND Brigade of the LAHORE Division will relieve the SEAFORTH HIGHLANDERS and 58th Rifles on night 11th/12th, and the BLACK WATCH and 2/8th GURKHA Rifles on night 12th/13th December. Details will be mutually arranged by Brigadiers concerned.

DIVISIONAL RESERVE.
4th Ind Cavalry
41st Dogras
107th Pioneers

5. The 4th Indian Cavalry, 41st Dogras and 107th Pioneers, will form the Divisional Reserve.
The 4th Ind. Cavalry will move to CROIX MARMEUSE on 11th December to be in new billets by 1.0 p.m.
The 41st Dogras will move into billets at LACOUTURE this evening 10th December 1914 after relief at RICHEBOURG St. VAAST by the Leicesters. Any transport with 41st Dogras can proceed to LACOUTURE at a convenient hour this afternoon, 10th December.
The 107th Pioneers will move to billets at LE TOURET at a date to be specified later.

ARTILLERY.	6.	No movements of batteries in relief will take place until after the 13th December 1914.
SAPPERS & MINERS.	7.	No. 3 Company, S. & M. will move from GORRE to billets to be selected by the G.O.C. Garhwal Brigade in the neighbourhood of LA COUTURE for work with the Garhwal Brigade. Move to be carried out on 12th December 1914 before 4 p.m. No. 4 Company S. & M. will stand fast at LE TOURET for work with the Dehra Dun Brigade.
COMMANDS.	8.	The G.O.C. Garhwal Brigade will remain in command of his present line till all the Dehra Dun Brigade troops are in position when the two Brigadiers concerned will, under mutual arrangements, report by wire that they have assumed command of their new areas. The G.O.C. Bareilly Brigade will hand over command of that portion of his line to form part of the Dehra Dun Brigade when all Dehra Dun Brigade troops are in position. The two Brigadiers will then, under mutual arrangements report by wire that they have handed over, and assumed command, respectively. The G.O.C. Bareilly Brigade will hand over command of the remainder of his ___ line to the G.O.C. Sirhind Brigade as soon as the troops of the latter Brigade are in position and will report the fact by wire. The G.O.C. Meerut Division will retain command of the present line till the G.O.C. Bareilly Brigade reports that he has handed over that portion of the line to be taken over by the Lahore Division, after which he will remain in command of the line held by the Garhwal and Dehra Dun Brigades.
BOMBS.	9.	All bomb-guns now in support of the right & centre sections of the Bareilly Brigade front will be handed over to the Lahore Division as the relieving troops take over on the night 12th/13th December. Those in support of the left section Bareilly Brigade will similarly be handed over to the G.O.C. Dehra Dun Brigade.
SIGNALS.	10.	Readjustment of the signal lines will be carried out under the orders of the Officer in charge Signals of the Indian Army Corps.
AMBULANCES.	11.	$\frac{A \& B}{19}$ British Fd Amb.) To open at MESPLAUX by noon 138 Indian Fd Amb.) 11th December. $\frac{C \& D}{19}$ British Fd Amb.) To open at ZELOBES by 2 p.m. on 129 Indian Fd Amb.) 11th December. $\frac{A \& B}{30}$ British Fd. Amb.) To move to VENDIN under orders 130 Indian Fd Amb.) of the A.D.M.S. Meerut Division in communication with A.D.M.S. Lahore Division. $\frac{C \& D}{30}$ British Fd Amb. Remains at LOCON.
SUPPLIES.	12.	Refilling will continue as at present up to the morning of 12th December inclusive. From 13th December inclusive the Division will refil on the BETHUNE - ESTAIRES Road between the cross roads at LOCON and the road junction at LES CHOQUAUX, at 8.30 a.m.
TRAIN.	13.	The train will move to billets in the vicinity of LOCON and LES CHOQUAUX after refilling is completed on the morning of December 13th.

C.M....
Colonel,
General Staff, Meerut Division

Issued by orderly at 4.0 p.m.
Copy No. 1 to Indian Corps.
Copy No. 2 to Bareilly Brigade.
Copy No. 3 to Dehra Dun Brigade.

OPERATION ORDER N° 8.
by
Lieutenant-General C.A.Anderson, C.B.,
Commanding M E E R U T Division.

Copy No. 6
APPENDIX 31

Reference Map:-
MERVILLE-LA BASSEE. 40,000

L O C O N 11th December 14.

4th CAVALRY.   1.   The 4th Cavalry will move to CROIX MARMEUSE at 11 a.m. tomorrow.

ARTILLERY.   2.   Artillery reliefs rendered necessary by readjustment of troops holding the line will now be completed by 12 noon tomorrow under arrangements to be made by the C.R.A. Meerut Division in communication with the C.R.A. Lahore Division.

SAPPERS & MINERS.   3.   No 4 Company, Sappers & Miners will move to LE CASSAN to day under arrangements to be made by the C.R.E.

PIONEERS.   4.   The 107th Pioneers will move from GORRE to LE TOURET to-morrow, via CHATEAU de GORRE-LOISNE road. Head of column not to reach CHATEAU de GORRE before 12-15 p.m.

BOMB-GUNS.   5.   General Officers Commanding, Dehra Dun and Garhwal Brigades will each detail an officer (British) to be in charge of the bomb-guns in their respective Brigades. These officers will report to Captain W.E. Fleming, 41st Dogras at Headquarters Dehra Dun Brigade for instructions.

AREAS.   6.   The boundaries of the Divisional Area will be as follows:-
NORTHERN BOUNDARY. From RUE du BOIS - LA BASSEE - ESTAIRE cross roads by a direct line North West to the "E" in FOSSE; thence ½ mile North West in the direction of the "R" in RUE du PONCH; ½ mile W. to the "L" in PONT LEVIS thence to the road immediately E. of the last "S" in HOUSSIERES; westward to the "H" in HOUSSIERES the line running below the letters of that word; thence N.W. to the road-junction at western extremity of village of LA BOUZAT-EUX; S.W. along the line from that point to the "D" of the CHEMIN de BETHUNE road along latter road to junction with road to QUENTIN, thence due west to HAMLET BILLET on the AIRE Canal. (Latter place not shown on map).

SOUTHERN BOUNDARY. From cross roads ½ mile N. of last "T" in FESTUBERT - FESTUBERT CHURCH - LES FACONS - LOCON road - LOCON - BETHUNE road - LES CHOQUAX - PONT LEVIS road - AIRE Canal Southwards. The area west of the canal about VENDIN and OBLINGHEM will be in Meerut Area and retained for infantry of Corps Reserve.

BRIGADE BOUNDARIES. The dividing line between the Brigades on the North and South fronts is from junction of LA QUINQUE RUE - RUE du BOIS, westward through "C" of CHAV-ATTES to the "T" headed road junction 1 mile North of LE TOURET; thence to bridge over canal at VASS'lle immediately North of LANNET.
The Western boundary of these Brigades is the LA LAWE Canal.

Issued at 6-30.p.m. by Orderly.

to:-
Indian Corps.   Copy No 1.
Bareilly Brigade.   2.
Dehra Dun Brigade.   3.
Garhwal Brigade.   4.   4th Cavalry.   No 8.
Lahore Division.   5.   107th Pioneers   No 9.
C.R.A. Meerut Divn.   6.   A.Q.M.G. Meerut. Nos 10 & 11.
C.R.E. Meerut Divn.   7.   A.D.M.S. Meerut. No 12.
   War diary and File No 13 & 14.

Major,
General Staff, Meerut Divn.

Operation Orders No 4.   Copy No ....30... **APPENDIX 32**
by
Brigadier General A.B. Scott, C.B., D.S.O.
Commanding Royal Artillery, MEERUT Division.

Reference map:- NERVILLE - LA BASSEE 1/40,000."   LOCON. 10th December 1914.

Intention 1. The MEERUT Division will hold the line from the cross roads at the junction of the RUE du BOIS and ESTAIRES - LA BASSEE road exclusive to the cross roads 1/4 mile E. of the x in RUE de CAILLOUX including the road. This line will be divided into 2 portions (1) Right Front (2) Left Front.

Left Front 2. The GARHWAL Brigade will hold the left front from the cross roads at the junction of the RUE du BOIS and the LA BASSEE - ESTAIRES road exclusive, to the Machine Gun post 200 yards S. of the junction of the RUE du BOIS and LA QUINQUE RUE - RICHEBOURG d'AVOUE road, inclusive.
Head Quarters of Brigade will be established at LA COUTURE by seven p.m. on 11th December.

Right Front. 3. The DEHRA DUN Brigade will hold the Right Front from the Machine Gun post, mentioned in paragraph 2, exclusive, to the cross roads one quarter mile E. of the x in RUE de CAILLOUX, including the road but excluding the Piequet House.
Brigade Headquarters will be established at Cse. du RAUX by seven p.m. on 11th December.

Corps Reserve. 4. The BAREILLY Brigade, less 41st Dogras, will, on relief, become Corps Reserve, and will billet about VENDIN and OBLINGHEM, W. of the LA BASSEE Canal.
Brigade Headquarters to be established at VENDIN.

Divisional Reserve. 5. The 4th Indian Cavalry, 41st Dogras and 107th Pioneers will form the
4th Indian Cavalry   Divisional Reserve, and will be billeted as follows:-
41st Dogras.
107th Pioneers.   4th Indian Cavalry........ CROIX MARMEUSE.
                            41st Dogras............... LA COUTURE.
                            107th Pioneers............ LE TOURET.

Artillery . 6(a) The Artillery will be grouped as follows:-
            with DEHRA DUN Brigade........ 9th Brigade R.F.A.
             " GARHWAL Brigade.......... 4th Brigade R.F.A.

This arrangement will come into force when G.O's.C. DEHRA DUN and GARHWAL Brigades take command of their portions of the line. Up to that time the G.O.C. GARHWAL Brigade commands the line and the present grouping remains in force.

(b) On relief (time will be communicated) the 13th Brigade R.F.A. will proceed to ZOBEEQ.

(c) The Headquarters and 2 Sections 56th Howitzer Battery R.F.A., 110th and 114th Heavy Batteries and 2nd Siege Battery R.G.A., will be under the G.O.C., R.A.

(d) Special orders will be issued to Section of 56th Battery at BURBURE.

(e) Divisional Ammunition Column:- Headquarters and No 1 Section will move to 1/4 m. S. of BOHEME.
Nos. 2, 3 and 4 Sections to TOMBE WILLOT.
This move must be completed so as to comply with paragraph 10 below.

(f) 114th Heavy Battery and 2nd Siege Battery Ammunition Columns will

P.T.O.

will remain as at present.

Ammunition Supply 7. Troops will draw ammunition as follows:—

GARHWAL Brigade.
4th Indian Cavalry
41st Dogras
No 3 Company, Sappers & Miners
} 4th Brigade R.F.A. Ammunition Column.

DEHRA DUN Brigade
107th Pioneers
No 4 Company, Sappers & Miners
} 9th Brigade R.F.A. Ammunition Column.

Corps Reserve . . . . 13th Brigade R.F.A. Ammunition Column } at ROBECQ

Ambulances 8.
A&B British Field Ambulance
128th Indian do
} To open at NESPLAUX by noon 11th December.

C&D British Field Ambulance
129 Indian do
} To open at ZELOBES by 2.P.M. on 11th December.

A&B British Field Ambulance
130 Indian do
} To move to VENDIN under orders of A.D.M.S MEERUT Division in communication with A.D.M.S. LAHORE Division.

C&D British Field Ambulance . . remains at LOCON.

Supplies 9. Refilling will continue as at present up to the morning of 12th December inclusive.
From 13th December inclusive the Division will refill on the BETHUNE – ESTAIRES Road between the cross roads at LOCON and the road junction at LES CAROUAUX, at 8.30.a.m.

Train 10. The Train will move to billets in the vicinity of LOCON and LES/CAROUAUX after refilling is completed on the morning of December 12th.

E.M. Geddes Newton, Major R.A.
Brigade Major R.A.
MEERUT Division.

Issued at Q.H.Q. P.M.
Copy No 1 to General Staff, MEERUT Division
Copies 2 to 6 to O.C. 4th Brigade R.F.A.
" 7 to 11 to O.C. 9th Brigade R.F.A.
" 12 to 16 to O.C. 13th Brigade R.F.A.
Copy No 17 to O.C. 11th Brigade R.A.B.
" No 18 to R.A. Group Commander BAREILLY Bde
" No 19 to R.A. Group Commander GARHWAL Bde
" No 20 to O.C. 56th How. Battery R.F.A.
" No 21 to O.C. No 11 Section Anti Aircraft Guns.
" No 22 to O.C. Divisional Ammunition Col:
" No 23 to O.C. 2nd Siege Battery R.G.A.

Copy No 24 to O.C. 110th H.A. Battery
" No 25 to O.C. 11th H.A. "
" No 26 to C.R.A. LAHORE Dn
" No 27 to B.M. BAREILLY Bde
" No 28 to B.M. GARHWAL "
" No 29 to B.M. DEHRA DUN "
" No 30 to WAR DIARY
" No 31 to File.

MESSAGES, SIGNALS ...
Army Form C. 2121. Modified for India.

APPENDIX 33

TO	RA Group Commander BAREILLY Brigade	

Sender's Number	Day of Month	In reply to number	AAA
RM 18	11·12·14		

Reference my CRA 1 dated 4/12/14 the action of 56th Howitzer Battery near GSE du KUILX temporarily grouped with the BAREILLY Brigade having accomplished the task for which it was then grouped comes under the orders of RA Group Commander of GARHWAL Brigade from 12 noon today AAA It will not be moved from its present position to-day AAA Addressed RA Group Commander Bareilly Bde repeated RA Group Commander Garhwal Brig for information and necessary action

FROM	Bde Major RA	Meerut
Place		
Time	10.45 a.m.	

"A" Form.   Army Form C.

MESSAGES AND SIGNALS.

APPENDIX 34

TO: C.R.A. Meerut Divn

Sender's Number: G.20/3
Day of Month: 11th

AAA

Indian Corps wires begins In modification para four (9.45 p redeployment of front) Indian Corps Lahore Divnl Artillery will relieve Meerut Divnl Arty by noon twelfth December aaa on completion of Artillery relief C.R.A Lahore Divn commands all artillery in Southern area address ends For information please

From Place: Meerut Divn
Time: 9-0 am

Davis Major
GSO II

APPENDIX 25

14.12.14

G.O.C. R.A Meerut Divn

Ind. Army Corps has asked me to arrange with you direct, about your support to Lahore Divn Operation tomorrow.

(2) Will you please direct the fire of your Heavy Batteries upon any German batteries that may open as our Infantry attack. The Infantry attack is being made by Ferozepore Bde, and will break out from Givenchy against the German trenches opposite, afterwards endeavouring to [gradual?] take the trenches W of RUE DOUVERT. German batteries near VIOLAINES, LES 3 MAISONS & neighbourhood, require special watching especially.

J. Johnson

Secret   APPENDIX 35

OPERATION ORDER No 15   Copy No 2
by
Br General F.E.Johnson, D.S.O.
Commanding Lahore Divisional Artillery
15-12-14

1. The 58th French Division will attack on the   on the
   front:- Junction of ANNEQUIN and MAZINGARBE RAILWAYS to
   railway juction on LA BASSEE-BETHUNE road.

2. Lahore Division will cooperate as follows:-
   (a) ~~One section of~~ 81st Battery 5th Brigade, R.F.A. ~~from a position near PONTFIXE~~ and 113th Hy Battery will open
       fire on the triangle formed by railways 1 mile East
       of GUINCHY, enfilading railway embankment which forms
       the Western side of the triangle -

   (b) 109th Hy Battery ~~and a section of 2nd Siege Battery~~
       will shell the centre and Eastern portion of the
       triangle -

   (c) 73rd Battery of 5th Brigade, R.F.A. will open fire on
       that portion of railway between Southern angle of
       triangle and the road crossing 500 yards to the
       South West -

   (d) A force under G.O.C. Jullundur Brigade will attack and
       hold the three bridges over the Canal and the Western
       angle of the triangle - and will be supported by the
       ~~section of the~~ 81st Battery ~~from PONTFIXE and also by~~
       the remainder of the 5th Brigade, R.F.A. ~~who~~ will direct
       its ~~their~~ fire on the German Trenches between CANTELEUX
       and the LABASSEE - BETHUNE road.
       As soon as this attack commences 113th Hy Battery will
       ~~cease firing at the triangle, 2nd Siege Battery will~~
       engage Eastern angle and 109th Hy Battery the Southern
       angle on LABASSEE - BETHUNE road.

   (e) The Ferozepore Brigade will carry and make good the
       enemy's advanced trenches N.E. of GIVENCHY in front of
       15 Sikhs and enemy's retired trenches in front of a
       portion of the Sirhind Brigade - and will be supported
       by one section of "N" Battery, R.H.A. and one section
       of 37th Howitzer Battery, R.F.A. from a position 500 yds
       N.W. of BURBURE ~~who will direct them~~ their fire being directed
       First (i) on the German trenches between CANTELEUX and CH11e
                  St ROCH -
       Later (ii) On German Trenches N.E. of GIVENCHY -
             Both the above sections will be grouped under
             G.O.C. Ferozepore Brigade - Artillery Group
             Commander Major HARDING NEWMAN O.C. 37th How Bty,
             R.F.A.

   (f) The remainder of the Jullundur Brigade and the Sirhind
       Brigade will occupy enemy's front with vigorus rifle
       fire and will meet any counter attacks made against
       Ferozepore Brigade - They will be supported ~~by a section
       of 81st Battery of the 5th Brigade~~ 11th and 18th Brigades of
       R.F.A.

   (g) The 113th Hy Battery, after the attack has commenced, and
       the Heavy Batteries of the Meerut Division ~~continued Battering~~
       will engage any German ~~Trenches~~ Batteries that may open
       fire -

3. ~~The order for~~ the commencement of the Artillery prepara-
   tion mentioned in 2 (a) and 2 (b) will be ~~given by G.O.C R.A. Lahore Division~~ - at 6 am & will continue
   till 8.2 am -

                                                        P.T.O.

4. Medical arrangements will be subsequently notified -

5. Reports for the Divisional and Divisional Artillery
Commander after   to the black pyramid
slate heap 400 yards South of the A in ANNEQUIN -

Copy No 1 Gen Staff Lahore Div
  -   2 Meerut Div Arty Hd Qrs
  -   3 B.M Jullunder Bde thro C R A of the Jullunder Bde Group
  -   4 B.M Ferozepore Brigade thro C R A of Group.
  -   5 B.M Sirhind Brigade thro
         C R A Sirhind Bde Group
  -   6 OC 109th Hy Bty.
  -   7 - 113rd Hy Bty
  -   8 - 2nd Siege Bty
  -   9 - 37th How Bty. R.A
  - 10 - "N" Battery R.H.A
  - 11 - Lahore Div Amm Col.

Amonton Maj
BMRA Lahore Div

Operation Orders. Copy No 1.

No. 5   by   APPENDIX 36

~~Secret~~

Brig. Gen. A.B. Scott
CB DSO
Commdg. Royal Artillery
Meerut Divn.

Place LOCON
Date 15.12.14.
Time 8 p.m.

Intention

(1) The LAHORE division is carrying out an attack on 16th Dec at 8 a.m, and the artillery of the Meerut Division will cooperate — the principle object being to keep down any artillery fire of the enemy directed towards GIVENCHY or the front. The FEROZEPORE Brigade is operating from GIVENCHY to the East and will also endeavour to take the trenches west of RUE d'OUVERT.

Orders

(2)(a) Batteries are to be ready to open fire at 7.50 a.m, 16th Dec, but should not commence until the LAHORE division does unless german batteries open fire on the LAHORE division when the enemy should be engaged at once.

(b) Should the fire of the LAHORE division not be observed fire should be opened at 8.15 a.m.

(3) 110th Heavy Battery will engage BEAU PUITS and 1 b.

114th Heavy Battery will engage 4 b, 125
3 MAISONS (47 or 17)
2nd Siege — 6 a, 25 or 40.

58th Battery should watch the front and take any opportunity of cooperating in the general scheme.

Operation Orders.

No.   by   Place

Date

Time

II

(4) The situation should be carefully watched and any opportunity seized of engaging any of the enemy's artillery that may open or reinforcements which may move towards the LAHORE division

[signature]
Major RA
issued at 7.45 p.m.   BdeMajor RA
by mounted orderly   Meerut Div

Copy No 1   retained ✓
No 2   110th Hy
No 3   Hy Bty
No 4   2nd Siege
No 5   58th Hy
No 6   Gen. Staff.

APPENDIX 3/6

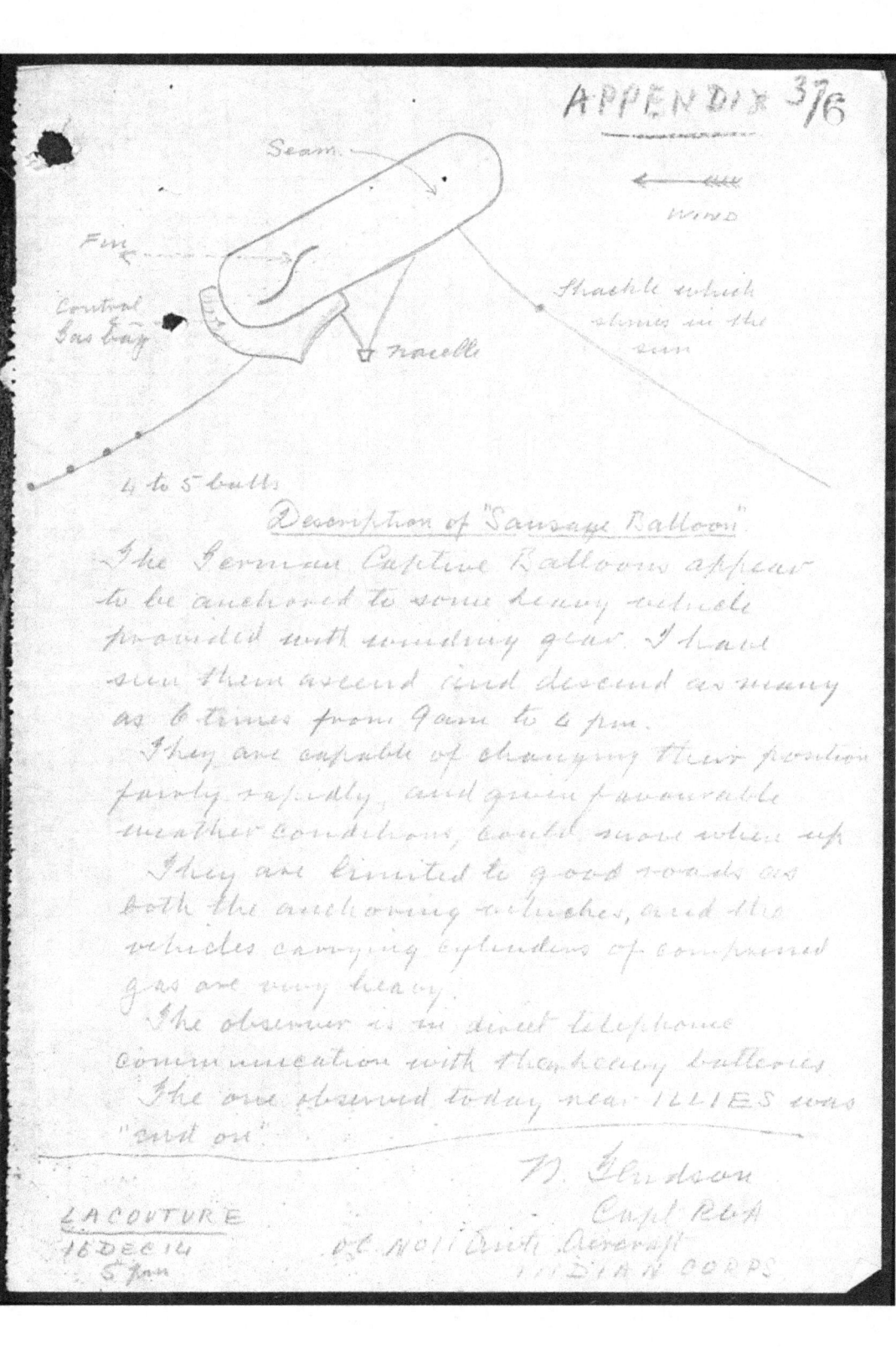

Description of "Sausage Balloon".

The German Captive Balloons appear to be anchored to some heavy vehicle provided with winding gear. I have seen them ascend and descend as many as 6 times from 9 am to 4 pm.

They are capable of changing their position fairly rapidly, and given favourable weather conditions, could move when up.

They are limited to good roads as both the anchoring vehicles, and the vehicles carrying cylinders of compressed gas are very heavy.

The observer is in direct telephone communication with the heavy batteries.

The one observed today near ILLIES was "cut off".

N. Glindon
Capt R.A.
O.C. No 1 Anti Aircraft
INDIAN CORPS

LACOUTURE
16 DEC 14
5 pm

SECRET

APPENDIX 38

Copy No. ...5...

OPERATION ORDER No. 9.
by
LIEUT.-GENERAL C.A. ANDERSON, COMMANDING MEERUT DIVISION.

LOCON, 18th December 1914.

Reference Map:- Merville - and Trench Map
Le Bassee, 1/40,000.

Information. 1. The C.inC. intends to attack vigorously today all along the front. The 2nd Corps is resuming the attack in the North in conjunction with the French.
A strong French attack is to be made in the vicinity of ARRAS and the IIIrd, IVth and Indian Corps are to demon--strate, and be prepared to take any favourable opportunity which may offer occur to capture enemy's trenches to their front.

Intention. 2. The Meerut Division will assist by demonstrating along its entire front and by special attacks as below.

Artillery. 3. Will maintain the ordinary slow fire during today and economise ammunition expenditure. This should cease by 4-30 at latest. Any necessary targets for the evening operations will be registered.
A heavy bombardment of the German trenches from the LA BASSEE Road to the North East of angle of the LA QUINQUE RUE triangle, along the front of the Garhwal and Dehra Dun Brigades, will commence at 5.0 p.m. today. This fire is not to be directed on the trenches close to our firing line. The bombardment should commence with a severe, sharp burst of fire, which will act as a signal to the Divisions on our right and left.

Dehra Dun Brigade. 4. The Dehra Dun Brigade will attack today as follows:-
(a) It will occupy the German sap in front of the "Orchard" and will connect it by a sap back to our firing trenches in the "Orchard".
If it is found possible this afternoon to explode the mine now being prepared into this sap saphead, this will be done at 5.0 p.m. and will be immediately fol--lowed by a rush on the enemy's sap-head. Should the explosion of the mine be found impossible, the attack on the sap-head is to take place at 4.45 p.m. 3-45a.m.
(b) Simultaneously with the above attack on the sap-head, the advanced post in the ditch in front of the right centre of the right battalion will be occupied and working parties will proceed to improve the bombproof cover over it and to connect it with our fire trenches by saps starting one from each end, and following the shortest line between the post and our trenches.
(c) The G.O.C. Brigade will arrange for heavy infantry and machine gun supporting fire to open from the right of his line as soon as the sap-head is rushed. Infantry and machine gun supporting fire from such other portions of his line as he may decide should open as soon as, but not before, the Garhwal Brigade attack on his left commences firing.
(d) If opportunity offers during the course of the GARH--WAL Brigade attack, the battalion holding the "Orchard" should cooperate by attacking the German trenches to its front. This cooperating attack is only to be initiated if the Garhwal Brigade attack is succeeding.

GARHWAL Brigade. 5. The Brigade Commander will arrange for an infantry attack by one battalion to break out from the re-entrant in our line on the left of the Dehra Dun Brigade at 4.45 p.m. against the German trenches in front of the southern portion of the re-entrant. After penetrating the enemy's line this attack will work along enemy's trench to both flanks making full use of bombs for the purpose of clearing out the enemy and occupying, with a view to holding it, such portions of the German trench as may be successfully cleared. He will support his attack, if it becomes necessary to do so, by a portion of another battalion. A working party of 2 Companies Pioneers and half No.4 Company S. & M. in addition to No.3 Company S. & M., already attached to his Brigade, is placed (vide para 7) at his disposal for the purpose of ada-ting the parapet of the captured trench to our require--ments and of opening a communicating trench between our

our front line and the captured trenches.

It is left to the discretion of the Brigade Commander, as should he find it possible in the course of the night, to inaugurate offensive action on a smaller scale from one of the piquets to the north of the re-entrant.

Cooperation by howitzer bombs, maxim gun and rifle fire will be arranged from such portions of his firing line as the Brigade Commander selects. The maxim gun and rifle fire from his left should be directed on points south and west of the ESTAIRES - LA BASSEE Road.

4th Cav. 6. Will move into close billets at LE TOURET, to be there by 4.0 p.m. this evening, and to remain in a constant state of readiness. Horses can be sent back to billets at CROIX MARMEUSE.

S. & M. 7. Half No.4 Coy S. & M and two companies 107th Pioneers
Pioneers. will be in the reserve trench "The Strand" in rear of the junction of the Dehra Dun and Garhwal Brigades at 3.30 p.m. today. They will be at the disposal of the G.O.C. Garhwal Brigade for work during the night. The G.O.C. Dehra Dun Brigade will arrange to have them guided into their position.

41st Dogras

41st 8. Have moved into close billets in RUE DU BOIS east of
Dogras junction of RUE de l'EPINETTE, and will remain in constant readiness from 5.0 p.m. today.

Bombs. 9. Brigade commanders are reminded that parties of bomb-throwers with a good supply of bombs should accompany all attacks. Also that full use should be made of their bomb-guns.

Signals.10. Arrangements will be made by G.O.C. Dehra Dun Brigade to hoist a red light close in rear of left of his Brigade as soon as the Garhwal Brigade attack commences firing. This light will act as a guide as to the direction of our lines to all concerned in the attack.

Reports.11. Reports to LOCON as usual.

R. Davies
Major
General Staff, MEERUT Division.

Issued by Motor Cyclist and
orderly, at 2.0 p.m.
to Indian Corps Copy No. 1.
Bareilly Brigade 2
Garhwal Brigade 3
Dehra Dun Brigade 4
C.R.A. 5
C.R.E. 6
4th Ind Cav 7
107th Pioneers 8
41st Dogras 9
Meerut Sig Coy 10
Lahore Divn 11
Eighth Division 12
A.A.& Q.M.G. 13 to 16 (including Medical and Train)
War Diary 17
File 18.

APPENDIX 39

Copy No. 10

OPERATION ORDERS No. 6.
BY
BRIGADIER GENERAL. A.B. SCOTT, C.B., D.S.O.   C. R. A. MEERUT DIVISION.

Reference:-
Skeleton squared map 1/20,000,   LOCON. 18th December 1914.

INFORMATION. 1. The Commander-in-Chief intends to attack vigorously today all along the front. The 2nd Corps is resuming the attack in the North in conjunction with the French. A strong French attack is to be made in the vicinity of ARRAS and the IIIrd, IVth and Indian Corps are to demonstrate, and be prepared to take any favourable opportunity which may occur to capture enemy's trenches to their front.

INTENTION. 2. The MEERUT Division will assist by demonstrating along its entire front and by special attacks communicated to Infantry Brigadiers.

ARTILLERY. 3. A heavy bombardment of the German trenches from the LA BASSEE Road to the North East of angle of the LA QUINQUE RUE triangle, along the front of the GARHWAL and DEHRA DUN Brigades, will commence at 4.a.m. tomorrow. This fire is not to be directed on the trenches close to our firing line. The bombardment should commence with a severe sharp burst of fire, which will act as a signal to the Divisions on our right and left.

2 Sections 56th How:Battery) On hostile trenches in
1 Gun 2nd Siege Battery R.G.A.) squares B 13 c and d and
) F 1 a, b, and c, also on
) cross roads in S.W.
) corner of F 1 c.

1 Section 56th How:Battery) On squares B 10 d, and
1 Gun 2nd Siege Battery R.G.A.) B 14 a, b, and c.

110th Heavy Battery R.G.A.
1 section on 39 and trenches in vicinity.
1 Section on cross roads in B 14 b.
This battery will also keep the following hostile batteries under observation and open on them immediately should they fire on our Infantry:-
8 a, 8 b, 46, 18 a, 18, 2 and 5.

114th Heavy Battery R.G.A.
1 section on 39 and trenches in B 13 c.
1 section on trenches in F 1 a, b, and c.
1 gun from one of the above sections will be prepared to engage enemy's searchlight in conjunction with the O.C. 9th Brigade R.F.A.
This battery will also keep the following hostile batteries under observation and open on them immediately should they fire on our Infantry:-

1 b, 4 b, 5 and 6 a.

P.T.O.

O.C. 2nd Siege Battery will send one gun to RUE de BERCEAUX
This gun should have 30 star Shell with it as well as
lyddite. Star shell only to be fired if requested
by G.O.C. GARHWAL Brigade, whose Headquarters will be
400 yards W. of top of B in RUE de BERCEAUX with whom
he should maintain communication. (MERVILLE-LA BASSEE m/p 1/40000)

Fire will be continued in bursts at intervals as required.

The 9th and 13th Brigades R.F.A. will act under orders
received from G.O.C's DEHRA DUN and GARHWAL Brigades,
respectively.

Any necessary registration for tasks allotted should be
carried out to-day.

SIGNALS 4. Arrangements will be made by G.O.C. DEHRA DUN Brigade to
hoist a red light close in rear of left of his Brigade as
soon as the GARHWAL Brigade attack commences firing. This
light will act as a guide as to the direction of our lines
to all concerned in the attack.

REPORTS 5. Reports to LOCON.

Major R.A.
Brigade Major R.A.
MEERUT Division.

Issued at 3.35.p.m. by motor cyclist.

O.C. 56th Howitzer Battery R.F.A.	Copy No.1.
O.C. 2nd Siege Battery R.G.A......	do. 2.
O.C. 110th Heavy Battery R.G.A.....	do. 3.
O.C. 114th Heavy Battery R.G.A.....	do. 4.
O.C. 9th Brigade R.F.A.............	do. 5.
O.C. 13th Brigade R.F.A............	do. 6.
G.O.C. GARHWAL Brigade..............	do. 7.
G.O.C. DEHRA DUN Brigade............	do. 8.
General Staff, MEERUT Division......	do. 9.
War Diary...........................	do. 10.
File................................	do. 11.

APPENDIX 40

G-163/11.   18th

The operations ordered in operation order No nine of dated are postponed for eleven hours AAA The following alterations should be made accordingly AAA para three line two for 4.30 pm to day read 3.30 a.m. tomorrow AAA line eight for 5.0 p.m. today read 4.0 a.m. tomorrow. AAA para 4 a for 5.0 p.m today read 4.0 a.m. tomorrow AAA and for 4-45 p.m. today read 3-45 a.m. tomorrow AAA para 5 for 4-45 p.m. read 3-45 a.m. tomorrow AAA para 7 for 3-30 p.m. today read 2-30 a.m. tomorrow AAA Acknowledge.

"A" Form.   Army Form C. 2121.

MESSAGES AND SIGNALS.

APPENDIX 41

TO: C.R.A. Meerut Divn

Sender's Number: G163/19
Day of Month: 18th
AAA

Under instructions from GHQ the amount of ammunition allotted for tomorrow is the same as that allotted for today AAA Please see GOC tomorrow morning.

From: Meerut Division
Time: 10-20 pm

P Darci Major GSO6

APPENDIX 42

Shewing arc of fire of 13 pr Anti Aircraft.

"A" Form.

MESSAGES AND SIGNALS.

Prefix	Code	m.	Words 38	Charge		Reed. at 5·30 p m.
			Sent At m. To By		This message is on a/c of: Service. GB (Signature of "Franking Officer.")	Date 20/12/14 From 2 B By R Burrows

APPENDIX 4

TO C R A DIVN

Sender's Number	Day of Month	In reply to Number	AAA
BM 47	20th		

Understand ~~heavy~~ heavies and other batteries are firing on second gurkhas vacated trenches aaa Please warn them to stop firing as soon as I let you know time of counter attack

From
Place DEHRA DUN BDE
Time

MESSAGES AND SIGNALS. "A" Form. Army Form C. 2121.

Prefix — Code — Words 28 — Recd. at 7.5 P.m.
Date 20/12/14
From 215
By E Burrows

This message is on a/c of: 364
Service: B

TO **CRA MEERUT DIVN**

Sender's Number: BM 51
Day of Month: 20th

AAA

Please stop guns firing on vacated second gurkhas trenches but should like fire continued to ground beyond

From Place: DEHRA DUN BDE
Time: 7 P.m.

Corporal Rogers
20th Battery RFA
9th Bde RFA states –

APPENDIX 27

About 12.50 pm on 20th Dec 1914 I was in the battery near ROE de BOIS.

I saw a German aeroplane making E and descending in a series of jumps, it finally suddenly disappeared when low down. Both myself and the men of my detachment thought it had fallen.

I should think he could not have been more than 3000 yds from us when we last saw him.

A Rogers

"A" Form.   Army Form C. 2121.
MESSAGES AND SIGNALS   No. of Message

Prefix ___ Code ___ m. Words Charge   APPENDIX 46   Recd. at ___ m.
Office of Origin and Service Instructions.   This message is on a/c of :   Date ___
                                Sent   From ___
                         At ___ m.   Service.
                         To ___   By ___
                         By ___   (Signature of "Franking Officer.")

TO { Meerut — Div — Art —

| Sender's Number | Day of Month | In reply to Number | AAA |
| 357 | 22 | | |

We are suffering from heavy
Artillery fire from 4.1 4.2
and Battery at SALOME J
A 6 a AAA can
you arrest

114 - 8rd

114 - n rds

From G.O.C R.A.
Place BETHUNE
Time 6.0 am

MESSAGES, SIGNALS AND FIELD TELEGRAPHS.

Army Form C. 2121. Modified for India.

APPENDIX 47

TO Lahore Dev? Arty

Sender's Number.	Day of Month.	In reply to number.	A A A
SM 124	29.12.14	357	

Have ordered 4.1 4.6 and Somme Battery to be engaged AAA No 4 in AAA Keep me informed of for the time being of progress in Zone AAA (this corr) I shall report copy tomorrow he by 5 am Arty

FROM R.A.
Place HQ
Time 7.52 am

MESSAGES, SIGNALS AND FIELD TELEGRAPHS.

Army Form C. 2121. Modified for India.

APPENDIX 47(a)

TO: Lahore Div? Art? Thro' Indian Corps

Sender's Number	Day of Month	In reply to number	A A A
BM 125	22.12.14		

Confirmation only PM 121 reply
Am heavy battery cannot reach
SALOMA by day this morning owing
to condition of roads AAA Am
trying to get in touch with
your troops

(Priority?)

FROM
Place: CRA Merut
Time: 8.40 a.m.

MESSAGES, SIGNALS AND FIELD TELEGRAPHS.

Army Form C. 2121. Modified for India.

APPENDIX 48

TO: BDE MAJ RA

White handkerchief is waving in orchard by men in the trenches now

About 10.15 a—

FROM: OC 2nd Siege Bty

MESSAGES, SIGNALS AND FIELD TELEGRAPHS.

Army Form C. 2121. *Modified for India.*

APPENDIX 49

TO — BDE — MAJ — RA

men	are	standing up	in
trench	trenches recommend		ascertain
who	they are	have	gone
now	infantry to	find	out
position			

FROM — O.C. — 2nd SEIGE

MESSAGES AND SIGNALS.

M APPENDIX 50

TO: B. M. R. A. from Brewery

Soldiers running back from trench to trench as hard as they could whether our men or german not quite sure have warned OC Sussex and am firing at orchard enemy shrapnelling a good deal

10-5 am

From: OC 2nd Siege

"A" Form. Army Form C. 2121.
MESSAGES AND SIGNALS.

P. SB Code KIA m.	Words 25/21	Charge	This message is on a/c of:	Recd. at 10.48 Am.
Office of Origin and Service Instructions. 215	Sent At m. To By		46 Service. (Signature of "Franking Officer.")	Date 12/12/14 From 215 By Dawson W

TO — CRA DIVN **APPENDIX 51**

Sender's Number	Day of Month	In reply to Number	AAA
BM18	22		

divl cmdr wishes to turn very heavy fire on to mackas orchard

(10-50 a~)

From — DEHRA JUN BJE
Place
Time — 10/30 AM

"A" Form.   Army Form C. 2121.

MESSAGES AND SIGNALS.

Prefix	Code	m.	Words	Charge		Recd. at 11.23 Am.
Office of Origin and Service Instructions.			25		This message is on a/c of:	Date 22/12/14
			Sent At ___ m. To ___ By ___		Service. (Signature of "Franking Officer.")	From 2nd By

TO — CRA DIVN

Sender's Number	Day of Month	In reply to Number	AAA
BM 25	22		

Situation as to orchard not clear with direct fire on trenches east of it and not on

11.30 am

From GEN ANDERSON
Place
Time 11/20 AM

The above may be forwarded as now corrected. (Z)

MESSAGES, SIGNALS AND FIELD TELEGRAPHS.

Army Form C. 2121. Modified for India.

APPENDIX 53

TO — BDE MAJ

Adjt of Seaforths and others confirm the fact that Germans have advanced into our trenches and hold Orchard I am resuming fire on orchard

G.P informs

11.30 am

2nd field told verbally ignore CRAs 9.8 am for OC to use his own discretion

FROM OC 2nd Seige

MESSAGES, SIGNALS AND FIELD TELEGRAPHS.

Army Form C. 2121. Modified for India.

APPENDIX 54

TO Bde Maj

Our troops just N of brewery are being infiladed from SE with shrapnel

g info

11.50 am

My bie to engage 41 +42 (12 rds each) and then return to squares.
110 told to engage AC and 110 observing station told to keep good look out.

FROM OC 2nd Siege

MESSAGES, SIGNALS AND FIELD TELEGRAPHS.

Army Form C. 2121. Modified for India.

APPENDIX 55

TO: Bde Major R A

Observation officer reports a coy of Infantry retired S.E behind White House

12.40 pm

G.S. informed

ack by telephone
fa 3 active
43

FROM: O C 110 H B

MESSAGES; SIGNALS AND FIELD TELEGRAPHS.

Army Form C. 2121. Modified for India.

APPENDIX 56

TO: B M   R A

So far as I can see only one man in trench in front of Orchard he keeps looking this way

GS informed

12.40 pm

FROM: O C 2nd Siege

"A" Form.   Army Form C. 2121.
MESSAGES AND SIGNALS.   No. of Message _____

Prefix ___ Code ___ m.	Words	Charge	This message is on a/c of:	Reed. at ___ m.
Office of Origin and Service Instructions:		Sent	APPENDIX 57	Date
_____	At ___ m.		Service.	From
_____	To		_____	_____
_____	By		(Signature of "Franking Officer.")	By

TO: OC 13th Bde R+A

| Sender's Number | Day of Month | In reply to Number | |
| CRA 99 | 22. | | AAA |

6a in action AAA Engage
immediately AAA inform GHARWAL
Bde

Also 114 tōrs W"
Sixth ads 43.
by telephone

(Priority)

12.45 pm

From: CRA
Place:
Time:

MESSAGES, SIGNALS AND FIELD TELEGRAPHS.
Army Form C. 2121. Modified for India.

APPENDIX 58

TO Bde Major

Observation party report hostile German battery shelling our trenches appears behind distillery

1 pm
HO told to engage and to take any similar opportunity that may occur

FROM O C
116

TO BM RA **APPENDIX 59**

Have just been forward to see situation there are half a dozen Germans reconnoitring in second trenches to West of orchard no one else so far as I could see AAA They are only just waking up to the fact that we have gone back AAA Am of opinion vigorous offensive would take trenches

2 pm

FROM O C 2nd Siege

MESSAGES, SIGNALS AND FIELD TELEGRAPHS.

Army Form C. 2121. Modified for India.

APPENDIX 6a

TO B M RA

Am	going	to	shell	second
trench	this	side	of	orchard
recommend		other	batteries	doing
same				

2 pm

FROM Place: O C 2nd Siege
Time: 1.12 PM

"A" Form.   J   Army Form C. 2121.
MESSAGES AND SIGNALS.   No. of Message _____

APPENDIX 61   Recd. a 61

TO   OC 9th Bde R.F.A.

Sender's Number: CRA 100   Day of Month: 22   AAA

2nd	Siege	wires	begin	am
going	to	shell	second	trench
this	side	of	orchard	recommend
other	batteries	doing	same	ends
For	information	and	Communication	
to	Divn	Dmn	Brigade	

Priority

2.10 pm

From   CRA
Place
Time

Signature: Jn MacFarlane

"A" Form. Army Form C. 2121.
MESSAGES AND SIGNALS.   No. of Message

APPENDIX 62

Words: 31   Recd. at 2.49 m.
This message is on a/c of: 152
Date 22/3/16
From

TO — CRA   MEERUT   DIVN

Sender's Number — Day of Month 22 — In reply to Number — AAA

Infantry very anxious for houses in orchard N E 21 c east of road and one just 200 yards north of these all is said to be loopholed to be shelled with HE also down an earthwork near picquet house into which enemy have been seen moving The orchard is also held by enemy I am using my howitzers for houses but orchard and earthwork require other guns and if possible houses as well

From 9th BDE RFA
Place
Time 2/20 PM

MESSAGES, SIGNALS AND FIELD TELEGRAPHS.

Army Form C. 2121. Modified for India.

APPENDIX 63

Words: 15

TO: BDE MAJ

| Several | germans | seen | in | trenches |
| just | north | of | Orchard | |

(3 pm)

FROM: O C Second Siege

APPENDIX 64

MESSAGES, SIGNALS AND FIELD TELEGRAPHS.

Army Form C. 2121. Modified for India.

APPENDIX 65

Words: 24

TO Bde Maj

Germans apparently coming from South RUE DU CAILLOUX are now in second trenches west of orchard.

Repeated G.S.

3.10 pm

FROM O C Second Siege
Time 2.20 pm

APPENDIX 66   13

OPERATION ORDERS No. ~~7~~   Copy No........
by
Brigadier General A.B. SCOTT, C.B., D.S.O. `C.R.A. MEERUT Division

LOCON. 25th. December 1914.

Reference 1/40000 map
Sheets MERVILLE-LA BASSEE and AIRE-LILLERS.

MOVES. 1. The artillery of the MEERUT Division less 114th. Heavy Battery, 1 Section 2nd. Siege Battery and No. 11 Section Anti-Aircraft will move tomorrow 26-12-14, after relief by artillery of 2nd. Division, to new billeting areas according to the attached march table.

BRIGADE AMMN. COLUMN. 2. Orders for 13th. Brigade Ammunition Column (18 pr. sections) and 9th. Brigade Ammunition Column will issue later but these units will probably remain in their present positions till 27-12-14 and must be prepared to continue supplying ammunition till relieved.

ATTACHMENTS. 3. 114th. Heavy Battery, 1 Section 2nd. Siege Battery and No. 11 Anti-Aircraft will remain in action in their present positions and be attached to 2nd. Division.

OFFICERS. 4. One officer per battery will remain behind with relieving battery until relieved by G.O.C. R.A. 2nd. Division.

TELEPHONES. 5. Existing lines of telephone wire will be handed over to relieving batteries. Instruments will not be handed over. Units should obtain as much wire as possible in return.

REPORTS. 6. Officers Commanding Brigades and Batteries will report by mounted orderly to G.O.C. R.A. MEERUT Division in LOCON immediately their relief has been carried out.

COMMAND. 7. G.O.C. R.A. MEERUT Division will continue to command the artillery holding the line until the last battery has been relieved.

HEADQUARTERS. 8. Headquarters of the G.O.C. R.A. MEERUT Division will be established at HAM from 7 p.m. 26-12-14.

MARCH DISCIPLINE. 9. The G.O.C. R.A. desires to impress the extreme importance of rigid march discipline on all units.

BILLETING. 10. Attention is invited to MEERUT Divisional Routine Order No. 340 dated 19th. December 1914.

R.N. Lynch Staunton
Major R.A.,
Brigade Major R.A.,
MEERUT Division.

Issued at 7-30 P.M.
Copy No. 1 to O.C. 13th. Bde. R.F.A.
"   "   2   "   4th.   "   "
"   "   3   "   9th.   "   "
"   "   4   "   Divsnl. Ammn. Col.
"   "   5   "   56th. (How) Batty.
"   "   6   "   2nd. Siege Batty.
"   "   7   "   110th. Heavy Batty.
"   "   8   "   114th.   "   "
"   "   9   "   O.C. Anti-Aircraft.
"   "   10   Bde. Major R.A. Mrut. Divsn.
"   "   11   ~~Bde. Major R.A. 8th. Divsn.~~ O.C. "N" Battery R H A.
"   "   12   Gen. Staff, Meerut Divsn.
"   "   13   War Diary.
"   "   14   File.
"   "   15   Bde Major GARHWAL Bde

MARCH TABLE

Unit	Place	Starting time	Destination	Route	Remarks
"N" Battery R.H.A.	Ch¹ du RAUX	1 p.m. to rejoin 19th Battery	BETHUNE		To rejoin SECUNDERABAD Cavalry Bde.
56th Hort Bty R.F.A.	RUE DES CHAVATTES	After relief after 1 p.m.	LESPESSES	BETHUNE, CHOQUES, LILLERS.	Will be relieved by a battery of 41st Bde. R.F.A. (between 12 and 1 p.m.)
17th Battery R.F.A.	do.	After relief after 1 p.m. relieving 56th Battery	Brigade area (AMES)	BETHUNE, CHOQUES, ALLOUAGNE, BUSNES.	do.............
20th } Battery R.F.A. 28th } Hd Qrs Q46 Bde R.F.A.	do.	After relief after 1 p.m. relieving 17th Battery	do	do	Will be relieved by batteries of 41st Bde. R.F.A.
2nd } Battery R.F.A. 49th } Battery R.F.A. Hd Qrs 13th Bde R.F.A.	RUE DES CHAVATTES, LICHERBOURG, SEVRAST in CAPTURE.	After relief	LIERES	LETOURET, ESSARS, BETHUNE, CHOQUES, LILLERS.	Will be relieved by 34th Brigade R.F.A. during the afternoon. 2-45 p.m.
8th Battery R.F.A.	CROIX BARBEE	After relief	do	do	Will be relieved by a battery of 36th Bde. R.F.A. during the afternoon. -3 p.m.
13th Bde R.F.A, A.C. S.A.A. Section	LACOUTURE	After relief 12 noon	do	do	Will move upon road outside present position immediately after the area (incoming Heavy Battery (97th Batte. R.G.A.) have passed the Cross Road ½ mile W.S.W. of L— LA COUTURE ready to move off en route of relieving S.A.A. Section.
Divisional Amm. Col. Nos 2,3 and 4 Sections	TOMBE WILSON ½ mile S.S.E. of PARADIS	12.30 p.m.	HAM.	HINGES, GONNEHEM, LILLERS.	Must not arrive at HINGES before 1.30 p.m.
Divisional Amm. Col. H² Qrs & No.1 Section	BOHEME	As soon as the Sections of the 2nd Division A.C. relieving N°2, 3 & 4 Sections have Campe over the Scarpe of Gonnehem Rd.	HAM.	do.	
110th Heavy Battery	½ m. E of last I in LEVERT LANNET	After relief 12.30 p.m.	LESPESSES	LE CASSAN, LOCON, LES CHOQUAUX, HINGES, GONNEHEM, LILLERS.	
4th Bde R.F.A. } Ecce Units Batteries. }	ROBECQ	9.a.m.	Billeting Area BELLERY	BUSNES, LILLERS.	Will be relieved by 35th Heavy Battery R.G.A. at noon.
114th Battery R.F.A.	PARADIS	6.30 a.m.	do	BOHEME, M¹ BEERNENCHON, ROBECQ, BUSNES, LILLERS.	

APPENDIX 67

OPERATION ORDER No 10.   Copy No. 6.

by

Lieutenant General C.A. ANDERSON, C.B., Comdg. Meerut Division.

Reference sheets 1/40,000   L O O O N 24/12/1914.
MERVILLE-LA BASSE and AIRE-LILLERS.

DIVISIONAL AREA.	The Division will commence to move into a new billeting area tomorrow. The boundaries will be as follows:- From LILERS (exclusive) northward to LA MIQUELLERIE and GUARBECQUE both inclusive, thence Southward through BERGUETTE exclusive to HAM, BOURECQ, LESPESSES, LIERES, AMES all inclusive, thence Westward to include AMETTES and FONTAINE-LEZ-HERMANS, thence South-east to include BAILLEUL and FLORINGHEM, thence Northward along main-road exclusive to LILLERS.

BRIGADE AREAS. BAREILLY & DEHRA DUN BRIGADES. The area South-west of the AUCHY-FERFAY GAUCHY road is allotted to the Bareilly & Dehra Dun Brigades, the dividing line running from the last "L" of BOIS de BAILLEUL to the "H" of BRUNEHO. The Northern portion is allotted to Bareilly Brigade, the remainder inclusive of FERFAY to the Dehra Dun Brigade.

ARTILLERY and TRAIN. The area allotted to Artillery units and the Train lies West of a line from "H" in BRUNEHAUT through the "O" in BOURECQ and "V" of LA NAVE to "M" of Gd HARAIS and thence North along railway. BOURECQ is allotted to the Train.

4th CAVALRY. The area allotted to the 4th Indian Cavalry lies North of a line drawn South-east from "L" of LOTERIE through "S" of CORNET BOURDOIS to Eastern boundary of Divisional area.

SAPPERS & MINERS and PIONEERS. Of the remaining portion of the Divisional Area, that portion lying North of the LILERS-BOURECQ road exclusive is allotted to the Divisional Engineers and the 107th Pioneers, that lying South of the LILLERS-BOURECQ road inclusive is allotted to the Garhwal Brigade.

MOVES.   2.   The moves into and towards the new billeting areas will take place tomorrow vide the attached table.

Major
General Staff.
Meerut Division.

Issued by orderly at 11.p.m. to:
Indian Corps.	Copy No 1.		
1st Corps.	" " 2.		
Dehra Dun Brigade	" " 3.	2nd Division	No 14.
Garhwal Brigade.	" " 4.	Signal Coy.	" 15.
Bareilly Brigade.	" " 5.	5h Brigade.	" 16.
C.R.A.	" " 6.	4th (Guards) Bde.	No 17.
C.R.E.	" " 7.	4th Seaforth Hrs.	No 18.
4th Indian Cavalry.	" " 8.	War Diary.	No 19.
107th Pioneers.	" " 9.	Fiel	No 20.
A.Q.M.G.	" " 10 to 13.		

MARCH TABLE

UNIT	TIME	DESTINATION	ROUTE	REMARKS
HR Cavalry	10 A.M.	LA MIQUELLERIE + LE CORNET BRASSART + Pad of OUARBECQUE		
to H Coy. S.A.M.	10 A.M.	MANQUEVILLE	via HINGES → GONNEHEM BUSNETTES + LILLERS	(i) To follow 104K Pioneers. (ii) Will billet in village to be reserved for N° 3 Coy SAM
104K Pioneers	10 A.M.	CORNET BOURDOIS		
1st Bn Seaforth Hrs	12 noon	VIELLE CHAPELLE	—a.l.to—	To occupy billets vacated by HR Seaforth Hrs.
4th Bn Seaforth Hrs	8 A.M.	ROBECQ	via LES LOBES	
14th Gurkha Rifles	9 A.M.	CROIX MARMUSE	via ZELOBES	
6R Jats	10 A.M.	CORNET MALO	via LE CASSAN + LOCON	
2/ Royal Hrs	10 A.M.	PARADIS	via LOCON + LE TOMBE WILLOT	
41st Dogras	10 A.M.	PARADIS	via FOSSE	

APPENDIX 67(a)

OPERATION ORDER No 11   Copy No......
BY
LIEUTENANT GENERAL C.A. ANDERSON, C.B. Comdg MEERUT DIVISION.

REFERENCE SHEETS 1/40,000   LOCON 25/12/1914.
MERVILLE – LA BASSEE and AIRE – LILLERS.

MOVES. 1. Moves as shown in Table below will be made tomorrow into, and toward, the new billeting area. Units are reminded that troops marching must give way to Mechanical Transport Columns.

RESERVES. 2. The 58th Rifles at RICHEBOURG ST VAAST will be in Brigade
58th Rifles   Reserve to the Garhwal Brigade.
1st Seaforth Hrs   1st Seaforth Hrs at VIELLE CHAPELLE and 41st Dogras at
41st Dogras.   PARADIS will be in Divisional Reserve.

                                                         C.M.Webb.
                                                         Colonel
                                                  General Staff Meerut Division.

Issued by Orderly at 11-30 am.
To
  Indian Corps   Copy No 1
  1st Corps   "   " 2
  Dehra Dun Bde   "   " 3
  Garhwal Bde   "   " 4
  Bareilly Bde   "   " 5
  C.R.A.   "   " 6
  C.R.E.   "   " 7
  4th Indian Cavalry "   " 8
  107th Pioneers   "   " 9
  A.Q.M.G.   "   " 10 to 13 (Medical Train included)
  2nd Divn.   "   " 14
  Signal Coy   "   " 15
  War Diary   "   " 16
  4th Seaforth Hrs   "   " 17
  File   "   " 18

P.T.O

MARCH TABLE 26th and 27th DECEMBER

UNIT	TIME	DESTINATION	ROUTE	REMARKS
13de R.F.A.	9 A.M.	Billeting Area		
4th Seaforth Hrs.	10 A.M.	Billeting Area		The Dehra Dun Brigade less 1st Seaforth Hrs will continue its march on 27th December to new billeting area
Dehra Dun Bde Headquarters	—	ROBECQ		
6th Jats	10 A.M.	ROBECQ	VIA HINGES, LEVERT ANNOY and LE CAUROY	
42nd Gurkha Rifles	11.30 A.M.	ROBECQ	VIA RIEZ DU VINAGE	
49th Gurkha Rifles	11.30 A.M.	ROBECQ		
1/2/19 B.F.A. and 128. J.F.A	10 A.M.	ROBECQ	VIA LOCON, HINGES and LE VERT - ANNOY	
Bareilly Brigade less 41st-Dogras & 58th Rifles(including Ambulances)	10.0 A.M.	ECQUEDECQUES and HURIONVILLE	VIA ROBECQ, BUSNES and LILLERS.	To continue its march on 27th December to the new billeting area.

Sketch & remarks by Maj. Archdale attached.

APPENDIX 68

8ᵗʰ Battery R.F.A.

Map Shooting on 10-XII-14.
Observed by O.C. 4ᵗʰ Battery at ~~Givenchy~~ Festubert.
Maj. Archdale

Series 1   Target No I. House (142h) A4b
House S. of Cross Road N.E. corner of Square.
Line laid out by M.a.B. Range given by map 3600
Corr. 154 T.S. – 162 H.E. A.S. zero.

Rds.				Obs. officer remarks	
1	T.S	no obs.	3625	–	Line laid out by wooden X
2	T.S	+25 yds	3625	–	protractor. very hard to
3	T.S	Range	3600	10' M.R.	read closer than 10-15 minutes.
4	T.S	Range	3608	10' M.R	
5	T.S	Target	3600	–	
6	H.E	Target	3600	–	

Series 2   House about 120 yds. S.
Fresh target 2° M.R 3575

				Obs. off. remarks.	
1	T.S	Target	3575	5' M.R	This correction was wrong
2	H.E	Range	3575	5' M.L	
3	H.E	Target	3575	–	
4	H.E	Target	3575	–	

J. St George Nikes
Major
Comdg 8ᵗʰ Bty R.F.A.

10-XII-14 / 12.5 p.m.

Target = **Direct Hit**

I would suggest with ref. to X above that a larger protractor with a Vernier & magnifying glass would still further improve the accuracy with which Targets could be taken on. This enabled that with good platforms the 18 pdr gun shoots as exactly as could be wished.

J. A. Tytler Lieut.
10/12/14   I. O. 135ᵗʰ Bty R.F.A.

11

Sketch of avenue by night.

[sketch of trees/landscape with annotations:]
- Today is still further back ↓
- + Today's yesterday's shell
- First yesterday's find at ↓
- First thing I find at 2nd round.
- light or lit ground's shells

Corner of Rue d'Ouest from Avenue Stratton left of Railway.

* Today's shell must have burst on passing through the wall as there was a great dust & explosion but light was not too good to see.

* All shell showers detonated. Those fired at afternoon Trier have fired at hitting soft ground fuses to clean (S?) TNA.

No. 120 R.A. (L)

HEADQUARTERS DIVISIONAL ARTILLERY,
MEERUT DIVISION.
15th December, 1914.

CIRCULAR MEMORANDUM.

In circulating these notes from the Officer Commanding, 8th Battery R.F.A., the G.O.C. Royal Artillery, Meerut Division, wishes to draw attention to the excellent results obtained by this battery in map-shooting, due to the careful practice of the points enumerated in these notes. He also once again wishes to draw the attention of Officers Commanding Brigades to the desirability of carefully calibrating all the guns in their Brigade.

R. K. LYNCH-STAUNTON, Major, R.A.,
Brigade Major, R.A., Meerut Division.

SHOOTING FROM MAP.

The large scale map $\frac{1}{20000}$, squared in 500 yds., issued for Artillery purposes is sufficiently accurate for shooting purposes provided certain points are carefully attended to. Both the Range and Line can be obtained by measurement to within 25 yds. Range and 5 min: Line.

In this country, which is almost flat, the question of the angle of sight may be neglected, or adjusted by a study of contour.

The points requiring special attention are:—

(a). Accurate resection of the Battery position with the No. III Director. Care should be taken when using this Director that it should be set up well away from the magnetic influence of the guns, and should also be carefully levelled. The operator should not wear spurs or jack-knife, &c.

Three or four bearings should be sufficient to give the position with accuracy.

In a late instance four bearings were taken, and when laid off on the map three met at a point and the fourth was within 10 yds. of it. The distance and bearing from the Director to the Battery is carefully measured and the Battery position can be plotted on the map.

(b). Gun platforms should be absolutely level for shooting at individual buildings at long ranges. A straight edge and Field Clinometer put across the wheels will enable the necessary accuracy to be obtained.

(c). A calm day should be selected, and a note taken of the Temperature and general condition of the atmosphere.

A frosty dry day at 2500 yds. requires corrector 142. On a damp warm day the corrector runs up to 158, and the Range may vary 50 yds.

(d). *Calibrating guns.*—I think it is highly important that all guns of a Brigade and Battery should range the same. This is at present purely a matter of adjustment, as guns are probably not worn very unequally at present.

I think also that they will shoot to the map on an average day, the sights being adjusted to bring gun and map the same.

As an instance on the 9th and 11th December, 1914, I took the Range and Line off the map at 3 different targets. The Range was correct in each case, and maximum correction for Line was in 1st case 10 ⋆, 2nd case 5 ⋆, and 3rd case nil. The distance between each gun is accurately measured, and displacement or concentration worked out accurately for each range. It is then possible to put all shells at 3600 yds. into a space of 10 × 20 yards.

At large targets the Officer Commanding Brigade ought to feel fairly certain that, if he sends down the square on the map and the portion of it requiring fire, he can turn on an effective fire at once from 1, 2 or 3 Batteries—all guns being calibrated alike one correction of Range or Corrector should suffice for all Batteries. I have never seen the guns of two Batteries shoot alike and the process of ranging is generally gone through separately by each Battery.

K. St. G. KIRKE, Major, R.F.A.,
Commanding 8th Battery, R.F.A.

APPENDIX 70

L O C O N
25th December 1914.

SUMMARY OF INTELLIGENCE UP TO 10.p.m. 24th December 1914.

1. 2 MINENWERFERS extremely active in vicinity of ORCHARD and SNIPER's House in E 4 d or E 8 a-142(h). Possibly one in trench abandoned by 2nd Gurkhas. These were temporarily silenced by 2nd Siege and 56th Howitzer Batteries.
2. 4a active at 9.50.a.m.
3. 5 active at 9.30.a.m. but eventually silenced by 110th Heavy Battery.
4. 3A active at 11.45.a.m. -position not located.
5. VIOLAINES batteries (4 b 4 d) appeared active, but were heavily shelled by 114th Heavy Battery.
6. It is reported that some Germans appear to be wearing our kit for attack purposes. Notably Khaki and Balaclava Caps ?.
7. Increase in the stack of CHEVAUX de FRISES at the "Redoubt". Also the line of these has been prolonged in front of the trenches.
8. Our Infantry reported that 4 machine guns were located in front of PLANTATION. These were engaged by 2nd Battery with H.E. shell.

AIRMAN's REPORT 24th December 1914.

1. 4 b appeared to be occupied to-day.
2. Section of guns at 4 c appears to have been removed.
3. A new battery is in action just North of the hedge running N.E. to S.W. in squares B 2 b and B 3 a-142(j) about two thirds of the battery to the E. of the dividing line between these two squares, and one third to the W. of it. This battery will be known as 4 d.

Major R.A.
Brigade Major R.A.
MEERUT Division.

TO ALL R.A. UNITS.

LOCON.
23rd December 1914.

SUMMARY OF INFORMATION UP TO 9.30.a.m.

1. <u>43</u> was active at intervals during the day (yesterday), firing in the direction of FESTUBERT. Weather prevented airmen putting our Heavy Batteries on to it.
2. <u>6 a</u> active about 11.a.m. yesterday.
3. A battery near DISTILLERY shelled GURKHA trenches- flashes not visible. Probably <u>8 b</u>, but possibly <u>46</u>.
4. 8th Division report enemy's "Archibald" in BOIS DU BIEZ.
5. LAHORE Divisional Artillery report enemy's heavy artillery much quieter during day, but another attack expected to-day.
6. At request of Infantry 56th Howitzer Battery and 2nd Siege Battery demolished houses in "Orchard" (E 4 c) and hostile "Redoubt" near PICQUET House.
7. Much very useful information received all through the day yesterday from the O.C. 9th Brigade R.F.A.- through his observing officers in the Infantry trenches- and from personal observation by O.C. 2nd Siege Battery R.G.A.
8. New trenches were being dug from a point 300 yards E. of the BREWERY to about 400 yards N. of CHARING CROSS during the night by our troops.

(approx.)

M Lynch-Staunton

Major R.A.
Brigade Major R.A.
MEERUT Division.

To ALL R.A. UNITS.

LOCON.
21st December 1914.

SUMMARY OF INFORMATION UP TO 10.p.m.

1. LE HUE (34) active to-day.
2. 43 active during day and is probably a heavy howitzer battery; it was reported shelling a field battery to-day. Was engaged by 114th Heavy Battery and made to cease fire.
3. 5 was active at about 5.30.p.m. and again at 6.50.p.m. probably fired on GARHWAL Brigade trenches.
4. 8.b was active in the evening.
5. 110th Heavy Battery fired on field guns in a line N.E. of 40.
6. 44th Battery engaged hostile battery located in S.E. corner of F 3 d-142(h) at 9.30.a.m. This battery ceased firing.
7. Airmen have located two new gun targets:-
    (a) 100 yards S. of bottom of last letter E in LA BASSEE (B 8 d-142(j).
    (b) N.W. corner of Western plantation in B 9 c-142(j).
8. A train with many trucks moved towards LA BASSEE at 10.5.a.m. and left at 11.40.a.m.
9. Two "Sausage" Balloons up to-day.
10. The MINENWERFER is reported to have been moved South, opposite the LAHORE Division.
    The 2nd Siege Battery got some good rounds into the trenches near PICKET House.

                                            Major R.A.
                                        Brigade Major R.A.
To All R.A. Units.   MEERUT Division.

L A T E R   22.12.14.

LAHORE Divisional Artillery reported that they were suffering from heavy Artillery fire at 8.a.m. from 41, 4 b, and SALOME (J-A6 a)

L O C O N.
30th December 1914.

SUMMARY OF INFORMATION UP TO 10.p.m.

1. 43 was active at 10.a.m.
2. 46 was active at 9.30.a.m. and was engaged by 110th Heavy Battery. Later again engaged by same battery with airman, when 3 hits were reported.
3. 7 a reported active at 10.40.a.m. but flashes not located. Later engaged by 114th Heavy Battery with airman, and located about 250 yards S.S.W. of 2 in F 2-142(h).
4. Either 22 or 23 was active during the morning.
5. 20th Battery report having engaged and silenced 7 a at 11.19.a.m.
6. Good effect obtained by 28th Battery on enemy's infantry attacking near PICQUET House.
7. A new "Sausage" Balloon seen up to-day (1.45.p.m.) S.S.E. of RUE du BOIS and about 15,000 yards range. Two ordinary balloons up to the S.
8. 20th Battery were shelled with H.E. for about 1 hour at 12.30 p.m. by battery thought to be No.5 (May have been 43 as 5 not seen by airman to-day.
9. 9.15.a.m. "Archibald" fired 25 rounds at a German "Albatross" - very nearly in ! 12.15.p.m. fired 28 rounds at another. 12.40.p.m. fired 12 rounds at another.
10. Our Heavy Guns much impeded in their shooting with aeroplane observation by hostile aircraft all through the day.
On two occasions Lieut Barratt R.A., who was observing in a single seater by himself, went off after an "Albatross" with his revolver; "Albatross" had the height of him each time and made off.
11. Captain Evans who was observing for 114th Heavy Battery fired 10 rounds with his rifle at the ILLIES "Sausage" when ever it.
11. FESTUBERT was heavily shelled about 2.p.m.

4.5.p.m. "Sausage" Balloon
Observed about MARQUILLES.

R.M. Lynch-Staunton
Major R.A.
Brigade Major R.A.
MEERUT Division.

To All R.A. Units.

LOCON.
20th December 1914.

SUMMARY OF INFORMATION.

1. The net result of the fighting which commenced at 4.a.m. 19.12.14 and lasted till about 7.p.m. was that the situation is now exactly as it was before the fighting began.
   The Leicesters captured about 300 yards of German trench in front of our line in E 4 and 2 machine guns, but owing to the heavy machine gun fire and bombing that they were subjected to they had to withdraw about 6.p.m.
   A considerable number of prisoners were captured in the first attack but unfortunately the majority of them got away and only four were brought in. The Bomb Gun used in the German trenches against the 2nd Gurkhas was a much more powerful weapon than we have yet had up against us in this line. Every endeavour should be made to locate it and knock it out.

2. As remarked in Summary up to 11.p.m. on 17.12.14 the trenches round No.26 house require attention with high angle fire from field howitzers, yesterday this was required but was not available.

3. "Sausage" Balloon up again near ILLIES.

4. 114th Heavy Battery registered 4 c with airman during day (new position of 4 b).

5. 2nd Siege Battery engaged 3 b with airman, obtaining 5 hits in Gun pits and communicating trenches.

6. 28th Battery R.F.A. did some effective shooting at parties of enemy's Infantry moving along VIOLAINES-LA BASSEE ridge at 11.30.a.m. yesterday.

7. Flashes were visible apparently in F 7 c from which direction 2nd Gurkhas were shelled with LITTLE WILLIES. This battery was silenced by 28th Battery soon after 2.p.m. (32 battery or section mentioned in (3) of 11.p.m. Summary dated 17.12.14.)

8. Our "Archibalds" made their debut this morning at 10.45.a.m. and made excellent practice at 2 German "Albatross" aeroplanes.

9. At about 1.p.m. a howitzer battery was seen to move down the ILLIES-LA BASSEE Road towards the latter.

R.M. Lynch-Staunton
Major R.A.
Brigade Major R.A.
MEERUT DIVISION.

To All R.A. Units.

LOGON.
16th. December 1914.

INFORMATION SUMMARY UP TO 6 P.M.

INFORMATION RECEIVED FROM LAHORE DIVISION:-

1. 33 is very active, also 41 and a battery near 4b (probably 4c vide to-day's summary.)
2. There is a German field battery at the Southern apex of the railway triangle East of CUINCHY. This is known as 50 a.
3. The ammunition supply of the French artillery is now practically unlimited.

Lieut. R.A.,
for Brigade Major R.A.,
MEERUT Division.

L O C O N.
19th December 1914.

AIRMAN's REPORT 10.a.m.

1. <u>1 a</u> is occupied.

2. <u>4 b</u> is un-occupied.

3. <u>3 b</u> is occupied and extends in a curved line to the N.E. from where he is marked on the map- total front about 100 yards.

4. The trenches opposite LA QUINQUE RUE, particularly the trenches S.E. of <u>a6</u> were very full of Germans.

5. <u>5</u> appeared to be empty.

6. <u>46</u> was in action behind the hedge 150 yards S.E. of where he is marked on the map facing N.W.

7. <u>6.a</u> was empty.

8. There is a semi-circle of newly dug gun pits facing N.W. in a green field about 100 yards S.W. of the DISTILLERY(B 14 d-142(h)).

9. Two guns were seen as in the sketch below at VIOLAINES(142(j)-B 3). They will be known as <u>4 c</u>.

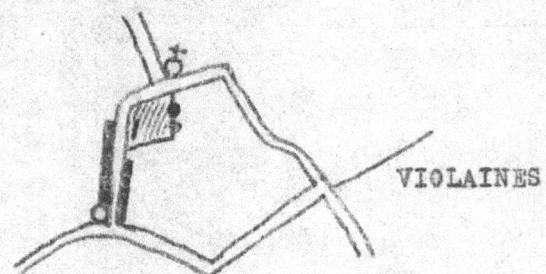

The guns are shown as two blobs on the E fence of a thick orchard which is shown shaded.

VIOLAINES

Major R.A.
Brigade Major R.A.
MEERUT Division.

To All R.A. Units.

LOCON.
18th December 1914.

SUMMARY OF INFORMATION UP TO 10.p.m.

1. No Artillery information received during the day.

2. At 11.30.a.m. O.C. 110th Heavy Battery reported a train left LA BASSEE.

3. Following message received from MEERUT Division:-

" Eighth Division wires begins twentythird Infantry report that Devons have captured and are holding enemy's trenches in front of C lines and have taken several prisoners ends for information AAA G.H.Q. also reports that French are making good progress along the line".

                                      Major R.A.
                            Brigade Major R.A.
                              MEERUT Division.

To All R.A. Units.

LOCON.
17th December 1914.

SUMMARY OF INFORMATION UP TO 11.p.m.

1. 8th Division reported to-day enemy fired H.E. shell both morning and afternoon; guns appear to be of larger calibre than have been used for some days.

2. "Sausage" Balloon up during afternoon near LE HUE(B 13 d-142(h)) descended and ascended again and remained up till dark.

3. 1.10.p.m. 110th Heavy Battery from its O.P. located section of field guns which had opened fire near BEAU PUITS. Engaged by 110th, range found. Position fixed in an orchard round an Estaminet, the southernmost house of the village on the LA BASSEE-ESTAIRES Road F 7 d-142(h)(about 300 yards E. of 32) Will be known as 32 b.

4. At 1.15.p.m. 2nd Siege Battery shelled a battery near BEAU PUITS. Apparently 200 yards N.N.E. of figure 7 in F 7 a-142(h). Target No.5.

5. Neighbourhood of BEAU PUITS requires keeping under observation. Haystacks and strange trees have been noticed to appear and disappear to the North of a line running E. and W. through the factory there, and a German telephone pole is handy.

6. 2nd Siege located what appeared to be a single howitzer pointing N.W. about 200 yards S.E. of DISTILLERY enclosure. A large green tarpaulin was spread in front of it, and a telephone pole and some earthwork close to it.

7. 25 and 40 appeared to be both un-occupied to-day.

8. 114th Heavy Battery with aeroplane observation registered 4 b, 1 b and 5.

9. 26(House N.E. of d in E 4 d -142(h)) shelled by 20th Battery with H.E. shell with good results to-day. Trenches round this however requires attention with high angle fire.

10. 8.45.p.m. Seaforths reported airship passed over our lines and sailed into beam of German searchlight, after which it returned.

Major R.A.
Brigade Major R.A.
MEERUT Division.

To All R.A. Units.

LOGON
17th December 1914.

SUMMARY OF INFORMATION RECEIVED FROM C.R.A. LAHORE DIVISION:-

1. 41 has moved 800 yards E. to the junction of the railway line and the vertical line dividing 142 j B 11 and 12.

2. FESTUBERT is being worried by 41 and 4 b.

3. In 148(K) A 2 C pits have been seen as shewn on the sketch below S.W. of No. 24:-

4. 42 is in action and is a Howitzer Battery.

5. The result of the fighting on the 16th December was:-
   (a) 2 german sapheads N.E. of GIVENCHY captured by the LAHORE Divn
   (b) The first line of german trenches in front of the 58th French Division on the LAHORE Division's Right flank were captured by the French 58th Division.

RECEIVED FROM OUR OWN AIRMAN:-

   a b is definitely unoccupied to-day.

RECEIVED FROM 8th DIVISION:-

   Ther german artillerie in front of the line held by the 8th Division E. of LAVENTIE was fairly active yesterday.

Major R.A.

Brigade Major R.A.
MEERUT Division.

Summary of information up to 3.a.m.
17th December

1. At 9.45.a.m. a German captive balloon of the "Sausage" type (see ascended in the neighbourhood of ILLIES. Some little delay occurred obtaining "true" bearings for accurate resection, but eventually the area and road in and from which it ascended was shelled by the Heavy Batteries. Result not known.

2. One gun plainly visible in emplacement at 4a, these guns now point further West.

3. At 2.p.m. the FACTORY chimney was shelled - reports say by 5's. (line of 5's, 14, and 5th 6ths from O.P. of 110th Heavy Battery). About 40 rounds fired at it. 1 blind 15 c.m. howitzer shell was found. O.C. 2nd Siege Battery however states the 105 m.m. field howitzer was used. About 20 feet of the top were knocked off.

4. A battery E of BOIS du BIEZ active at 6.50.a.m.

5. 6a reported active at 6.55a.m. (? as 2nd Siege were then shelling it).

6. 25 manned their guns in the morning - shelled by 66th Battery - time not stated.

7. Enemy's artillery fired today as follows:-

   9.5.a.m..... 10 rounds light shrapnel on FESTUBERT.
   9.20.a.m.} 20 rounds H.E. and shrapnel from high angle - gun of big
   to   } calibre and long range on centre square E6a-142(h) - possibly
   9.45.a.m.} from VIOLAINES.
   10.15.a.m... 7 more rounds from the same gun, but 400x shorter, and
   2.p.m..... 5 more again at 2.p.m, 150x shorter still - These 32 rounds were probably fired at a battery somewhere in square E5a or E1c-142(h).
   2.10.p.m... Light shrapnel were again fired again at FESTUBERT.

8. LORGIES showed signs of occupation.

9. Enemy appear to have some fresh troops, many men in trenches seem to have new clean uniforms.

10. O.C. 2nd Siege Battery states "Not only is the German Artillery fire very much less in volume but it is much inferior in power to what it used to be. The shrapnel bursting near our trenches E of FESTUBERT seemed to have very little velocity, probably being from a field howitzer at long range; bursts of "universal shell" are now rarely seen; the shelling of R.t.E du BOIS silk factory this afternoon was carried out by field howitzer shell when heavier shell would obviously have been more effective.

THE "SAUSAGE" BALLOON.

[Diagram showing sausage balloon with labels: Wind, Fin, Control Gas bag, Nacelle, Shackle which shines in the sun, 4 to 5 balls.]

By Captain W. HUDSON. R.G.A.
O.C. No II Section Anti Aircraft Guns.

Description of "Sausage Balloon".

The German Captive Balloons appear to be anchored to some heavy vehicle provided with winding gear. I have seen them ascend and descend as many as 6 times from 9.a.m. to 4.p.m. They are capable of changing their position fairly rapidly, and given favourable weather conditions could move when up.

They are limited to good roads as both the anchoring vehicles, and the vehicles carrying cylinders of compressed gas are very heavy.

The observer is in direct telephonic communication with their heavy batteries.
The one observed today near ILLIES was "end on".

To. All units (R.A)

G.E. Lynch-Staunton. Major R.A.
BRIGADE MAJOR R.A.
MEERUT DIVISION.

LOCON.
15th December 1914.

SUMMARY OF INFORMATION UP TO 9.p.m.

1. 40 was active at 10.30.a.m.; was engaged by 66th Battery which put one H.E. and 1 persussion shrapnel into an emplacement.

2. GARHWAL Brigade reported at 1a.40 a.m "hostile" guns firing from N.E. of BEAU PUITS village near ESTAIRES-LA BASSEE Road towards LA QUINQUE RUE. Our guns reported firing but apparently falling short ! Para 1 above probably explains this. BEAU PUITS battery is probably in ol position of No.5 or possibly flashes of 1 b observed by GARHWAL Brigade.

3. 1 b active at 10.15.a.m. and engaged by 110th Heavy Battery.

4. 19th Battery reported flashes at 12.noon on bearing of 6 a, but this may have been a battery near BEAU PUITS.

5. 20th Battery saw column of about 50 Infantry on track in F 2 a - 142(h) marching S.W. and got well into them. They eventually went to ground in and around position of 7 a. O.C. 9th Brigade R.F.A. places 7 a 300 yards E.S.E. of position marked on map.

6. RICHEBOURG Distillery is reported as being used as an O.P.

7. 41 occupied and active early morning 16.12.14. also 4 b

8. Horses seen in and around 8 c morning 16.12.14.

Major R.A.
Brigade Major R.A.
MEERUT Division.

To All Units.

LOCON.
14th December 1914.

SUMMARY OF INTELLIGENCE UP TO 10.P.M.

1. 8 b was active at 9.30.a.m. and shelled O.P. of 66th Battery, 110th Heavy Battery and other batteries. Shelling probably due to ~~observing~~ Observing Officer of ~~—~~ Battery up chimney exposing himself unnecessarily and drawing fire. (one report attributes the shelling to 25 ?).

2. Activity noticed at the "Redoubt" in B 14 c-149(h) at 3.p.m. and it was shelled by 110th Heavy Battery.

3. Flashes were noticed from a field battery in an orchard round the Southern most house in BEAU PUITS, and more were seen going into houses near by.

4. 2nd Siege Battery engaged 40 and made a detachment run away along the trench.

5. The Germans were seen to be baling water out of firing line trench today.

6. 60 horses and riders were seen walking into LORGIES from BEAU PUITS between 8 and 9.a.m.

7. FESTUBERT and its near vicinity was shelled in the morning.

Major R.A.
Brigade Major R.A.
MEERUT Division.

To all units.

LOCON.
15th December 1914.

INFORMATION SUMMARY UP TO 11.p.m.

1. 40 still occupied (position F 2 d, diagonally across N.W. corner of square, centre of battery about 800 yards from the corner). There were 4 guns visible to-day.

2. 25 This battery now reduced to 4 guns, which are dug in so deep that only the muzzles appear above the ground, and to-day they were covered all over with tarpaulins, which made them practically invisible. It was firing at 8.a.m. today.

3. Either 6 a or 4 a (on same line from O.P. from which reported) was firing today.

4. It is suggested that LE HUE battery (34) is split up, and that one section has gone to LES 3 MAISONS (or possibly to 47) one section to neighbourhood of LA MOTTELETTE.

5. A dummy gun was visible at 1 c (LE TILLEUT) firing 'puffs'.
1 b reported active yesterday.

6. German's shelled the old position of 114th Heavy Battery at 3.p.m. to-day, for about the tenth time. Shrapnel and a few heavy shell were used.

7. 7th Battery Observing Officer noticed two bombs fired by our Infantry to be most effective on German trenches.

8. A field gun followed by its wagon, and then by another limbered vehicle (gun or wagon) was seen moving S.E. from ILLIES this morning.

9. Reference (a) of yesterday's summary:- the 4 CHEVAUX de FRISES lying near the "redoubt"(?) in B 14 c-142(h) yesterday have been placed in front of enemy's main trench N.E. of "White House". There is a fresh collection of logs at the "redoubt".

10. Many horses and cyclists observed during the day on the LORGIES-BEAU PUITS Road, going in both directions. A certain number on ILLIES-LA BASSEE Road.

Major R.A.

Brigade Major R.A.

MEERUT Division.

To ALL UNITS.

LOCON
13th December 1914.

SUMMARY OF INFORMATION UP TO 8.a.m. 12.12.14.

Feature of yesterday's operations was the very marked increase of activity on part of the German Artillery.   Following reports received of hostile guns:-
1. No.25 active) engaged by map and
2. No.24 active) bearing.
3. No.1b active, flashes located by 110th Heavy Battery and engaged by 114th Heavy Battery by map.
4. Battery somewhere S. of White House, probably along road bank on E. of road in square F1b-14%(H) or F1c.
5. A Battery reported to be firing from somewhere E. of LORGIES.
6. A Battery behind the BOIS du BIEZ.

Other objects located:-
(a) A mound or redoubt in square B14c-14%(H), just N.W. of road appears to be where enemy make Chevaux de Frix.
(b) Presumed(?) O.P. of 24 at the Distillery, as hostile gun fire from 24 ceased when this was shelled.

Note:- The following are probably worth the expenditure of a few H.E. or Lyddite shell:-
Distillery
Chateau "A"
Other houses at cross roads in B14b.
While a few shrapnel at odd intervals at the ruins of White House night also deter snipers from using it.

Major R.A.
Brigade Major R.A.
MEERUT Division.

To All units.

LOCON.
12th December 1914.

Information Summary up to 10.a.m.

1. The "NUREMBERG" one of the two cruisers which escaped from the action off the FALKLAND Islands has been sunk and the one remaining cruiser is still being chased.

2. The Russians are continuing to do well in E. PRUSSIA particularly round CRACOW.

3. Large bodies of German troops passed E. through CHARLEROI and LOUVAIN between November 29th and December 5th.

4. 2nd Siege Battery report much timber being brought up by Germans to the works in the neighbourhood of the 'Snipers' and 'Picquet' houses. This is presumably to afford overhead cover against a possible repetition of the previous day's bombardment.

5. The same battery also shelled No.25 where a gun or limber was visible.

Major R.A.
Brigade Major R.A.
MEERUT Division

To All Units.

L.C.C.O.M.

INFORMATION SUMMARY UP TO 10.a.m 11th December 1914.

1. It is stated on good authority that the Germans frequently place their guns in pits which are covered over with canvas sheets, one side of which is earthcoloured and the other green. The pit is deep, the canvas is on ground level and only leaves enough space for the actual firing of the gun.

    A very extensive use is made of field telephones. Every Brigade headquarters has several lines leading into it. In many instances every haystack near the firing line has an observer with a telephone on the top. The observers are very cleverly concealed. German illustrated papers give pictures of observers hidden by straw.

2. NIEUPORT was heavily bombarded by the Germans yesterday.

3. Black water-proofs have been issued to the Germans.

4. Certain German Regiments appear to have been duplicated, i.e. Two Regiments are given the same number and one may be found in E. PRUSSIA while the other is on the North Front. This is probably an attempt to fog our intelligence.

5. A long official communique from PETROGRAD contains the following points:-
    (a) The Germans have reinforced their Eastern Front with 6 Corps and 5 Cavalry Divisions.
    (b) The Austrian troops about CRACOW are supported at most points by German troops. The Germans do not seem to place much confidence in the Austrians by themselves.
    (c) The recent operations in E. PRUSSIA and POLAND may be briefly summarised as follows:-
    First the Germans very nearly turned the Russians right flank and broke through their centre.
    Then the Russians extricated temselves and narrowly escaped demolishing the whole German force which had penetrated their line.
    The line is now fairly straight.
    The loss of LODZ is of no importance. It formed a dangerous salient and the Russians abandoned it voluntarily. The Russian troops are fighting extremely well- wading through icy cold rivers up to their necks in the attack etc; and the Germans have undoubtedly lost enormously.

6. The 44th Battery observing station was shelled about 11.a.m. yesterday by Shrapnel(possibly 8a).

7. The Germans shelled W. FESTUBERT near the old 8th Battery position with H.E. (Field Howitzer) just after the above.(May have been 4a or 4b).

8. Yesterday's bombardment of the enemy's saps and trenches near XXXXIXXXXX QUINQUE RUE was very successful.

                                Major R.A.
                            Brigade Major R.A.
                            MEERUT Division.

To All units.

Information Summary 10/12/14

1. Indian Corps wires begins G 533 tenth Admiralty wires that German squadron of SCHARNHORST GNEISENAU DRESDEN NUREMBERG LEIPZIG was sighted at 7.3 a.m. December eighth near Falkland Island by Admiral STURDEES squadron AAA An action followed in which SCHARNHORST GNEISENAU LEIPZIG were sunk AAA DRESDEN and NUREMBERG are being chased AAA British casualties reported very small AAA

2. The large amount of transport converging on MENIN is remarkable, there is also a considerable reduction of the rolling stock at that place and at COMINES, and these observations may possibly indicate a withdrawal of units from the front north of the LYS.
    The comparatively large amount of rolling stock at LA BASSEE may perhaps indicate a clearance of material from that town, which is threatened by the capture of VERMELLES and RUTOIRE.

3. PARIS, 7th. December 1914.
    A communique issued this afternoon states:- "There is nothing new on the Eastern frontier where the positions of the proceeding days have been maintained.

GENERAL. It is reported that the LANDWEHR and LANDSTURM units in Bruges are armed with old pattern rifles without magazines.

                                            Major R.A.,
                                         Bde Major R.A.,
                                         MEERUT Division.

LOCON.
9.12.14.

Information Summary up to 9.a.m.

(1) The whole of VERMELLES and LE RUTOIRE are now in the hands of the French.

(2) The Russians have driven back the Turks in the CAUCASUS with heavy loss.

(3) A large quantity of rolling stock was seen yesterday by an airman in various stations behind the German lines on our front. A certain number of columns on the roads were also seen. They seem to have been moving chiefly in a N.E. direction.

Reference Information Summary of 8.12.14:-

(a) At 5.20.p.m. the 66th Battery fired salvos at the Germans who were endeavouring to remove the debris of No. 40.

(b) O.I. 2nd Siege Battery reports that the Germans have sunk a shaft or sap about 30 yards to the West of "Sniper's House" (E8a-142(h) centre of square at bottom) in the plantation towards the 9th Gurkhas trenches.

(c) 2nd Gurkhas yesterday worried by snipers in tower of "White House". 110th Heavy Battery only partially destroyed this tower.

*A house knocked down by us a few days ago.

E. F. Eyre de Brandon
Major R.A.
Brigade Major R.A.
MEERUT Division

LOCON.
8.12.1914.

Information Summary up to 7 p.m.

1. The Germans have taken LODZ.
2. 2nd Siege Battery knocked out two (possibly three) guns of a German Field Battery near No. 40. Line and range to 4b were also obtained with the help of an aeroplane.
3. 7th and 66th Batteries also shelled battery near 40. Also German trenches and working parties.
4. 110th Heavy Battery also shelled battery near 40 and hit tower on 39 twice.
5. Reference 9 p.m. summary of 5.12.14 - the house near "a" was shelled today by one of our 18 pr. batteries and the flag has gone. It appeared today, judging by the movements of orderlies etc; to be a German Headquarters of some kind.

J.M.Macfarlane
Lieut R.A.
for Brigade Major R.A.
MEERUT Division.

LATER.

Extreme accuracy of squared map for Artillery purposes conclusively proved by 8th Battery R.F.A today. In first instance a house reported as Brigade Headquarters by airman in square E 4b was hit by a H E shell at second round, at range of 3625 yards although invisible from battery. A second house just North of this was then switched on to; first round just off for line, second round direct hit. Error of range of map and guns worked out to 25 yards at 3625 yards.

It may be added that 8th Battery observing officer was unable to see these targets and only observation obtained was through linking up with O.P of 44th Battery.

LOCON.
4.12.1914

Information Summary up to 7 p.m.

① The French have made considerable progress at VERMELLES. There is no change on the British front.

② No change in E. PRUSSIA.

③ The artificial wood described in para 5 of today's summary issued at 11.a.m. will be known as N° 47.

④ The two houses near 46 are obviously used as billets.

⑤ 48 is occupied.

⑥ 8a, 8b and 25 seem to be occupied as alternative positions by not more than one Battery.

⑦ 2nd Siege Battery got two direct hits today on 6a.

⑧ Reference 142(R) E4d and 8b

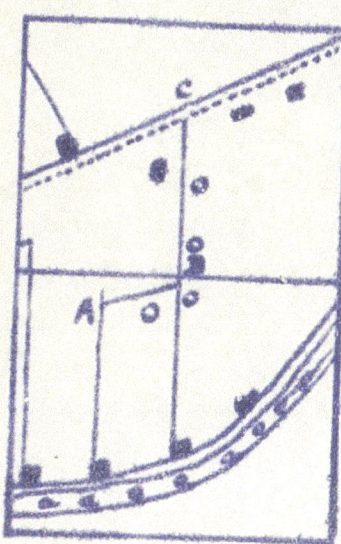

There is a fence "AB" not shown on the map and there are four circular emplacements as shown on the sketch.

There is a trench just E of the hedge ABC running all along it in front of the emplacements.

H. A. Eyston Shaunton
Major R.A.
Brigade Major R.A.
Meerut Division

LATER.

Reference the flashes seen by O.C. 19th Battery on 4.12.14 mentioned in Summary of that date under "Later (2)". It is evident from further report that the flashes seen were not those of 4b, but may have been those of guns in or near 6a. See also information summary dated 5.12.14.

LOCON.
6.12.1914

Airman's Morning Report   11.a.m.

1. 8a and 8b both have guns in them this morning although all the emplacements of each are not occupied.

2. 25 does not appear to be occupied this morning.

3. 1a, 1b, 41, 42 empty.

4. At 8.30 a.m. this morning a wagon (possibly ammunition?) and about 12 men were noticed on the road about 200ˣ S.E. of 4b (B.3.d 142(j)).

5. There is an artificial "wood" newly "planted" 100ˣ N.E of eastern house above b in B.4b - 142(j). (Les 3 MAISONS). There is very probably a battery concealed here.

6. This morning's reports place 34 in orchards either (a) 100ˣ S.S E of E in HUE or (b) in apex between two roads 400ˣ East of E in La BOUCHAINE.

                    H.W. Lynch-Staunton
                            Major R.A
                    Brigade Major R.A
                        Meerut Division

LOCON.
5.12.1914.

Information Summary up to 9 p.m.

The advanced enemy's trenches on our front are much more weakly held than formerly.

The presence of Austrain and Bosnian Troops on our front is suspected and it is possible that the 7th Corps is going or has gone to E. PRUSSIA.

News from RUSSIA continues to be good.

The road from F^e du BIE to LORGIES and the ground about LE TILLEUL is frequently flooded in winter.

From local information it has been heard that there is a large vaulted mound with door facing N.W. (used for storing inflamable chemicals) in the angle of the LE HUE-ILLIES, LE TRANSLOY-ILLIES roads about where the top lines of 142 (K) 1a and 1b meet. It is suggested this may contain a gun.

25 and 34 were active today.

A flag was flying on a house 200x from house "A" on the road running N.E. from it.

There is apparently a dummy gun in the centre of 142(k) F2d.

Reference information summary of yesterday it seems more probable that the flashes supposed to come from guns run down from 6a were really from 4b which is known to be occupied and is in continuation of the line to the flashes from 19th Battery observing station.

The following localities were shelled by the enemy today:-

① RICHEBOURG St VAAST and } by 34.
   N. end of RUE du BOIS.

② 66th Battery in 142 (K) A.11 a.

③ RUE de BETHUNE and MARAIS neighbourhood from direction of 6 a.

R. Y. Lynch-Staunton
Major. R.A.
Brigade Major R.A.
MEERUT DIVISION.

To.
All units.
Brigade Major R.A. LAHORE DIVN.
    "   "   "   8th DIVN.

LOCON
4.12.14

Information Summary up to 6.p.m.

1. 8a, 8b and 25 are active from time to time.
2. There is a field battery at 4b or the RUE de TRONCHANT position of 14.
3. 34 is in the fork of the roads by the windmill in 142(K) E/a.
4. 32a, 22, 23 and 4b are probably in action.
5. 1a and 1b are unoccupied.
6. There has been a considerable amount of digging about 33.

         [signature]
         Major R.A.
         Brigade Major R.A.
         Meerut Division.

To,
All units.

Later.

1. O.C. 2nd Siege Battery reports No. 25 opened fire during the day, but ceased when he fired on it. (no time given).
2. 19th Battery R.F.A. fired on flashes of a hostile battery firing towards FESTUBERT, located by him 100x East of figure 6 of square F6 - 142(h), just North of line dividing F6b & d - 142(h). (possibly guns run down from 6a).
3. O.C. 110th Heavy Battery reports that No. 8(a) was firing during the morning (no time given). Seemingly towards houses in the RUE du BOIS.

APPENDIX   APPENDIX X.2

War DIARY

December 1914
Hd. Qrs. Divisional Artillery
MEERUT division

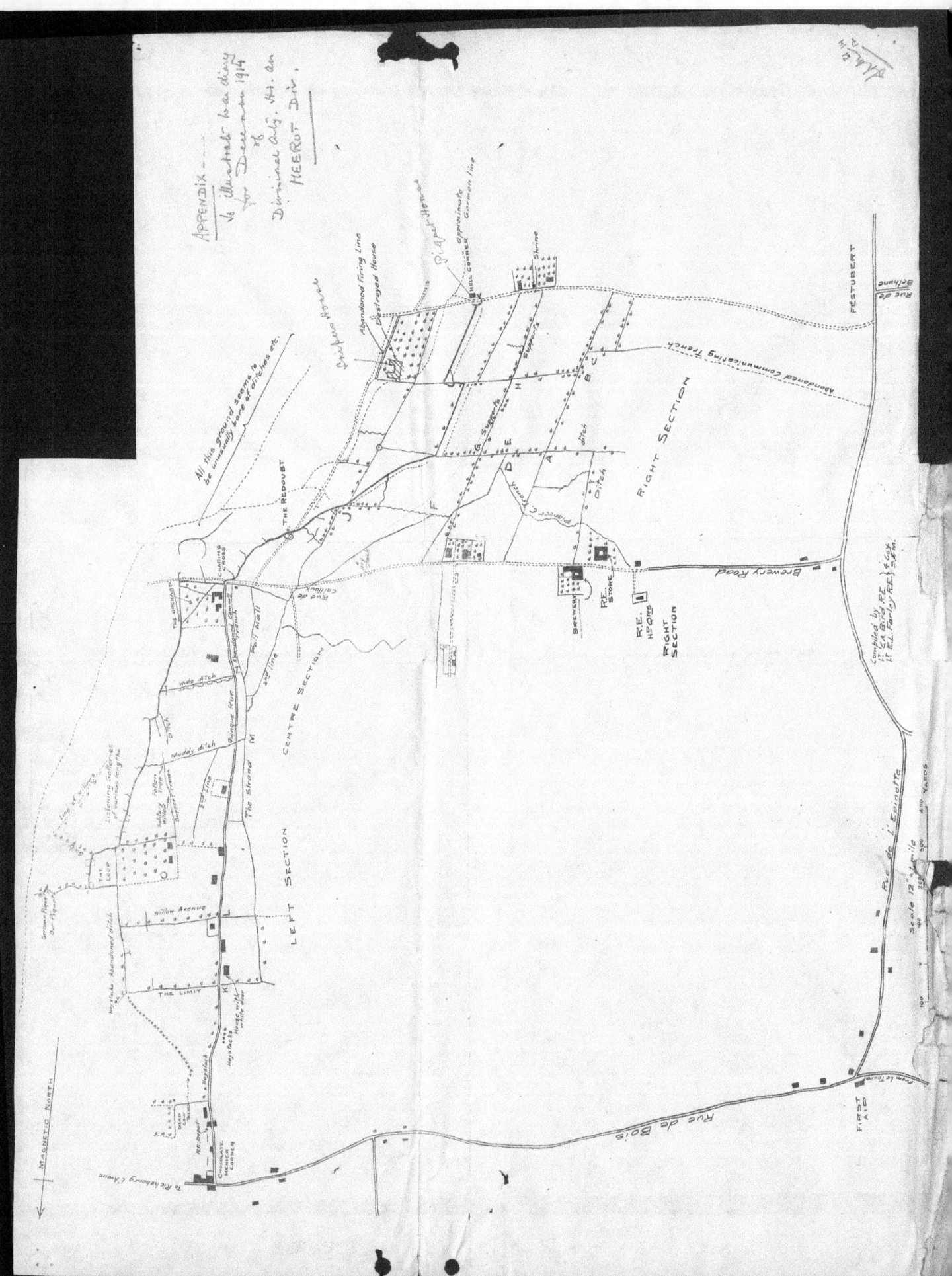

APPENDIX

WAR DIARY

December 1914

Hd Qrs Divisional Artillery

MEERUT division

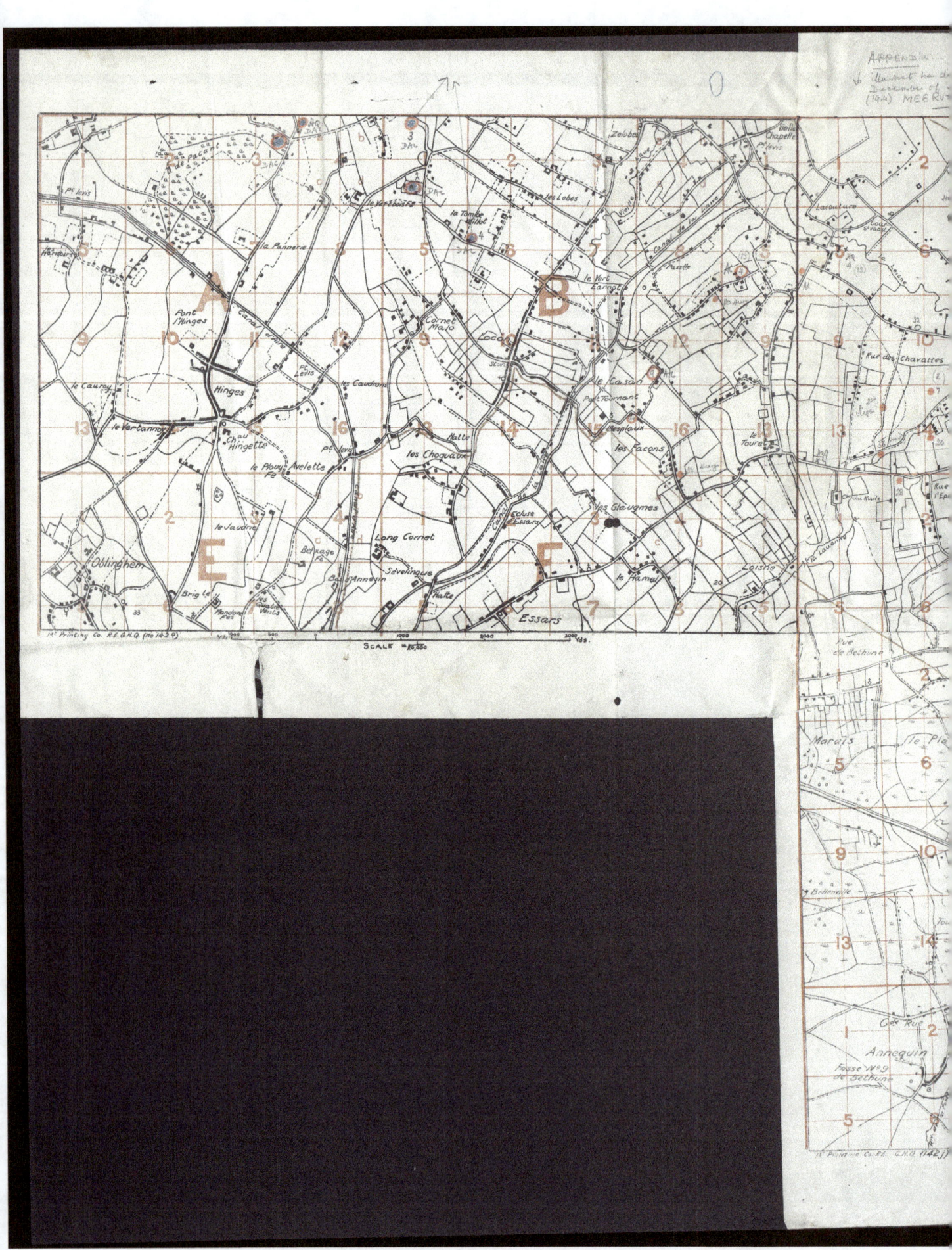

APPENDIX

APPENDIX 71

WAR DIARY

December 1914

Hd. Qrs Divisional Artillery

MEERUT division

www.ingramcontent.com/pod-product-compliance
Lightning Source LLC
Chambersburg PA
CBHW080908230426
43664CB00016B/2755